Perspectives on the Holocaust

Holocaust Studies Series

Randolph L. Braham, Editor
The Jack P. Eisner Institute for Holocaust Studies

The Graduate School and University Center
The City University of New York

The Holocaust Studies Series is published in cooperation with the Jack P. Eisner Institute for Holocaust Studies. These books are outgrowths of lectures, conferences, and research projects sponsored by the Institute. It is the purpose of the series to subject the events and circumstances of the Holocaust to scrutiny by a variety of academics who bring different scholarly disciplines to the study.

Perspectives on the Holocaust

Randolph L. Braham, Editor

Kluwer·Nijhoff Publishing
Boston The Hague London

Distributors for North America:
Kluwer·Nijhoff Publishing
Kluwer Boston, Inc.
190 Old Derby Street
Hingham, Massachusetts 02043, U.S.A.

Distributors outside North America:
Kluwer Academic Publishers Group
Distribution Centre
P.O. Box 322
3300AH Dordrecht, The Netherlands

Library of Congress Cataloging in Publication Data
Main entry under title:

Perspectives on the holocaust.

(Holocaust studies series)
Bibliography: p.
1. Holocaust, Jewish (1939–1945) — Addresses, essays, lectures.
I. Braham, Randolph L. II. Series.
D810.J4P49 1983 940.53'15'03924 82–17916
ISBN 0–89838–124–X

Printed in the United States of America.

Contents

Preface

The number of books and articles dealing with various aspects of World War II has increased at a phenomenal rate since the end of the hostilities. Perhaps no other chapter in this bloodiest of all wars has received as much attention as the Holocaust. The Nazis' program for the "Final Solution of the Jewish Question" — this ideologically conceived, diabolical plan for the physical liquidation of European Jewry — has emerged as a subject of agonizing and intense interest to laypersons and scholars alike. The centrality of the Holocaust in the study of the Third Reich and the Nazi phenomenon is almost universally recognized.

The source materials for many of the books published during the immediate postwar period were the notes and diaries kept by many camp and ghetto dwellers, who were sustained during their unbelievable ordeal by the unusual drive to bear witness. These were supplemented after the liberation by a large number of personal narratives collected from survivors all over Europe. Understandably, the books published shortly after the war ended were mainly martyrological and lachrymological, reflecting the trauma of the Holocaust at the personal, individual level. These were soon followed by a considerable number of books dealing with the moral and religious questions revolving around the role of the lay and spiritual leaders of the doomed Jewish communities, especially those involved in the Jewish Councils, as well as God's responsibility toward the "chosen people." The theological-metaphysical works were in the course of time complemented by empirical studies aimed at identifying and analyzing the causal relations between the various historical, political, socioeconomic, psychological, and cultural factors that were clearly discernible in this tragedy. Some of these studies focused primarily on the perpetrators — the Nazis and their accomplices — emphasizing their racial-ideological motivations, bureaucratic techniques, and efficient killing operations. Others concentrated on the victims, highlighting their helplessness, defenselessness, and suffering in the camps and ghettos, as well as their acts of heroism and resistance. Still others were devoted to the onlookers — the Allied and neutral powers, the Vatican, and the nongovernmental agencies, including the International Red Cross — documenting their essentially passive and indifferent attitudes toward the destruction of European Jewry. In recent years, there has appeared an encouraging number of synthetic studies, which focus on all three collective actors in this unparalleled historical drama. A few of these comprehensive studies cover the Holocaust in Europe as a whole; the others (the majority) are devoted to individual countries or communities.

Practically all the major works on the destruction of European Jewry appeared in the Western world, especially the United States and Israel, which have by far the most prestigious centers for Holocaust studies. However, it is also in the West that a new "revisionist" school of history came into being. Its representatives, consisting primarily of rabidly anti-Semitic pseudo-historians and academic charlatans both here and in Western Europe, are associated with a network of "institutes" that are generously financed by well-endowed extreme Rightist and neo-Nazi organizations. Their primary objective is to "prove" that the Holocaust was a "myth," a "hoax" invented by the Jews and their allies for reasons of their own.

Another and potentially more dangerous challenge to historical truth is evident in many of the Islamic and Soviet-bloc nations. The institutionalized challenge from the pro-Soviet Left is particularly ominous. In the USSR and most of the Soviet-bloc nations, the Jewish component of the Holocaust is largely ignored or at best distorted. The large number of books and articles published in these countries about the Nazi era and World War II simply ignore the "Final Solution" theme (in the sense that there is minimal if any acknowledgment that Jewry was singled out for total extermination) and tend to consolidate the staggering losses in Jewish lives into the overall losses of the particular nations. This attitude of the pro-Soviet Left toward the Holocaust is a logical extension of the campaign that was launched in 1948 against cosmopolitanism and Zionism (read Jews), which culminated in the 1970s in the identification of Zionism with racism.

The dangers inherent in these developments and the need to counteract them by scholarly means were recognized by many institutions of higher learning, including the Graduate School and University Center of The City University of New York. It was partially in pursuit of this objective that President Harold M. Proshansky persuaded Jack P. Eisner, the founder and president of the Holocaust Survivors Memorial Foundation, to help bring about the establishment of the Institute for Holocaust Studies that bears his name. The Institute began operations in 1979 with a variety of research, teaching, and lecture programs. This book — the first in a series of studies on the Holocaust — is an outgrowth of the regular and special lectures given under the auspices of the Institute.

Reflecting the expertise, interests, and approach of the individual lecturers, some of the eleven studies in the book are scholarly in the traditional sense, while others are more popular or personal in nature. The book is divided into two parts. Part I, "Philosophical and Psychological Perspectives," consists of five chapters. The first of these is by Alan Rosenberg of Queens College and deals with the philosophical implications of the Holocaust. The next two studies deal with psychological problems: Leslie Berger of Queens College presents a succinct overview of psychological perspectives on the Holocaust, probing whether mass murder is indeed part of human behavior, and Stanley L. Rustin of Queensborough Community College documents the "survivor syndrome," focusing on the post-Holocaust generations. The remaining chapters in Part I deal with Christian responses to the Holocaust. Franklin H. Littell of Temple University presents a broad historical overview of Christian anti-Semitism, tracing its responsibility for the climate that made the Holocaust possible. Ruth Zerner of Herbert H. Lehman College focuses on German Protestant responses to the Nazi persecution of the Jews, emphasizing the positive role of a number of clergymen and especially of the Lutheran pastor-scholar, Dietrich Bonhoeffer.

Part II, "From Within: A Variety of Responses," leads off with a piece by Yitshaq Ben-Ami, one of the Jewish *dramatis personae* of the Holocaust era, in which he presents his evaluation of the role of the *Irgun* in the struggle for the rescue of European Jewry and contrasts it with the alleged passivity of the "establishment" Jewish leaders of the free world. The second study, by Jonathan I. Helfand of Brooklyn College, presents an interesting historical perspective on Jewish law (*halakha*) and the Holocaust. Helfand's analysis is based on the response by rabbis to hundreds of *halakha*-related questions concerning the implications and consequences of the Holocaust that were raised during and immediately after the war. The next three chapters are devoted to literature. Ellen S. Fine of Kingsborough Community College presents a succinct yet comprehensive overview and analysis of the memoiristic literature of the Holocaust. Frieda W. Aaron of Brooklyn College contributes a study on poetry in the Holocaust dominion, dealing, among other things, with the role of the poet in the landscape of death and the constriction of language and image when faced with Holocaust themes. Rosette C. Lamont of Hunter College presents a fascinating glimpse of Holocaust imagery in contemporary French literature, focusing on the writings of Léon Blum, Charlotte Delbot, Jorge Semprun, and Elie Wiesel. The last chapter in the book is by Jack P. Eisner, who reviews the Holocaust experience through the perspective of a survivor. While more personal in tone than the other papers, this presentation raises a number of fundamental issues relating to the Holocaust and provides many valuable insights.

Acknowledgments

The publication of this book would not have been possible without the generous support and collaboration of many people. I would like to thank, first of all, the contributors who agreed to share their wisdom and expertise by participating in the lecture series as well as by submitting their studies for publication. I am also grateful to the leadership of the Graduate School and University Center, and above all to President Proshansky and Dean Solomon Goldstein, for their consistent support of the Institute and its endeavors. Finally, I would like to acknowledge the generous support received from the Holocaust Survivors Memorial Foundation for making the publication of this volume possible.

PHILOSOPHICAL AND PSYCHOLOGICAL PERSPECTIVES

1 THE PHILOSOPHICAL IMPLICATIONS OF THE HOLOCAUST

Alan Rosenberg

There are issues in the conduct of human affairs in their production of good and evil which, at a given time and place, are so central, so strategic in position, that their urgency deserves, with respect to practice, the names ultimate and comprehensive. These issues demand the most systematic reflective attention that can be given. It is relatively unimportant whether this attention be called philosophy or by some other name. It is of immense human importance that it be given, and that it be given by means of the best tested resources that inquiry has at command.

— John Dewey

The literature on the significance of the Holocaust contains a number of enigmas and paradoxes. We are told that we must understand the Holocaust so that it will not happen again, but we are also told that it is a unique event beyond comprehension. We are told that the event is a historical aberration, and yet we are asked that it be taught as part of history. We are often reminded by survivors that the only true response to the event should be silence; yet this point is made with thousands of words. We are told that the horrors and violence of the Holocaust have rendered language inadequate; yet the same language is used in many attempts to convey the significance of the event.

The author wishes to express special thanks to Alexander Bardosh for assistance in the preparation of this paper, and to Professor Ralph Sleeper for his invaluable comments and suggestions.

Such paradoxes as these are typical of the way the Holocaust has been discussed. They are all interesting and raise important questions, but one is especially important to philosophy. Indeed, it is a central problem for any philosophy of history or culture attempting to shed light on the meaning of the Holocaust. This paradox arises from the frequent warning that the Holocaust cannot be given meaning; that is, any attempt to attribute meaning to it is futile.[1] And yet we are also told that the Holocaust is a transformational event of epochal significance for Western culture. Just how any event that cannot have meaning can also be understood as having a transformational impact on history remains unclear.

For instance, historian Henry Feingold writes that "the Holocaust is a central event for our time in history . . . because what died at Auschwitz was the promise and hope embodied in Western civilization."[2] In a similar vein, Emile Fackenheim, the philosopher and theologian, states that "the Holocaust is not only a unique event; it is epoch making. The world . . . like the Jewish world . . . can never be the same."[3] And literary critic Alvin Rosenfeld, together with Rabbi Irving Greenberg, writes that "the Holocaust . . . like other singular and transforming events . . . has changed our way of being in the world and looking at it."[4] Finally, the novelist and lecturer Elie Wiesel makes the point with macabre drama: "At Auschwitz," he claims, "not only man died but also the idea of man."[5] Such thoughts are represented in the literature, thus creating the paradox of whether the Holocaust is an event that meaning can be associated to or whether it is meaningless.

Clearly, these writers claim that the Holocaust has somehow transformed Western civilization and culture in some extremely fundamental way. Each claims that the epochal event in question brings an end to a historical era and asserts that it has altered the very idea of the nature of man. These are dramatic claims. But are they substantiated? Disappointingly, the answer must be that they are not. We are not told how our lives have been affected and changed, owing to the Holocaust, by the "transformation" in the culture. We are not provided with evidence to convince us that this great change has indeed taken place. Why not? Perhaps we are unconvinced because, on the one hand, they are telling us that the Holocaust has transformed the meaning of history, while on the other hand they are telling us that the Holocaust is a meaningless and unique aberration of history. But, we may ask, isn't it precisely the transformational quality of the event itself that is meaningful? Perhaps this confusion is what prevents these writers from spelling out the basis of their claims?

On the contrary, it appears that these writers simply take it for granted that the Holocaust is a transformational event of enormous significance. This is quite remarkable, for seldom, if ever, has another historical event of magnitude been perceived and described in this manner; not even World War II itself has been considered and discussed in this way. Yet, despite the emphatic but unclarified manner in which the claim of transformation is made, there exists something peculiarly demanding of our hearts and minds about it: The "shattering effect" of the annihilation of about 11 million people, of whom more than half were Jews,[6] does not appear to have appreciably affected the behavior and thinking of people in our time and our world so as to demonstrate signs of genuine change.

If we accept the message in these statements, that the Holocaust is a transformational event, then we must conclude that the Holocaust has somehow transformed the world we live in without having transformed us as people. This astounding, paradoxical point is driven home by Elie Wiesel's statement in *One Generation After,* that to the disappointment of survivors, "nothing has been learned: Auschwitz has not served as a warning. For more detailed information, consult your daily newspapers."[7] Wiesel's remark raises an important question: Is it possible that — in a manner not sufficiently understood — the Holocaust has transformed the *objective* conditions of our world in some fundamental ways, without having a profound impact on the *subjective* consciousness of people. To put it differently, is it possible that the Holocaust has transformed the hopes and dreams of Western civilization without having had a profound impact on the conscience or the moral world of people?

Implicit in this theory is the question, If the Holocaust is as significant as it is claimed to be, then why hasn't it been absorbed into our consciousness? As Emil Fackenheim has stated, "only when [the events] are assimilated by the historical consciousness of succeeding generations are they capable of transforming the future and thus become historical in the deeper sense."[8] If the Holocaust is assumed to be as transformational as these claimants state, then we must confront it and try to make sense out of it.

There are, of course, some obstacles in accomplishing this task. One such obstacle may be the problem of time. After all, the Holocaust is only about 40 years past, and on the scale of history that is a relatively short time. More than a few decades are necessary before the impact of a transformational event becomes absorbed into the cultural patterns of a civilization. Such an assimilation may be even more difficult and complicated if the event is, like the Holocaust, unprecedented in many of its features.

Nonetheless, this excuse is not satisfactory. Though 40 years may not be enough for *all* the transformational implications of the Holocaust to have penetrated our awareness, it is surely enough time for at least *some* of it to have been absorbed into our commonsense knowledge. By now we should recognize some apparent signs of its transformational significance in the lives of people, and in the behavior of their leaders, if the claims are true. Fackenheim expresses this expectation in this manner:

> The passage of time has brought [the Holocaust] closer rather than moving it farther away, disclosing that the world has thus far shied away from it but must at length confront it with unyielding realism and, if necessary, despair.[9]

Conversely, passage of time has a negative effect. It can be argued that the increased passage of time following the event hinders, rather than assists, the assimilation and understanding of the event. In time memory dims, except for those of the survivors themselves; the shock of the event loses its impact as the details of the event blur and disappear in the flux of other events, thus losing its distinct identity. The world, though in reality it may never be the same again, resumes its mundane continuity. The passage of time, furthermore, assists in the corruption and misuse of the language by which we identify and signify historic events, through overuse and indifferent application. We have seen, accordingly, an increased debasement of the word "holocaust" through various misapplications of its use. The exact historical meaning of the word, and the event which it signifies, thus lose their centrality. Yet, neither the passage of time with its corrosive effects, nor the inadequacy of it to assimilate the total impact of the transformation the Holocaust has wrought, should prevent us from seeking an understanding of it.

Perhaps the way in which the transformational aspects of the Holocaust are presented to us contributes to our failure to absorb its impact into our subjective consciousness. One such prevalent and popular mode of presentation is the treatment of the Holocaust as a horror story. Certainly, such treatment is understandable in light of the fact that the nature of the Holocaust is filled with horror. However, the problem with such presentations lies in their inability to proceed beyond the horror as such and to offer meaningful insights about the event. This sort of treatment limits itself largely to recounting the atrocities and brutalities, without attempting to extract significance beyond the plight of victims. This kind of portrayal prevents our thinking about the significance of the event since the enormity of the horror itself overwhelms us. The piling up of the details of horror, which assault and numb our emotions, eventually prohibits the event from becoming a part of our moral and intellectual worlds. These results are unintended, but they nevertheless impair our perception of the event and stunt our understanding. Alice and Roy Eckardt stated the case well in their "Studying the Holocaust's Impact":

> There is the danger that the Holocaust will be appropriated only as a nightmare, a horrible episode that erupted within a brief span of years as part of a special ideological development or political tragedy or whim of an insane man, a nightmare from which we have long awakened. There is the temptation to reduce [the Holocaust] to an aberration, a kind of cultural-moral mutation. In consequence, a needed comprehension of the event as the logical and even inevitable climax of a lengthy and indestructible ethos-tradition and theological obssession may be lost.[10]

To enable us to make an event a part of our world, some kind of conceptual framework is required to allow us to feel the event as part of something that has a "logic" to it, no matter how perverse that logic may be. Obviously the integration of the facts of the Holocaust into our lives, or into the context of our daily existence, both as Jews or Gentiles, would have to be difficult and intellectually and psychologically painful. But still, if we are to understand what has happened and why, and what it tells us about our culture and civilization, as well as what it tells us about ourselves as human beings — we would have to construct a logical context for it so that we might apprehend its meaning.

> Our cultures help give us ways of thinking about and dealing with the tragic death of a child or even our own incapacitation or untimely impending death. But no cultural framework provides a way to encompass genocide.[11]

Such an understanding is not easy to acquire. Understanding involves a rigorous effort to identify not only the causes and effects and the conditions, analogies, and disanalogies of an event, but also the meaning and significance of the event. Just a knowledge of the pertinent facts are not enough: One must also have a conceptual structure in order to make the facts meaningful. The dismaying fact is that, with the exception of Hannah Arendt, postwar philosophers generally seem to have failed to examine the Holocaust with an eye to seeing what implications this event might have. Even a number of major thinkers who were among the witnesses of those shattering events failed to, or preferred not to, investigate and consider what had taken place.

Were they afraid to confront the problem, or were they fearful of possible forthcoming answers? The names of those major thinkers who have failed to study systematically the implications of the genocides of World War II constitute a pantheon of contemporary twentieth century philosophers: Sartre, Heidegger, Camus, Jaspers, Adorno, Buber, and many others.[12] Martin Buber is a particularly glaring example since nowhere in the body of his works do we find a systematic investigation of the meaning of the Holocaust, even though Buber was a Jew who also was a witness to a major part of its historical unfolding.[13]

Why the problem has been avoided so consistently by philosophers is unclear, especially when we consider that their discipline has always been concerned primarily with the analysis of events that have presented society with major crises in its value structure. Saul Friedländer, in his stimulating essay "Some Aspects of the Historical Significance of the Holocaust," states the problem:

> Three decades have increased our knowledge of the events as such, but not our understanding of them. There is no clearer perspective today, no deeper comprehension than immediately after the War. Indeed we know that any attempt to assess the historical significance of the Holocaust means trying to explain in a rational context events which cannot be encompassed in rational categories alone or described solely in the usual style of historical analysis.[14]

Another claim might be made that philosophers' reluctance to undertake a systematic and thorough analysis of the problems of the Holocaust is based on their belief that such a study will add nothing substantial to its collective meaning. The horror of those events stands by itself, it might be said, transformed by its magnitude to the level of a metaphysical universal with a substance and meaning all its own.[15]

Perhaps the silence of the philosophers is the manifestation of a critical epistemological impasse; as the Holocaust contained elements in its makeup that were without precedent, philosophers may be lacking the necessary analogies to help put the matter into perspective, out of which could evolve categories of meaning and thus understanding. Philosophers might have failed to conceptualize what appears as unknown to them for the reasons that John Hermann Randall, Jr., suggested as being the process of philosophy:

> Men can work only upon what they have inherited. Fresh experience and novel problems they must understand with the instruments they have learned from those who came before them. New ideas they must grasp in the concepts they already know, for they have no others; new habits they must work slowly into the accustomed pattern of their lives.[16]

After all, philosophers are confronted with the same problem that the rest of us encounter while contemplating the Holocaust. As Robert Jay Lifton writes in *Living and Dying,* "The mind cannot take in or absorb those experiences that cannot be meaningfully symbolized and inwardly re-created."[17] In other words, another possible reason why contemporary philosophers have failed to respond to the questions raised by the Holocaust is because, like most humans, they have not been able to assimilate aspects of the event into their categories.

Nevertheless, the problem posed by Friedländer is not insurmountable. We must keep in mind that the primary task of philosophy always has been concerned with the analysis of events and phenomena — especially those with transformational implications — that present society with questions of meaning. The aim of philosophy is to make sense, that is, to understand. John Dewey made the following observation on the nature of philosophy:

> The life of all thought is to effect a junction at some point of the new and the old, of deep-sunk customs and unconscious disposition, that are brought to the light of attention by some conflict with newly emerging directions of activity. Philosophies which emerge at distinctive periods define the larger patterns of continuity which are woven in effecting the enduring junctions of a stubborn past and an insistent future.[18]

Indeed, unless we undertake a systematic philosophical effort and analyze what took place with regard to the Holocaust, we will never be able to comprehend the essential meaning of one of the most important events in all history, and we will fail to learn what it says about human conduct and thought, both within the context of its period and for all time to come. Yehuda Bauer has stated the matter succinctly: "The crucial problem is how to anchor the Holocaust in the historical consciousness of the generation(s) that follow it."[19]

In *Philosophy and Civilization* Dewey explains that one of the major tasks of philosophy is to understand the meaning of historic events and to define their significance for the present and the future of our civilization. For Dewey the truth or falsity of the account of an event is not the sole or even most important element in the formulation of meaning. What is truth or what is not merely offers but one kind of meaning; certainly especially with regard to a philosophy of culture, and even more specifically a philosophy of culture concerned about the meaning of transformational events, the establishment of this level of meaning is not the most crucial task that philosophy could set for itself. Dewey is not suggesting that the truth or falsity of an event or a fact is not important, but rather important only with regard to telling us that something has occurred, or that something *is*. Once this elementary level of meaning is reached, the hard task of seeking the significance of an event begins. As Dewey has stated:

> Beyond this island of meanings, which in their own nature are true or false, lies the ocean of meanings to which truth and falsity are irrelevant . . . In philosophy we are dealing with something comparable to the meaning of Athenian civilization or of a drama or a lyric. Significant history is lived in the imagination of man, and philosophy is a further excursion of the imagination into its prior achievements.[20]

In other words, when philosophy confronts the question of meaning in relation to something, it is engaged in an imaginative and meditative act. It is not immediately concerned with the scientific accuracy of the claim of verifiability concerning something but with its significance. So, when we consider the Holocaust we are not probing into what happened in factual terms. The fact of the event stands before us as recorded in live history. It cannot be denied. But we are concerned with the significance of it, by what it tells us about ourselves, about our culture and civilization, and about the possibilities in our future. We look for meaning by interpreting aspects of the event, by postulating plausible ideas from the context of its records. Thus, we proceed by at first stating that one of the meanings of the event, one of its significant aspects, is that it is transformational. To put it differently, Dewey indicates that the proper function of philosophy is to signify or mark precisely those changes in civilization that are purported to be transformational.

Once we have identified the transformational aspects of an event — which, of course, become parts of the overall meaning of the event — it then becomes imperative for philosophy to indicate how those transformational aspects demand new responses from our culture; that is, if the event is transformational, it should force us to reevaluate the taken-for-granted assumptions that dominate both the way we think and act in the world. Once again, to quote Dewey, "philosophy marks a change of culture. In forming patterns to be conformed to in the future thought and action, it is additive and transforming in its role in the history of civilization."[21]

The context of Dewey's prescription for the proper function of philosophy, therefore, is precisely what philosophy ought to be doing in confronting the meaning of the transformational aspects of the Holocaust. It can do so in the following manner: First, depending on the insights of a variety of other disciplines in addition to that of its own, philosophy can help in the development of a theoretical structure for understanding the event. This kind of a structure will be a conjoining of the new and the old, placing the event within the perspective of a historical process, and a search for interpretive meanings. Such meanings will, and should, incorporate or involve all categories of meaning appropriate to the event, ranging from political and artistic to economic and scientific and from subjective to objective.

Second, philosophy in the course of fulfilling this stated role can provide an analysis of the key concepts used to articulate the event and can indicate by either their novelty, or by the context in which they are used, the transformational impact that the event has had — such concepts and terms as the words "Holocaust" and "genocide." Even more traditional terms have acquired novel connotations in the face of the transformational impact of the Holocaust and with regard to the context of the event. Concepts like "uniqueness" and "resistance" seem to possess connotations that differ from their original meanings, or from their historic references, when applied to the Holocaust. The analysis of concepts and terms in this regard is important since the varied and undefined ways these terms are used and interpreted often cause confusion.[22] Hence, to understand the transformational meaning(s) of the Holocaust, we must clarify the meanings of these key terms and evolve a vocabulary that is applicable and comprehensible.

Third, and this is the most important task of philosophy in trying to understand the specific transformational nature of the Holocaust, it can examine the event in relation to the established value structures and categories of our civilization. In this way, it can provide a ground map of criticism in light of the Holocaust for probing into our long-standing moral traditions and ethical values that have formed the definitions of our culture. Thus, in following the percepts set by Dewey and along the lines suggested here, philosophy may help us understand in what manner the Holocaust can be considered as an unprecedented transformational event. When looked at as an event that has actually transformed Western civilization, the Holocaust presents Western culture with certain implications. While the intention of this paper is not to identify and diagnose all or many aspects of this civilization that have been transformed by the impact of the Holocaust, some preliminary suggestions may be offered. These aspects seem to be plausible when the event is regarded from a philosophical perspective, especially in the context of a philosophy of culture.

To begin with, we must have a plausible definition of what is meant when an event is called transformational; the definition offered here is both tentative and exploratory in nature. Nevertheless, an event like the Holocaust can indeed be said to be transformational in its import when it has managed to change both the objective conditions and the categories by which the world we live in are understood, so that the context in which we exist is no longer the same as the context of lives lived prior to its occurrence, *and* when it has therefore altered our subjective perceptions of the world around us — or as it *should have* altered them. In other words, the impact of the event has been so great as to shatter or impair the categories and assumptions by which people understand their world and negotiate their ways in it. Now, if the Holocaust is a transformational event as I believe it is, then it must have done something to destroy or shatter some of the most cherished assumptions of our culture.[23]

It is plausible to claim that the Holocaust has helped to shatter, if not destroy, the dominant motivating force in Western civilization, a force that has been in effect since the Enlightenment. What it directly challenged is the cultural belief that science and technology, grounded in functional reason, would inevitably lead to progress. One could call these notions and the belief in ideas of progress that they would give rise to the major paradigm of modernity. Ever since the Enlightenment these notions have been taken, consciously or unconsciously, as defining the essential character of Western civilization.

These views are so deeply rooted in our culture and so central for our own personal belief structure that they are almost not open to the possibility of criticism. For instance, speaking of technology in general, Charles Drekmeier makes the following observation:

> Technology has invaded our lives to a degree that makes it extremely difficult for us to view it critically. Our basic values have been shaped by a conception of progress rooted deeply in technological development, but in obscuring the very idea of humanity, technology has rendered ambiguous that tradition of enlightened values from which the concept of progress emerged.[24]

This is probably why the transformational aspects of the Holocaust with regard to what they have done to this paradigm have not penetrated our historical consciousness and conscience. This failure is due in part to the continuing spell that the promises of science and technology still hold over our imagination. As Henryk Skolimowski has astutely observed in a recent essay, the spell of science and technology "has become an overriding principle with the force of a moral imperative expressed in one commandment: One must not be against progress."[25] The threat that the Holocaust poses to this paradigm is monumental in scope.

My intention is not to debunk the myth of progress or, as it has become fashionable in some quarters to do, to minimize the role it has played in the betterment of the human lot over the past couple of centuries. My purpose, rather, is to show the relationship of science and technology to the actualization of the

Holocaust so that we can explore the ramifications of this event on the modern paradigm.

Most people continue to believe in progress in a positive sense because they have failed to integrate transformational implications of the Holocaust. However, to sustain a belief in the idea of progress as an inevitability is difficult when we recognize that the Holocaust was made possible largely by both science and technology. I agree with George Iggers when he states that "the Final Solution, which in a sense symbolized the high point of the application of modern science and technology in the service of inhumanity, appears to spell the total absurdity of progress."[26] Irving Greenberg echoes a similar sentiment: "No assessment of modern culture can ignore the fact that science and technology — the accepted flower and glory of modernity — . . . climaxed in the factories of death."[27]

Facts are indisputable: Technology and modern science gave us the tools that in the twentieth century made mass destruction possible. The prominent symbol of the idea of progress for humanity in the Enlightenment, the smokestack, became the symbol of Auschwitz. The facilities of modern science and technology helped to generate vast bureaucratic procedures that made the processing of millions for extermination into a relatively orderly routine. Thus, instead of aiding humanity in its quest for perfection, science and technology taught it newer and easier means of murder and destruction of large numbers of people; in the twentieth century the art of murder has become the science of murder. Killing was made another means of mass production; processing or recycling bodies of the dead was another form of industrial output. As Richard Rubenstein has written in *The Cunning of History,* "Bureaucratic mass murder reached its fullest development when gas chambers with the capacity for killing two thousand people at a time were installed at Auschwitz."[28]

Along with the methods of mass killing, science also legitimized the ideological basis, or the motivating cause, for mass murder. The Jews, along with Gypsies, Slavs, and millions of others, were "scientifically" decreed as inferior races or designated as "subhuman." The fact that these claims were advanced and even believed in the name of science, and were expounded by scientific authorities, lent a high degree of credence to popular prejudices and made the acceptance of the idea of mass extermination so much easier for a large number of people. After all, under these "scientific" claims, what was taking place was not killing for killing's sake. Rather, it was a deliberate "scientific" undertaking to correct the errors of the past by removal of the causes of these errors, and to improve the best in the racial stock of a nation so that it would become better and stronger in the future. It was a "progressive" effort toward the attainment of the holiest of the Enlightenment ideals: perfection. In recognition of this factor Hannah Arendt has written that "there is very little to doubt that the perpetrators [of the Holocaust] committed [these crimes] for the sake of their ideology which they believed to be proven by science, experience and the laws of life."[29]

Since these unforeseen implications of modern science and technology have not yet been assimilated into our consciousness and its lessons have not been absorbed into our conscience, I am extremely fearful that today, with even more complex and accessible technological means at our disposal, we can evolve even more sophisticated methods of mass destruction than the Nazis could ever have imagined. For instance, we have in our hands the computer, with its infinite possibilities. One day it may not take anything more violent than the observation of certain crossed signals glimpsed on a computer board for us, even unknowingly, to get caught in another process of mass destruction. The presence of technology, the capabilities of the computer, can easily translate false perceptions or rash emotions into drastic actions, and we can rest smugly afterward — that is, if we survive the new holocaust — with the satisfaction that comes from feeling that our superior science and technology have justified our faiths in them by ridding the world of our enemy. In his essay "The Scientific World View and the Illusions of Progress," Henryk Skolimowski has written: "One of the most important among the causes that prompted us to develop science and technology, as we see them today, was the ideal of the earthly paradise, of the fulfillment of man here on earth instead of there — in some transcendental heaven."[30] Unfortunately, the Holocaust has demonstrated, beyond a shadow of a doubt, that such a conception of progress can lead to hell on earth instead of earthly paradise. This, I believe, is one of the transformational implications of the event.

In *The Holocaust and the Crisis of Human Behavior,* while George Kren and Leon Rappoport strongly implicate science and technology as culpable agents in the formation of the Holocaust, the stress is properly directed at the mode of mentality that underlies it:

> The science and technology which had been increasingly celebrated for almost a century as the bastion of Western rationality and had become synonymous with liberal-progressive thought turned out to be a major factor contributing to the feasibility of the Holocaust . . . In a number of ways, the evidence surrounding the Holocaust suggests emphatically that from its . . . origins . . . to its final large-scale industrial actualization in Auschwitz, the scientific mode of thought and the methodology attached to it were intrinsic to the mass killings.[31]

Although the position of Kren and Rappoport may be too sweeping, their statement forces us to the realization that we must reassess not only science and technology in light of the Holocaust but the very mode of thought on which they are based. This point cannot be stressed enough since this mode of thought still tends to dominate our thinking — our faith in science and technology as paths to utopia remains largely unshaken despite the fact that is has been challenged with increasing frequency and cogency ever since World War II.

This form of mentality has been variously described and labeled as pragmatic reason, scientific reason, or instrumental reason. The last, attributable to the critical mode of thought analyzed by the philosophers and sociologists of the Frankfurt school, is well known. However, since the use of this term by the Frankfurt school has other connotations and implications, I have chosen to employ a more neutral term, "functional reason," which will be sufficient to identify the kind of mentality referred to by Kren and Rapporport.

Functional reason is distinguished by a number of characteristics. The first thing to notice about it is that it separates the emotional from the intellectual. Next, it is amoral and concerned with means, not ends. It claims to be value-free and outside of moral considerations. It is "task-oriented;" that is, it is concerned with techniques and not with substance. It is preoccupied with projecting an image of efficiency; it must be cost-effective. To achieve its ends and to fulfill its own image it must reduce human beings to quantified objects, thus eliminating their troublesome qualities of humaneness, which interferes with the neat, surgical precision that this mode of reason tries to achieve in its results. Functional reason must treat people as objects, as things, as mere numbers that can be easily manipulated and casually disposed of if the occasion should arise. As Lionel Rubinoff has commented, functional reason must dispense with ethics, for ethical considerations merely stand in the way of efficiency.[32]

Functional reason has allowed individuals to manipulate fellow human beings as things until they were done away with when no longer perceived as useful or needed. The task at hand, the duty to be performed, becomes the only category for approval and merit. Inevitably, functional reason leads to the bureaucratization of problems. It considers all problems as solvable, provided that they can be pegged to the right bureaucratic order, or technical mechanism, or category.

In the Holocaust the bureaucrats, utilizing functional reason, discovered a technical solution to the "Jewish problem." What must be reckoned with here is that in the Holocaust a mode of reasoning that became dominant during the Enlightenment, as a means of solving practical problems that stood in the way of human perfection, had become the means of eliminating masses of human beings.

Furthermore, the use of functional reason has led to the gradual bureaucratization of problems. According to this mode of thinking, all problems can be resolved, provided that the right technique can be found. For a large number of German bureaucrats the Jewish question was merely a problem of finding the correct Final Solution. Undoubtedly, without the utilization of functional reason in the technology of death and bureaucracy, the Holocaust would not have been possible. It is this scientific-technical–bureaucratic dimension engendered by functional reason that distinguishes the Holocaust from the pogroms of the past.

The mentality that extolled functional reason and ultimately reduced science and technology, and consequently the once noble ideal of progress, into means of mass death also gave birth to a new kind of killer, the desk-killer. For the first time in history those responsible for the killing of millions never saw the consequence of their acts, or even the faces of their victims, for they were removed from the implementation of the actual deed by the bureaucratic refinements that science and technology, plus the machinations of functional reason, had procured for them. The "desk-killer" is an executive type, a functionary in a vast bureaucratic organization, who kills from behind a desk without wielding any weapons more lethal than a typewriter that issues reports dealing out death, signed and processed along deliberately anonymous channels or through a labyrinth of bureaucratic routines and apparatus. The desk-killer operates from within a network of other faceless functionaries radiating in every direction and in which the sense of responsibility could be passed along from faceless bureaucrat to faceless bureaucrat with the greatest of ease, as if it is nothing but an item passed along a conveyer belt on a mass-production line. For the desk-killer the act of killing is only a method of problem solving, of pegging the right solution to the right ideological or political niche. Desk-killers have mastered the art of functional reason so much — or it has mastered them so well — that the killing of millions of people is, for them an act totally devoid of any moral responsibility; it is merely a matter of correct logistics, of carrying out an order given by higher authorities in the name of the state; the people being killed are just disposable objects. As Rubinoff stated:

> The Final Solution was a carefully planned, bureaucratically organized application of means to ends. It was, in fact, a prime example of what Max Weber and Karl Mannheim have called "functional rationality."[33]

Furthermore, the bureaucratization of the mechanics of mass murder allowed desk-killers to retain their status or role in society as normal persons; in their job category as merely a functionary carrying out orders and doing their work diligently; and outside of it as ordinary citizens with families, a respectable and unpretentious member of the community. Functional reason was thus able to effect a fundamental split between the public persona and the private person, public service and private lives. This split has profound implications for our culture. Eichmann, of course, is the archetypical representative of "desk-killers." So was Himmler. Indeed, nearly all the Nazi hierarchy can be classified as desk-killers.

What makes the notion of the desk-killer even more extraordinary, however, is that many ordinary people also served and participated in the processes of mass murder as desk-killers in various capacities among the lower echelons. Indeed their involvement was necessary for the fulfillment of the Final Solution envisaged by the Nazi leaders. Without them, the Final Solution would never have been transposed from theory into praxis.

What distinguishes desk-killers from other ordinary murderers is the degree of efficiency that their mode of killing has achieved through the refinements of bureaucracy and the organizational skills thus mastered in the service of functional reason. As Rubenstein has noted:

> As we know, the twentieth century has witnessed extraordinary ''progress' in the unlimited intensification of human destructiveness and the radicalization of the forms of human domination. Nevertheless, it was the organizational skills of the Nazis rather than their new weapons that made the society of total domination a reality.[34]

The society of total domination, in which problems could be resolved by recourse to functional reason and ideology, was a first step toward the society of total death represented by Auschwitz. By referring each action to the prerequisites of an ideology, desk-killers can place a convenient distance between this conscience and the consequences of their acts, in a way similar to how they distance themselves from the actual killings through bureaucracy.

Perhaps because it is hard to think of reason and its manifestations under any form as something possibly less than a positive force, we have not as yet come to terms with the presence of the desk-killer as an important element in the modern world. In *Angel in Armor,* Ernst Becker states this problem thus:

> We simply cannot allow ourselves to believe in and to live with disinterested bureaucratic evil. . . . It is just too much to believe that simple bureaucratic decision, simple paperwork expediency, can abstractedly grind up six million lives.[35]

The phenomenon of the desk-killer, the corruption of rationality into ideological forms of functional reason as manifested by the Holocaust, indicates that the kind of underlying mentality presents us with a new, radical notion of evil. As Rubinoff has stated it, in the world of the Holocaust, ''men acquired the capacity for engaging in evil without experiencing it as such. They learned how to perform evil acts as part of their job description . . .''[36] To put it differently, in the wake of the Holocaust we can no longer entertain conventional notions on evil. The idea of evil is one of the things that the Holocaust has transformed, irrevocably. In the words of Hannah Arendt, it ''has brought into the world a *radical* evil characterized by its divorce from all humanly comprehensible motives of wickedness.''[37]

Prior to the Holocaust evil was generally perceived as a spiritual malignancy or failure in humanity stemming from ignorance, hate, envy, false pride, or from some kind of innate aggression. In its manifestations involving overt brutality, evil was usually regarded as the behavior of bullies. But such perceptions fail to explain the systematic, rational, technologically implemented destruction of millions in factorylike buildings and facilities. Whereas the pogroms of old could be explained away by reference to bully mentality, greed, prejudice, and the like, the bureaucratic-technological dimensions of the Holocaust cannot. As Rubenstein has observed, ''it was only when the bureaucrats took over from the bullies that mass murder became possible.''[38]

In other words, the Holocaust has created a new form of evil based upon the calculating ideological rationality of functional reason, practiced by ordinary men and women isolated from both the clamor of their conscience and the consequences of their deeds by barriers of desks and bureaucratic agencies, put into effect with the aid of science and technology, and in a perversion of the Enlightenment idea of progress. One of the challenges of the Holocaust's transformational impact on our cultural values and categories is the need for a new understanding and definition of evil that will incorporate all that has been mentioned above.

How, then, can we give succinct summary to the philosophical implications of these events? How can we say what the Holocaust means in terms of philosophy? What changes in our fundamental assumptions are required as we attempt to deal with the problem of meaning in history and culture? What are the messages of the Holocaust transmitted to us across the years, which we have yet to absorb into our consciousness? These questions have no easy answers, but, clearly, we must struggle to find them. For if we do not, our philosophy will remain groundless and sterile. By ignoring them our philosophy becomes irrelevant, and our efforts to capture the meaning of human life and culture in our time are but empty gestures, destined to become themselves but meaningless postures in the face of history.

If, as argued here, the Holocaust must be grasped as a genuinely transformational event, at least one conclusion is inescapable: We can no longer afford the assumption that science and technology offer an unambiguous path to human progress. The eighteenth century faith in the inevitability of cultural advance through the application of "scientific" reason to human problems lies in ruins. We must recognize that scientific methods may give implementation to evil intentions, that technical innovation may support with brilliant efficiency the worst designs of man's inhumanity to man. We must absorb the lesson of what happens when ends and means are separated, when subjectivity is obscured in favor of a mindless "objectivity." As philosophers we must never again assume that values and facts occupy separate and ontologically distinct categories. We must never again subscribe to the myth that science is "value free" and that the "mores" of a particular culture can provide an adequate moral justification for whatever practices that culture may engage in.

Yet, at the same time that we must be wary of "cultural relativism," we must be equally wary of the assumptions of "moral absolutism." For the ancient belief in the absolute and intrinsic worth of human beings that sustained the Enlightenment faith in reason has itself been challenged. We can no longer assume as beyond question that "man is measure" of all things and an "end-in-himself." Or, even, that "God's in his heaven and all's right with the world." For such "absolutes" crumble in the face of the facts of Auschwitz and Treblinka. Above all, perhaps, the Holocaust has clearly exposed the fallacy of ideology, its inevitable tendency toward a mindless moral absolutism of its own making. As philosophers we must remain skeptical of any and all ideological programs and, perhaps especially, of those that place science and technology at the disposal of their ideological aims. In the end we must remain even skeptical of the ideological implications in the idea of progress itself. For, as Roger Shinn has pointed out, "the faith in progress, sorely battered in this traumatic century, still holds its allure for mankind. This generation, which more than most has looked destruction in the face, has no shortage of reformers, manipulators, and utopians who are confident that they know the secret of progress."[39]

As ordinary men and women we still face the awful and awesome possibility that one day we shall be drawn into the vicious cycle of yet another genocidal holocaust. And if this happens, it will be in the name of some charismatic ideology of progress, just as ordinary men and women were drawn into a similar cycle only a few decades earlier. Unless, of course, we are able to absorb the truly transformational implications of the Holocaust into our consciousness and conscience — and to learn from what we have experienced.

Notes

1. The following quotations are offered as examples that indicate the extent of the dilemma:

> The [Holocaust] . . . resists explanation — the historical kind that seeks causes, and the theological kind that seeks meaning and purpose. [Emil Fackenheim, *The Jewish Return into History* (New York: Schocken Books, 1978), p. 279.]

> Though accustomed to search for meaning in human experience, as in literature, we must be content to find none [in the Holocaust]. [Lawrence Langer, "The Writer and the Holocaust Experience," in *Holocaust, Ideology, Bureaucracy, and Genocide,* ed. Henry Friedlander and Sybil Milton (New York: Krauss International, 1980), p. 321.]

> Although [historic crises like the Holocaust] involve events that can be described . . ., understood in terms of individual or group psychological process, and even placed in some plausible context of historical development, their larger meaning . . . remains . . . ambiguous . . . [and indeed] at the level of personal knowledge . . . their ultimate meaning appears unknowable. [George Kren and Leon Rapporport, *The Holocaust and the Crisis of Human Behavior* (New York and London: Holmes and Meier, 1980), p. 127.]

2. Henry Feingold, "Four Days in April: A Review of NBC's Dramitization of 'The Holocaust,'" *Shoah* Vol. 1, I, no. 1, p. 16.
3. Fackenheim, *The Jewish Return,* p. 279.
4. Alvin Rosenfeld and Irving Greenberg, *Confronting the Holocaust: The Impact of Elie Wiesel* (Bloomington: Indiana University Press, 1978), p. XI.
5. Elie Wiesel, *Legends of Our Time* (New York: Holt, Rinehart and Winston, 1968), p. 190.
6. Cf. Alan Rosenberg, "Genocidal Universe," *European Judaism* 13, no. 1 (Autumn 1979): 29–34. Reprinted in *Genocide and Human Rights,* ed. Jack Nusan Porter (Washington, D.C.: University Press of America, 1982), pp. 46–58.
7. Elie Wiesel, *One Generation After* (New York: Bard Books–Avon, 1970), p. 15.
8. Fackenheim, *The Jewish Return,* p. 210.
9. Ibid., pp. 106–07.
10. Alice and Roy Eckardt, "Studying the Holocaust's Impact Today: Some Dilemmas of Language and Method," *Judaism* 27, no. 2 (Spring 1978): 227.
11. Patricia Bender, Ethel Roskies, Richard Lazarus, "Stress and Coping Under Extreme

Conditions,'' in *Survivors, Victims, and Perpetrators,* ed. Joel Dimsdale (New York: Hemisphere Publishing, 1980), p. 253.

12. To be fair, most of these philosophers have, with the obvious exception of Heidegger, dealt with various aspects of what happened. However, none of them has taken the destruction as anything like a major theme or problem in their writings. Heidegger's complete silence with respect to the Holocaust may speak volumes.

13. In an essay titled ''Buber's Concept of Holocaust and History,'' David Glanz had this to say about Buber's silence: ''It is disturbing to observe how little Martin Buber, a man considered by some as the leading 'Jewish' philosopher of the twentieth century, himself an escapee from this modern *mabul,* this Noahidian flood, had to say about it. His inability to grapple with this problem has serious implications for his view of history and of evil . . . Even in his social and political works after the Nazis, Buber's thought flows on, unperturbed by the Holocaust.'' (*Forum* 30–31 (Spring–Summer 1978): 142.)

14. Saul Friedländer, ''Some Aspects of the Historical Significance of the Holocaust,'' *The Jerusalem Quarterly* 1 no. 1 (Fall 1976): 36.

15. Jacob Katz makes this point very explicit in his article, ''Was the Holocaust Predictable?''

> To Auschwitz and Treblinka there was no historical analogy, no philosophical or for that matter, theological framework in which they might be accommodated. This was an absolute *novum,* unassimilable in any vocabulary at the disposal of the generation that experienced it. And it remains so today, despite the tremendous effort to investigate all its aspects. . . . Given the radically transcendent nature of the Holocaust, what significance can there be to the mere historical recording of its events, let alone attempting to lay bare their roots in a more or less remote past? What enlightenment can be possible derived from tracing the history of anti-Semitism, or Jewish–Christian relations in past centuries, if indeed the Holocaust has to be conceived as an absolute *novum,* unparalled in previous generations? . . . What is the use of rehearsing these horrors in historical retrospect? Is it not a kind of masochism, a form of useless penitence for not having shared the fate of the victims? [*Commentary* 59, no. 5 (May 1975): 45]

This kind of an argument, if taken seriously, is an invitation for philosophers and others to continue to ignore the problem. George Steiner raises in part a similar point, but in a more sensible manner. In writing about the Holocaust he states:

> We are not — and this is often misunderstood — considering something truly analogous to the other cases of massacres, to the murder of the Gypsies or earlier, of the Armenians. There are parallels in technique and in the idiom of hatred. But not ontologically. But not on the level of philosophical intent. That intent takes us to the heart of certain instabilities in the fabric of Western cultures, in the relation between instinctual and religious life. [*Bluebeard's Castle* (New Haven: Yale University Press, 2nd printing, 1972), p. 36]

16. John Herman Randall, Jr., *The Career of Philosophy* (New York: Columbia University Press, 1962), p. 9.

17. Robert Jay Lifton, *Living and Dying* (New York: Praeger, 1974), pp. 32–33.

18. John Dewey, *Philosophy and Civilization* (New York: Capricorn Books, 1963), p. 7.

19. Yehuda Bauer, *The Holocaust in Historical Perspective* (Seattle: University of Washington Press, 1978), p. 45.

20. Dewey, *Philosophy and Civilization,* p. 5.

21. Ibid., p. 8.

22. For more detailed treatment of this topic of comprehensibility, see Alan Rosenberg, ''Philosophy and the Holocaust,'' *European Judaism* 14, no. 2 (Winter 1980–Spring 1981): 31–38.

23. On the question of transformational events, see Kren and Rapporport, *The Holocaust,* pp. 131–43; and Alan Rosenberg and Alexander Bardosh's critique of the same in *Modern Judaism* 1, no. 3 (December 1981): 337–46.

24. Charles Drekmeier, ''Knowledge as Virtue, Knowledge as Power,'' in *Sanctions for Evil*, ed. Nevitt Sanford and Craig Comstock and Associates (Boston: Beacon Press, 1971), p. 220.

25. Henryk Skolimowski, ''The Scientific World View and the Illusions of Progress,'' *Social Research* 41, no. 1 (Spring 1974): 53.

26. George Iggers, ''The Idea of Progress: A Critical Reassessment,'' *American Historical Review* 71, no. 1 (October 1965): 15.

27. Irving Greenberg, ''A Cloud of Smoke, Pillars of Fire,'' in *Auschwitz, Beginning of a New Era?* ed. Eva Fleischer (New York: Ktav, 1977), p. 15.

28. Richard Rubenstein, *The Cunning of History* (New York: Harper & Row, 1975), p. 25.

29. Hannah Arendt, ''Social Science Techniques and the Study of Concentration Camps,'' *Jewish Social Studies* 12, no. 1 (1950): 62.

30. Skolimowski, *The Scientific World View*, pp. 52–53.

31. Kren and Rapporport, *The Holocaust*, p. 133.

32. Lionel Rubinoff, ''Auschwitz and the Pathology of Jew-Hatred,'' in *Auschwitz, Beginning of a New Era?* ed. Eva Fleischer (New York: Ktav, 1977), p. 355.

33. Ibid.

34. Rubenstein, *Cunning of History*, p. 79.

35. Ernest Becker, *Angel in Armor* (New York: Free Press, Macmillan, 1975), p. 140.

36. Rubinoff, *Auschwitz*, p. 361.

37. Hannah Arendt, ''The History of the Great Crime: A review of Leon Poliakov's *Harvest of Hate*,'' *Commentary* 13, no. 3 (March 1952): 300–04.

38. Rubenstein, *The Cunning of History*, p. 27.

39. Roger Shinn, ''Perilous Progress in Genetics,'' *Social Research* 41, no. 1 (Spring 1974): 83.

2 A PSYCHOLOGICAL PERSPECTIVE OF THE HOLOCAUST: *Is Mass Murder Part of Human Behavior?*

Leslie Berger

In May 1945, Hitler's military machinery was crushed by the Allied forces and the Third Reich collapsed, bringing 12 years of brutalizing Nazi terror to an end. By then, however, some six million Jews — two-thirds of the Jews living in occupied Europe — and millions of non-Jews were already murdered. The liberated prisoners and the thousands of unburied corpses in the concentration camps presented a shocking sight. The horrifying reality — man's inhumanity toward his fellow man — could no longer be ignored or denied.

Close to 40 years have passed since the end of the Nazi Holocaust. Many of the adults of that period have already passed away; the children are already in their forties and fifties, and a new generation of post-Holocaust adults lives. For the Jews in German-occupied Europe, the Nazi Holocaust resulted in the destruction of their homes, their families, and their lives. Although Hitler did not succeed in murdering all the Jews, he did destroy Jewish life and Jewish culture in much of Europe. He came close to achieving his goal of making Europe *Judenfrei*.

Persecution of Jews, however, did not start with Hitler. Jews had had a long history of brutalization. The Nazis perfected only the methods of destruction by introducing industrial technology to mass murder — a first in human history. The technical resources of a "cultured" people were redirected for a long period, over four years, toward the destruction of an entire other people for nothing more than their racial identity. The Holocaust, unlike the murders of Jews in Eastern Europe, was a long-term systematic extermination with thousands of passionate and impassionate active participants and millions of passive observants and supporters.

A great deal had been said and written about the Holocaust since 1945, including "scholarly" statements denying that it had ever taken place. Among the survivors are those who insist that only those who were present could ever comprehend the meaning of the Holocaust; their strictly emotional response, while fully understandable, represents an extremely narrow perspective that helps no one. Still others refer to the Holocaust as mind boggling, beyond human understanding or incomprehensible. This writer, a psychologist by profession and a graduate of four concentration camps — Auschwitz, Mauthausen, Melk, and Ebensee — believes that the Holocaust and the behavior of its participants — victims and perpetrators — can be analyzed and must be understood.

At this point, it is important to emphasize explicitly that an understanding of human behavior is different and separate from justifying or forgiving it. There is no way to minimize a possible recurrence of the Holocaust, moreover, without a thorough understanding of all the elements and forces that contributed to that complex event. Understanding human behavior is in the domain of psychology. Assessing responsibilities and deciding on punishment is dependent on the philosophy and social and judicial values of the individual and society.

Let us begin our analysis with the most critical piece of the Holocaust puzzle. In all probability, a Jewish Holocaust would not have happened in Germany at that time without Hitler. The destruction of Jews for Hitler was a dominant passion, with malignant hatred of these people occupying the center of his world until the very hour of his death. He ended his last will and testament just hours before his suicide, in his Berlin bunker, as follows: "Above all I charge the leaders of the nation and those under them to scrupulous observance of the laws of race and to merciless opposition to the universal poisoner of all people, international Jewry."[1] This last act proved that Hitler's anti-Semitism was not a practical political ploy but a deep-seated pathological part of the man. A number of explanations are possible for Hitler's violent hatred of the Jews, but none can be proved definitively.

The most ironic of the explanations connects Hitler's hatred of Jews to his family background. Hitler's father was born a bastard in Victorian Austria. Maria Schicklgruber, Hitler's grandmother, gave birth to Alois — Hitler's father — out of wedlock. Hans Frank, governor general of German-occupied Poland, stated in writing while awaiting execution at Nuremberg as a war criminal that Hitler's half brother, Patrick, threatened to divulge their Jewish ancestry. Supposedly, Hitler asked Frank to investigate confidentially the charge. According to Frank he found evidence that Hitler's grandmother was impregnated by the 19-year-old son in the Jewish household she had been employed as a domestic. Investigation of local records after 1945, however, could not locate any Jews living in that area at that time.[2] Were the incriminating records destroyed? Was Frank's story a hoax? While we may never have a conclusive answer, Hitler's paternal grandfather remains unidentified. The man who had required Aryan verification for all Germans supposedly did not know who his grandfather was.

Another theory connected Hitler's anti-Semitism to events relating to his half-niece Geli Raubal, who had been his mistress and supposedly died by committing suicide — or perhaps she had been murdered by Hitler in a fit of rage over her infatuation with a Jewish artist. Following her death Hitler fell into a state of depression and started a kind of mourning cult — her room remained undisturbed as long as he lived in Munich, and he revisited it every Christmas. At the time of her death Hitler stopped eating meat, thus suggesting a severe psychological crisis possibly related to intolerable feelings of intense hatred.[3]

Still another explanation related Hitler's anti-Semitism to his mother's death from cancer while being treated by her Jewish physician. Hitler's love for his young mother and hate for his old father — he was 23 years older than his wife — assumed morbid proportions. According to Eric Erikson, it was this conflict that drove Hitler to love and hate and compelled him to save or destroy people who really were substitutes for his mother and father.[4]

This writer could continue with additional examples that may have contributed to Hitler's virulent anti-Semitism and mental imbalance — many articles and a number of books have been written on the subject. This paper is more concerned, however, with providing an approach for the study and understanding of the Holocaust than with proving any specific point.

Unfortunately, Hitler was something over and above his psychopathology. He had an unusual ability to compensate for and in fact exploit his mental illness. Consequently, instead of being recognized and treated as a mentally deranged individual, he had succeeded in transforming the realities of his environment around him in such a way that he had become the idealized norm. His greatest strength was his ability to understand the mood of the German masses at that time. As a charismatic leader he could hypnotically mesmerize his audiences and turn them into fanatically loyal followers. Consequently, in 1933, the man who in his late teens sank to the depths of the soup kitchens and the men's shelters in Vienna — he was an Austrian — was named by Hindenberg the chancellor of the Weimar Republic.

Hitler came into power through legal means, and when he swore "I will employ my strength for the welfare of the German people, protect the Constitution and laws of the German people, conscientiously discharge the duties imposed on me and conduct my affairs of office impartially and with justice to everyone,"[5] dressed in top hat and tails, he had succeeded in fooling not only the Germans but the whole world. The die was cast in 1933 when Hitler was placed in a position of power from which he could manipulate, control, and release the forces of destruction and thus create the necessary environment for mass murder.

Hitler's ability to consolidate his power was greatly facilitated by the psychological, social, political, and economic conditions of Germany. The 1920s and early 1930s were a period of desperate hopelessness. The loss of World War I and the Versailles Treaty that followed were not only experienced as a national shame but also resulted in complete economic collapse, unemployment, hunger, and political and social chaos. The Weimar Republic was a trial in democratic government that did not work, and the Nazis and Communists succeeded in sabotaging the system to the point where by 1932 the government was paralyzed and could rule only through its emergency powers. The police and the military were powerless in maintaining law and order, and Germany was in a state of collective anxiety; the paramilitary mobs of Nazis and Communists were battling on the streets and could no longer be contained.

The German people, wanting security, were ready and open to be exploited by any demagogue, and Hitler was a master of the craft. His explanations for the misfortunes of the people — blaming the Jews for most — were distorted lies, but his promises were simple and concrete solutions for their future. This was soothing music to their ears, for the hopeless masses did not want to hear about the complexities of human problems. They only wanted a "leader" who could bring them out of the tunnel and save them from their miseries. Hitler promised them a "national awakening" and an end to their "shameful past."

Once in office, Hitler and his entourage cleverly exploited and speedily expanded their legal base. Within days of his appointment as chancellor, Hitler convinced Hindenburg, who was failing physically and mentally, to utilize his presidential authority and sign a decree under Article 48 of the Weimar constitution, thereby invoking emergency powers to protect the state from overthrow. The decree provided for police detention, prohibition of public meetings, and suppression of publications that endangered public safety. And so the road was open for the establishment of absolute power and authority. The Nazis, "in defense of the state," brutally crushed any opposition by imprisoning and/or ruthlessly murdering potential opponents. The first inmates of the newly created concentration camps were primarily Aryan Germans.

When in March 1933 Hitler succeeded in having the Reichstag pass the Enabling Act, giving the government — Hitler — the power for four years to legislate even if it was in conflict with the Weimar Constitution, he had "legally" created a basis for the transformation of the democratic Weimar Republic into a totalitarian dictatorship that would soon provide absolute power for him as Führer of the Nazi Third Reich. So by July 1933 the government was able to declare the National Socialist Party the only political party in Germany. Any attempt by any other party to function or to form a new party was punishable by a minimum of three years imprisonment, unless it was covered by any other regulation imposing a higher punishment.

All these changes were brought about with little internal or international reaction. Thus by July 1933, or perhaps by February 1933, the point of no return was reached in Germany. From then on, effective internal opposition was no longer possible. The people in Germany surrendered en masse to the Nazi terror — with the exception of some two million potential opponents who had already been eliminated.

And thus a "new reality" was created, and that new reality had become the second essential component of the Holocaust puzzle: Hitler and his close associates, especially Goebbels, were keenly aware of the importance of controlled communication in the effective manipulation of people. They instituted total censorship over all media, and they were bombarding the people with their propaganda messages directed toward the establishment of the New Order with its new values and new morality. The eyes and the ears of the people had become captivated by the state — the Nazi Party. They read and heard only what Hitler wanted them to see and hear.

The Nazis were completely ruthless but, unfortunately, they were also clever and the conditions were very much in their favor. They combined brutal intimidation of those who would dare to question with rewards for those who unquestionably accepted and supported the Führer.

The Jews had become a special target not only because of Hitler's pathological hatred of them but also because they provided an especially convenient target to channel the passion for pogrom of the rank-and-file anti-Semites into action. In addition to harassment and violence against individual Jews by individual Nazis, the persecution of Jews became government policy, beginning with legislation in early 1933 to eliminate Jews from government service and public life. It was followed in April 1933 by a large-scale, centrally organized, violent boycott of Jewish businesses. When these atrocities against the Jews brought on protests outside of Germany, the Jewish organizations were pressured to respond and neutralize the criticism. One of the typical messages was sent to the American Jewish Committee by the Berlin Jewish Community:

> According to newspaper reports, atrocity and boycott propaganda against Germany is continuing overseas, apparently in part also by Jewish organizations. As Germans and Jews we must enter a decisive protest against this. The dissemination of untrue reports can only bring harm, affecting the reputation of our German fatherland, endangering the relations of the German Jews with their fellow citizens. Please try urgently to see to it that every atrocity and boycott propaganda report is halted.[6]

The brutalization of the Jews and the oppression and violence against the other "enemies of the state" did not stop the Vatican from ratifying the Concordat with Germany, providing a diplomatic victory and implicit moral support for Hitler.

After years of chaos even the brutal totalitarian control appeared reassuring to many Germans. By tradition and personality, the Germans were perhaps more accepting of an absolute authoritarian leadership than others would have been, but to assume that the rest of us are invulnerable to oppressive manipulations would be a mistake. Too many examples in our recent history make one stop and think with humility.

Hitler and his inner circle, masters of taking advantage of the insecurities of the German people and their needs for approval, cleverly provided for them a substitute — superpatriotism. The people redirected their anger, caused by the political and economic collapse, toward their internal and external enemies. They blamed the Allied countries and the internal traitors — the Marxists and the Jews — for Germany's defeat. This displacement helped to reintegrate and unite the society that had been on a verge of collapse. The pageantry at the Nazi rallies reached out to the deepest and most primitive emotions, and the high-pitched ethnocentric patriotism helped the people overcome their insecurities, fears of failure, and lack of self-esteem by identification with the glorious and powerful nation. As the Nazis incited national mobilization against their "enemies," cohesiveness and morale increased, making it extremely difficult psychologically for the individual to resist Hitler's policies.

Patriotism reached a high pitch as Hitler flaunted the allied countries. He repudiated the Versailles Treaty by reestablishing universal compulsory service and marching into the demilitarized Rhineland — the British and the French stood by while the German masses were hysterically shouting "Heil Hitler," "Heil Hitler." The work programs instituted by Hitler also began to show results: Unemployment decreased and the economy was improving.

With his popularity rising, in August 1934 Hitler added the presidency to the chancellorship and also assumed the supreme command of the armed forces. Germany had become a completely centralized state with Hitler as the legalized absolute dictator. He had succeeded in less than two years to transform the intimidated German masses into fanatically enthusiastic and loyal followers.

The "spontaneous" and the legalized persecution of Jews continued, and in 1935 the "Nuremberg Laws" legitimized racial anti-Semitism by the establishment of a legal category of the "purity of German blood." This new legislation disenfranchised those subjects who were not of "German blood" and forbade marriage and extramarital relations between Germans and Jews. Jews were also forbidden to employ Aryan female domestics under 45 years of age. One cannot help but wonder about the possible connection between Hitler's bastard grandfather and this legislation.

The persecution of the Jews and the virulent oppression of the "enemies of the state" who were being tortured and murdered in the concentration camps did not stop the thousands of admiring foreign visitors who flocked to Berlin in 1936 to join the Nazis in celebrating the most spectacular of pageantries, the Olympic games. Once more Hitler's internal policies were ignored by the world. The cries of the Nazi victims remained unanswered. Unbelievable as it seems today, the Olympic games in Berlin were celebrated with no protest from anyone — even Jewish athletes participated as members of the various national teams. Thus by acquiescence the free world not only provided international recognition and prestige for Hitler but also implicitly condoned his brutal oppression.

The Nazi propaganda machine continued to saturate the German mind with fear, horror, and hatred of the Jews. The propaganda was effective, in part because of the long history of anti-Semitism, and because of the clever packaging of the message — partial truth was distorted and/or mixed with vicious lies. The Nazi propaganda was aimed at separating the Jews from their fellow Germans and presenting them as *untermenschen,* as subhumans. To make the "enemy" non-human was an important prerequisite for their eventual mass murder.

A good example of simplistic distortioins is the *Nazi Primer,* used for the indoctrination of the Nazi youth.[7] In just a few sentences, starting out with some obvious though irrelevant facts, the writer differentiated the Jews from other white men as dishonest and undesirable and concluded with an open-ended justification for ominous corrective action:

> The foundation of the Nationalist outlook on life is the perception of the unlikeness of men. If at first, we relate this unlikeness solely to the physical appearance, no one will wish to contest it. For it is all too apparent that the red skin, the yellow, the black and the white are very different. Moreover, within the family of white men all people are not the same. Every attentive observer can recognize distinction in physical size and shape. The coloring of eyes and hair and the skin is also very different. There are also distinctions among men with respect to mental and spiritual traits. This becomes very clear to us whenever different types of men converse about one and the same subject. To one person for example, work is a curse from Heaven, a punishment of God, and a burden to be avoided as much as possible. For another, on the contrary, it is a necessity of life which first given the human being his true meaning. Again, for some courage and loyalty are the very marks by which they treasure and value man. For them a promise once made is binding. They stick to it through good times and bad. They cannot live without honor and prefer death to cowardice.
>
> There are men, therefore, who are differentiated from others not alone because of physical characteristics. Just as deep and impossible to bridge are the differences in spirit and soul. Body, spirit and soul primarily constitute the complete man because they form a unified whole. Men therefore, must be considered with respect to their inner makeup. For the great difference which separates those of German blood from Jews is clearly evident, although physical characteristics seem to designate both as members of the family of white men. We suit our actions accordingly and evaluate what happens according to this knowledge.[8]

The twelve commandments published in the same primer give additional flavor of the values and "new realities" of the Third Reich:

1. The leader is always right;
2. Never violate discipline;
3. Never waste time in idle chatter nor in self-gratifying criticism, but take hold and help;
4. Be proud but not arrogant;
5. The program is your dogma; it demands your complete surrender to the cause;

6. You are a representative of the party; govern your behavior and appearance accordingly;
7. Loyalty and unselfishness are the first commandments;
8. As a true socialist you must be a real comrade;
9. Do to your comrades as you would have them do to you;
10. In battle be standfast and discreet;
11. Courage is not recklessness;
12. Whatever serves the interest of the movement, and through it Germany and the German people, is right.[9]

Hitler appeared to be "right" — the world acquiesced to his persecution of Jews and other internal "enemies" and to his aggressive, militaristic, expansionist, international posturing — and consequently his popularity with the German masses kept rising. Hitler succeeded in turning his fantasies into reality. With his creation of an environment in which his insecurities appeared as strengths, he turned his shame into pride. He created a "new reality" in which the environment, instead of confronting him with his psychological conflicts, fulfilled his inner needs. Consequently, the young man of the Vienna flophouses and the madman from 1942–1945, during the 1933–1940 period, became the trusted, charismatic leader who provided the German masses with a religiouslike superpatriotic identification. He created a Nazi Third Reich with a "new purpose" and "new values."

Human behavior is dependent on some kind of frame of reference. Our behavior toward our fellow human beings is affected usually by the attitudes and values of our families and society. In general, when a discrepancy between societal and family values arises, the resolution is dependent on the relationship with our families. The Nazis, however, not wanting the family ties to interfere with their indoctrination, placed loyalty to the Führer and state explictly above that of the family.

Hitler succeeded in transforming "conventional reality" and "conventional morality" as practiced in Germany before 1933 into the Third Reich "reality" and "morality" as controlled by the Nazi propaganda apparatus. The circle was complete; Germany had become a morally insulated island. The German people became "prisoners" in the system they had helped to build — they had completely disconnected from the realities of humanity and they had replaced the Ten Commandments with Nazi commandments, which placed obedience and loyalty to the Führer as the highest moral requirement. From that point on, change could come only from outside the borders, from the free world. Perhaps there was still some possibility of reawakening the conscience of the German people and providing reality testing if the "free people" and especially if the Pope cared. The entire world remained silent, however, and the last opportunity to confront the German people with their immorality and destructiveness was lost.

Let us turn to the last part of the Holocaust puzzle. Why did so many Germans actively or passively participate in the implementation of the Holocaust? Was this a singular, deviant event in human history caused by certain abnormalities in Nazi Germans that the rest of humanity therefore need not be concerned of, or is there a volcano capable of erupting into destructiveness under the right conditions in all of us?

What are the fundamental aspects of humankind — aggression and destructiveness? This question is eternal, going back to the archetypal murder of Abel by his brother Cain. History reveals a long and uninterrupted record of war, invasion, torture, and destruction; during the 5,600 years of recorded history, according to Ashley Montagu, more than 14,600 wars have occurred. During this period, of the roughly 185 generations of people, only 10 seem to have enjoyed uninterrupted peace.[10]

There are many, many examples of purposeless killings. The Greeks, in 1184 B.C., upon capturing Troy executed all males over age of 10 and sold the remaining children and women as slaves. The Roman legions after defeating Carthage in 146 B.C. massacred all defenders who surrendered and burned the city. Ganghis Khan's hordes massacred many thousands, perhaps millions, of civilians. And during the Spanish Inquisitions from 1420–1498, thousands of men, women, and children were burned alive at the stake for heresy and "other" crimes against the Church and state. More recently, the Armenians, the Bangladash, the Biafrans, and the Vietnamese at Mylai were some of the victims of wanton destructiveness. The list goes on and on.

What does all this violence represent? Is destructiveness inherent in man or is it a habit we acquire from our society? According to Lorenz[11] man's aggressive behavior as manifested in war, crime, and all kinds of destructive and sadistic behavior is the consequence of phylogenetically programmed innate instinct, which presses for discharge and breaks through whenever there is a proper occasion. Consequently, since our violence stems from our animal nature, we can't do much to change it.

Freud also explained aggression as an instinct. "Men are not gentle, friendly creatures wishing for love, who simply defend themselves if they are attacked; the powerful measure of aggression has to be reckoned as part of their instinctual endowment."[12] Later in a letter to Albert Einstein he wrote:

> "According to our hypothesis human instincts are of only two kinds: those which seek to preserve and unite which we call erotic, . . . and those which seek to destroy and kill, . . . as a result of a little speculation, we have come to suppose that this instinct is at work in every living creature and is striving to bring it to ruin and reduce life to its original condition of inanimate matter. Thus it quite seriously deserves to be called a death instinct while the erotic instinct represents the effort to live."[13]

He claimed, however, that parents and society could manage and rechannel these primitive drives.

Similar pessimism was expressed by Nietzche, who stated that each man struggles for his own good without consideration of the well-being of others. Bonds between men are based on common fear and common hatred; the fittest survives.[14] While recognizing how widespread human destructiveness is, Fromm is more hopeful about humankind. "It is not unlikely that inhibitions against killing also exist with regard to other humans provided there is a sense of identity and empathy."[15]

Other psychologists argue that even if human genes carry the potential for aggressive behavior, they do not determine the social pattern — at least that part is learned in a social environment.[16] Experimental evidence points to low self-esteem and feelings of social inadequecy as a basis of prejudice. Prejudice is often the precursor and determinant of the intensity and object of aggression. Injury to narcissism seems to result in aggression also. A close relationship between frustration and aggression is also suggested.[17] Still others argue that all behavior is learned; consequently, a person can learn to behave aggressively as well as nonaggressively.

The question of whether destructiveness in humanity is instinctual or learned is significant because an acquired form of behavior is open to modification whereas any behavior motivated by an instinctual drive may be more resistant to change. But, regardless of the underlying origin, aggressive behavior is observable not only in historic events and in everyday living and it can also be studied under experimental conditions.

One classic experiment was conducted by Milgram. In his study under the pretext of a learning experiment to study the effect of punishment on learning, one person was ordered to deliver an electric shock of progressed intensity to a second person. Whenever this second person erred on a learning task, a series of 30 switches ranging from 15 volts to 450 volts in 15-volt intervals was utilized. The learner — an experimenter in reality — grunted at 75, 90, and 105-volt levels and gave increasing distress signals as the level of shocks increased. Sixty-five percent of the people participating in the experiment obeyed the authority's orders to continue, despite the protests, screams, and then silence of the learner, and ultimately delivered the maximum level of shock possible — marked "XX" following the previous one marked "Danger: severe shock." It must be noted, however, that the surrounding social context did affect behavior.

The results were varied, depending on the social conditions that surrounded the person who delivered the shock. When in the same room with the victim, the person had to keep the victim's hand on the electrode, but when the authority was removed from room, the number of disobediences to continue the shock increased. When the person was allowed to select the level of shock only one out of 40 delivered the highest possible level. According to Milgram, "For a man to feel responsible for his actions, he must sense that the behavior flowed from the self. . . . In these experiments the subjects had precisely the opposite view of their actions; namely, they see them as originating in the motives of some other person."[18]

In a study by Zimbardo, students playing the role of prison guards exhibited unexpectedly destructive and sadistic behavior toward other students who were playing the role of prisoners, many of them friends. According to Zimbardo, "conditions that reduce a person's sense of uniqueness, that minimize individuality are the well springs of antisocial behavior such as aggression, vandalism, stealing, cheating, rudeness as well as general loss of concern for others. Conversely, prosocial behaviors are encountered by environmental and interpersonal conditions which enhance one's sense of recognition and self-identity."[19]

It appears that when individuals become part of a group they loose their identity, and thus the potential for violent behavior increases. Freud identified the "group mind" with minds of primitive people, neurotics, and children. He saw governing similarities in them. He likened them to a herd that "could never live without a master. It has such a thirst for obedience that it submits instinctively to anyone who appoints himself its master."[20]

As a group solidifies, it usually becomes more exclusive, and consequently a corresponding intensity of hatred develops toward those who are outsiders. As self-interest is promoted, the lack of investment in those outside gets further justified, and the group may become increasingly more menacing to the outsider. As the group focuses more on self-interest, furthermore, the more intensely it anticipates the hostility of those whom it previously alienated. Whatever threatens the particular egocentricity of a group, which gives it its distinction, is experienced as an attack on its narcissism, thus mobilizing its defenses. And important among these defenses is the readiness to violence.

The evidence for aggressiveness and potential violence in men is overwhelming. Its origin — instinctual or learned — cannot be determined based on current knowledge. This lack of knowledge must not be understood to mean, however, that the expression of violence cannot be limited or controlled.

Hitler was skillful in exploiting man's potential for aggressiveness and channeled a major part of that energy into the destruction of Jews in order to satiate his own pathological hatred of these people. The Jews' destruction was accomplished in sequential steps. Once the Nazi propaganda machine reduced the Jews to "nonpersons," they became convenient targets for increased aggression. Their abuse was facilitated by being described, among other things, as international enemies, foreign spies, blood polluters, and bacilli. Their murder was facilitated by involving many individuals, including other prisoners, each contributing only one more step in the chain of destruction. Participation in only one segment of murder minimized "responsibility" and maximized pressure and "support" for the activity. The Nazis created a perfect environment for the rationalization of mass murders. The Holocaust was implemented with satanic cleverness.

An attempt was made in this paper to explore from a psychological perspective, within the limitation of current psychological knowledge and space of an article, three significant components of the Holocaust. The evidence for potential destructiveness in men, whether based on instinctual drives or social learning, is overwhelming. A volcanic capacity for destructiveness appears to be present in most of us. Consequently, any one of us could become not only a victim but also under certain conditions a murderous beast — this thought deserves considerable humility.

Hitler's rise to power was made possible by Germany's defeat in World War I and the political, economic, social, and psychological conditions that resulted from the Versailles Treaty. Once he achieved uncontested dictatorial powers, Hitler created a "new reality" with complete control over the bodies and minds of the German people. The Jews were made into dangerous and despicable "nonpersons;" thus the necessary conditions for the Holocaust was ready.

It must be emphasized, however, that the "new realities" of the Third Reich remained unchallenged, at critical times, by the Free World and especially by the Pope, and their acquiescence to the Nazis' beastialities significantly contributed to the development of the New Order. If we are to understand the Holocaust, we must not limit ourselves only to the forces within the borders of Germany — the space within which the event took place includes the Western world. We cannot ignore the potential effect of a challenge against Hitler even on the enslaved German mind, and also on the people in Eastern Europe — mostly Catholics — where most of the Jewish victims lived.

We may ask now whether there is a chance for another Holocaust in the future? Any event that happened once obviously could happen again if the conditions are conducive. We must therefore ask, how can we control or channel man's destructiveness? Freud suggested that aggression be harnessed by developing an elite stratum of men, not open to intimidation who "would give directions to the dependent masses."[21]

More recently Kenneth Clark,[22] in his presidential address to the American Psychological Association in 1971, proposed that "the psychological and social sciences must enable us to control the animalistic, barbaric and primitive propensities in man." He believes that the "redirecting of power . . . must be seen as a responsibility and goal of science and psychotechnology." Clark stated his belief that "psychotechnological intervention can, within a few years, remove the basis for wars." Clark assigned a level of responsibility to science that based on current knowledge is not warranted.

This writer would be quite pessimistic about human survival if the control of the masses would be the responsibility of an elite cadre. Counting on an elite cadre is utopian. Who is to select the elite? Could it have prevented Hitler from assuming dictatorial powers?

This writer believes that the Holocaust could have been prevented only if Hitler was stopped before he assumed dictatorial powers or if his credibility and behavior were challenged during the early phase of his power. His unchallenged successes not only permitted him to maintain a resemblance of sanity but created in the German people a passionate admiration and blind and unquestioned loyalty for Hitler.

Continued butchering of man could be avoided only if we could bring ourselves to face all the facts, including the destructiveness in ourselves. The control of human aggressiveness is the responsibility of all people and must never be delegated to any small group — whether political or scientific elites. Rather, societies need to be structured with sufficient checks and balances that prevent any individual or small group from gaining absolute power. The Weimar Republic lacked this capacity. Moreover, our educational system should consider human survival as an equivalent or perhaps a more important subject — for understanding and teaching — than technical knowledge.

Finally, we must recognize that events take place in a context larger than the immediate borders. The same way that behavior within a family under certain conditions is interfered with by the state, we must assume a level of responsibility as a family of nations for events that take place within the borders of any one state. The theoretical framework for this is already in place within the United Nations. As we know, however, the United Nations is considerably influenced by the prejudicial self-interests of various political blocs.

The control of human aggression in the nuclear age, both within states and between nations, is an absolute necessity for the survival of the human race. Hopefully, men will rise to the challenge and will provide structural controls, thereby limiting the possibility of anyone assuming dictatorial powers, and education for the people — responsibility toward one's fellow man.

Notes

1. L.S. Dawidowicz, *The War Against the Jews, 1933–1945* (New York: Holt, Rinehart and Winston, 1975), p. 22.
2. Ibid., p. 6.
3. E. Fromm, *The Anatomy of Human Destructiveness* (New York: Holt, Rinehart and Winston, 1973), p. 404.
4. E.H. Erikson, *Childhood and Society* (New York: W.W. Norton & Company, 1963), pp. 328–29.
5. L.S. Dawidowicz, *The War Against the Jews*, p. 48.
6. Ibid., p. 53.
7. Fritz Brennecke, *The Nazi Primer* (New York: Harper Brothers, 1938), pp. 5–12.
8. Ibid., pp. 5–7.
9. Ibid., pp. XXIII–XXIV.
10. A. Montagu, *The Nature of Aggression* (New York: Oxford University Press, 1976), p. 302.
11. K. Lorenz, *On Aggression* (New York: Harcourt, Brace & World, 1966), pp. 270–74.
12. S. Freud, *Civilization and Its Discontents* (London: Hogarth Press, 1927), p. 85.
13. S. Freud, "Why War?" in *Collected Papers* (New York: Basic Books, 1959), vol. 5, p. 282.
14. O. Levy, ed., *The Complete Works of Friedrich Nietzshe* (New York: Russell & Russell, 1964), vol. 10, pp. 31–35.
15. E. Fromm, *The Anatomy of Human Destructiveness*, p. 121.
16. Ibid., p. 167.
17. N.E. Miller, "Frustration-Aggression Hypothesis" *Psychological Review* 48 (1941): 337–42.
18. S. Milgram, *Obedience to Authority* (New York: Harper & Row, 1974), pp. 143–45.

19. P.G. Zimbardo, ''Transforming Experimental Research into Advocacy for Social Change,'' in *Applying Social Psychology: Implications for Research, Practice and Training,* ed. Morton Deutsch and Harvey A. Hornstein (New Jersey: Lawrence Erlbaum Associates, 1975), p. 53.

20. C. Rochlin, *Man's Aggression: The Defense of the Self* (Boston: Gambit, 1973), p. 261.

21. S. Freud, ''Why War?'' p. 284.

22. K.B. Clark, ''The Pathos of Power: A Psychological Perspective,'' *American Psychologist* 26 (1971): 1047–57.

3 THE POST-HOLOCAUST GENERATIONS:
A Psychological Perspective

Stanley L. Rustin

Survivors of the Holocaust of World War II have been described in the psychiatric literature as suffering from a "survivor syndrome."[1] In this paper I would like to discuss the implications of the survivor syndrome on the postgenerations of Holocaust survivors. While the survivor syndrome appears to exist to some degree in *all* survivors of the Holocaust, the degree to which it has influenced the relationship between the survivors and their offspring varies greatly. The survivors' post–World War II adjustment may be envisioned as being on a continuum from the least psychopathological reactions to very intense psychopathological reactions. In this paper I will therefore first define the survivor syndrome, discuss the variables affecting survivors' coping mechanisms, then deal with the second generation's experience with parents, and conclude with some thoughts on the early findings and implications for the third generation of the survivors.

In their papers on the survivor syndrome, Krystal and Niederland have described a clinical picture of acute anxiety, nightmares, survivor guilt, depression, hypochondriacal fears, and a lifelong sense of heightened vulnerability to and increased awareness of dangerous situations.[2] This description is very similar to the diagnostic category of "Post-Traumatic Stress Disorder." In the American Psychiatric Association's *Diagnostic and Statistical Manual* the diagnostic criteria for the Post-Traumatic Stress Disorder is described as follows:

Diagnostic criteria:

A. Existence of a recognizable stressor that would evoke significant symptoms of distress in almost anyone.

B. Reexperiencing the trauma as evidenced by at least one of the following:
   1. recurrent and intrusive recollections of the event;
   2. recurrent dreams of the event;
   3. sudden acting or feeling as if the traumatic event were reoccurring, because of an association with an environmental or ideational stimulus.

C. Numbing of responsiveness to or reduced involvement with the external world, beginning some time after the trauma, as shown by at least one of the following:
   1. markedly diminished interest in one or more significant activities;
   2. feeling of detachment or estrangement from others;
   3. constricted affect.

D. At least two of the following symptoms that were not present before the trauma:
   1. hyperalertness or exaggerated startle response;
   2. sleep disturbance;
   3. guilt about surviving when others have not, or about behavior required for survival;
   4. memory impairment or trouble concentrating;
   5. avoidance of activities that arouse recollection of the traumatic event;
   6. intensification of symptoms by exposure to events that symbolize or resemble the traumatic event.[3]

From this criteria one may see that the Holocaust survivor has inevitably suffered from some aspects of the posttraumatic stress disorder. The crucial point here is that the degree of trauma and of the ego defenses adopted to cope with the truama varies considerably among survivors. There are, I would suggest, differing degrees of trauma experienced among the survivors — among those in hiding during the war, the partisans, those in labor camps, those in concentration camps, and, lastly, those in extermination camps. Survivors who were partisans and therefore given an opportunity to fight the Nazis may have experienced the horrors of war in a less vulnerable psychological state than the inmates of an extermination camp who had no control over their fate. In the former instance, survivors, in retrospect, could see themselves as fighters and, in relating stories of the Holocaust, be perceived by their children as heroes. In the latter instance, survivors have often seen themselves as victims and communicated this perception to their children.

Another factor influencing the degree of trauma experienced by survivors is the age of the survivor during the Holocaust. Survivors' age is an obvious factor in their determining previous levels of adaptation, as well as determining their role in their family and whether they were the heads of a new nuclear family. Chodorff,[4] Rustin,[5] and Davidson[6] have suggested that the younger the age of the survivor during the Holocaust, the better the level of adaptation after the Holocaust. While this theory may contradict our intuition about older people better coping with trauma, it does not seem to have been the case. Many survivors who were heads of families had spouses and children killed, losses frequently more overwhelming than the loss of parents and siblings. The survivor's inability to protect one's spouse and children often led to feelings of inadequacy and a profound sense of survivor guilt. Following the war, the loss of one's children frequently drove survivors, with a desire to have children to replace the children who had been killed, into hasty marriages. As Danieli has pointed out:

> Many survivors gave birth in DP camps as soon as it was physically possible. For some who had lost spouses and children during the war, these were second families. Almost without exception, the newborn children were named after those who had perished. In their eyes, these children were a replacement for the agonizing losses of the past and were to realize the lost years and opportunities of their parents. The children, often viewed as a blessing, miracle, gift, or symbol of victory over the Nazis, were to be the future-secure, normal, capable, happy, proud members of the human race.[7]

Another variable affecting the coping mechanisms of the survivors was the culture the survivor emigrated to after World War II. Many survivors emigrated to newfound homes in the United States, Israel, South America, and Canada, each of which presented varied problems and challenges. Perhaps the most hospitable environment was provided in Israel, where the survivor was treated as an important manpower resource and potential contributor to an emerging nation. In an earlier paper Klein has described the salutary effects of the kibbutz structure on the new immigrants: "The kibbutz served as an attempt to bridge the gap in their existence and seems to have enabled them to continue the former identities as members of a closely knit 'super family.' The kibbutz provides a feeling of resituated family and has given each member a clearly defined positive role."[8] In addition to the kibbutz structure, Israel as a nation, has been supportive of the survivor by enabling the survivor to engage in collective mourning remembrance days, and by providing an avenue for new identifications as productive members of a society that emerged as a by-product of the carnage of the Second World War.

Within the United States and Canada, survivors tended to move into areas where other survivors lived. These survivors frequently became friendly and formed surrogate families. In times of crises, particularly when a family member died, the survivors, by banding together, provided a network for consolation and support. Also, many survivors formed organizations that focused on remembrance of the Holocaust as well as on the education and transmission of the Holocaust experience to the society at large and to their children. Recently the media in the United States has been quite supportive of the educational goals of survivor groups. Television programs such as "The Holocaust," "Skokie," and "The Wall" have presented a docudrama approach to the Holocaust, which has provided the survivors and the second generation a format through which they may exchange ideas and reactions to the Holocaust.

In summary, then, we can see that the survivors are not a homogeneous group. Where practically all survivors display some aspects of the posttraumatic-stress disorder, the degree of symptomatology may vary greatly. Depending upon a number of variables, survivors may communicate to the second generation a perception of themselves as hero or victim or, by engaging in a conspiracy of silence, completely minimize their involvement in the Holocaust. The manner in which survivors elect to portray themselves, consciously or even unconsciously, therefore has great impact on the second generation. I would now like to turn to some of the variables that condition the second generation's reactions to their parents' experiences and its means of coping with its unique legacy.

The major variables influencing the second generation's development that may differ from a nonsurvivor population appear to be the following: parental preoccupation with the Holocaust; parental affect, particularly when discussing their past lives; the child's birth order and number of siblings; the parents' involvement with flashback phenomena; and hypernestic moments.

Sigal has discussed the role of parental preoccupation with the Holocaust as sabotaging the forming of attachment and "emotional engagement" between parent and child.[9] The parents have been so preoccupied with their loss that they therefore have been unable to extend themselves and be emotionally involved with their post-Holocaust children. This phenomenon appears to be particularly true in the older survivors whose previous children were killed. The consequence of parental preoccupation with unresolved, interminable mourning leads children to feelings of inadequacy to make their parents happy and frequently to personal feelings of loss and depression. Conversely, it follows that when parents are *not* overly preoccupied with their sense of loss and depression, the offspring are less oppressed by the burden of the Holocaust.

The parents' affect is of crucial importance in all families. When parents exhibit excessive depression, anxiety, or "affect lameness," an obvious contamination factor results in their children's development. To the degree that survivor parents exhibit constricted or depressed affect, the second generation may be affected. However, as mentioned previously, the degree of affective damage varies considerably among survivors; the degree of contamination to the second generation, therefore, is of considerable variation. If the attachment had been symbiotic, then one may expect a continuation of the parental depression into the next generation. Conversely, when parents employed effective coping skills and utilized appropriate repression of traumatic episodes, the second generation may not be burdened by the distant past.

We may consider here the positive value of repression since it allowed some survivors to keep from consciousness those horrible experiences that could cause only pain. Through repression, rather than emotional depletion, survivors turned their emotional energies to building a new life with a new family. Therefore, the role of parental effect is really not very different from the general population. Just as alcoholics, psychotics, and depressives affect their children, so may the excessively depressed or psychotic survivors affect their children. We cannot automatically assume, therefore, that *all* survivors, having experienced loss, are depressed and contaminate the next generation with this depression.

The role of birth order for the second-generation child is important since the firstborn child or an only child is frequently the object of great emotional investment. Here again, this is true for a nonsurvivor population as well. The difference is that survivors, because of their losses, frequently became overinvested in their children, who thus feel that they must compensate their parents for what they have lost. Frequently the unspoken communication is for the child to replace the deceased sibling or deceased aunt, uncle, or parent. Furthermore, because survivor families are small, the child feels a responsibility to accomplish more than does the nonsurvivor child. The need to accomplish, to please one's parents, is frequently accompanied by excessive anxiety regarding failure or acute guilt if one fails or disappoints one's parents. In this area the second generation carries a burden that is somewhat different than the general population.

Another area in which the second generation may be different than the general population, but similar to the children of veterans or other survivors of catastrophy, is the extent to which other parents suffer from "flashback phenomena" or hypernestic moments. To illustrate this phenomena I would like to report the following three episodes and their impact on the second generation.

In the 1970s adolescent women, as part of the fashion of the period, wore wooden clogs. In psychotherapy two second-generation women reported almost identical maternal reactions to their wearing these wooden shoes. Each mother went into a rage reaction and both physically and verbally attacked their daughters for wearing the clogs. After their rage had been spent, they explained that they had to wear similar shoes when they were inmates in the concentration camps. The sudden reminder, and seeing their own children wear the shoes associated with the horrible episode of their lives, elicited the rage reaction with subsequent displaced aggression onto the children.

An illustration of hypernestic images and their role in fostering behavior in the present is a woman who prepared cabbage soup whenever there was a happy family occasion or when she felt depressed. When her adult children finally asked why she associated cabbage soup with happy events, she reported the following: When she and many other concentration camp inmates were selected for transfer to a labor camp, they were told to prepare for a long march. Prior to the march they were given a very hearty cabbage soup with meat and potatoes, rather than the thin watery broth that barely sustained them in the camp. The survivor recalled with accompanying aromas and mouthwatering relish the joy of eating the cabbage soup. For her, cabbage soup and happiness became indelibly paired. Whenever she felt depressed or anxious, without even realizing it, she would buy the ingredients for cabbage soup as a means of warding off her depression and as a device for feeling better.

The third example of these phenomena was that of parents who were canine phobic. They not only refused to allow their children to have dogs as pets but became extremely agitated and anxious whenever they saw stray dogs or even dogs on a leash. The phobic reaction became especially intense whenever a Doberman pinscher or German shepard appeared. The children, in time, acquired their parents' phobic reaction to dogs. The connection between dogs and the parents' imprisonment in the concentration camps became linked to such a degree that the survivors could not separate the sight of dogs from their painful memories.

These examples are culled from clinical experiences with survivors and the second generation. I must stress, however, the fallacy of generalizing to all survivors or to all second-generation children based on these clinical samples. We have ample evidence from other sectors, Porter, Epstein, and Leon and Butcher among others, that many survivors and the second generation have not demonstrated especially aberrant reactions to the Holocaust. Porter suggests that the second generation has a high degree of social and political consciousness, which may come from its awareness of the parents' experiences.[10] Epstein has discussed the wide range of second-generation reactions, which run the gamut from political conservatism to liberalism, from religious orthodoxy to antireligious attitudes.[11] While some of the second generation have degrees of survivor guilt, and manifest aspects of their parents' survivor syndrome, many do not. Leon and Butcher et al., in a well-documented study comparing children of survivors with a control group of similar European and religious backgrounds, found "no significant differences between the survivor and control group children on any of the psychological variables or on their attitudes and behaviors toward their parents."[12] Based on the analysis of their data, they concluded: "Despite the presence of chronic physical problems, restlessness, reports of occasional nightmares, and preoccupations about their war-time experiences, these persons truly survived and adjusted remarkably well. It, therefore, seems a great disservice to them, and there is no evidence from the present study, to automatically assume that children of survivors, as a group are psychologically impaired because of their parents' experiences."

As the second generation has matured, married, and become parents, the question then arises, What impact, if any, has the Holocaust had on the third generation? In Porter's article alluded to earlier in this paper, he suggests that there are sociopolitical characteristics of the second generation that may cause them to be activists in the political and religious sectors. Some of the second generation are forming "generation after" groups. Others, active in the Jewish Defense League, are involved in militant activities and quite aware of aspects of anti-Semitism in the culture. Some of the second generation have chosen to assimilate and, in some instances, married Gentiles.

In the first clinical paper describing the effects of the Holocaust on the third generation, the Rosenthals reported on the multigenerational dynamics of a survivor grandmother's depression, her suicide, and its impact on her six-year-old grandson.[13] The family history discussed in her paper illustrates many of the more severe psychopathological reactions to the Holocaust. The survivor in this case had been preoccupied with her husband's death during the Holocaust and "after viewing a televised documentary on the Auschwitz concentration camp experience had leaped to her death from her sixth story apartment." Her grandson in subsequent sessions said: "He knew that the 'Germans killed her' and drew pictures of Snoopy and the Red Baron bombing soldiers."

Since the literature regarding the third generation is sparse, drawing conclusions from one case history would be premature. As the third generation matures the impact of the Holocaust may manifest itself as psychological problems or may serve as an impetus toward social, political, or religious action. Because the multigenerational consequences are still to a large degree unknown, the great need for systematic and careful research becomes evident, lest we stigmatize the past Holocaust generations with inaccurate, premature conclusions, which would cause them a disservice.

Summary

Virtually all survivors of the Holocaust appear to suffer from some aspects of the survivor syndrome. This syndrome has distinct similarities to the Post-Traumatic Stress Disorder. The literature suggests that a wide range of survivor reactions may have been communicated to the second generation.

The impact of the Post-Traumatic Stress Disorder on subsequent generations varies considerably and is related to parental preoccupation with the Holocaust, parental emotional impoverishment, as well as other variables. The second generation may or may not show evidence of the effect of the Post-Traumatic Stress Disorder. In some instances the second generation becomes involved in social, political, and religious activities as a means of coming to grips with their families' role in the Holocaust.

The impact of the Holocaust on the third generation is just beginning to be felt and conclusions in this regard are premature at the present time.

Notes

1. H. Krystal and W. Niederland, "Clinical Observations on the survivor Syndrome," in *Massive Psychic Trauma,* ed. H. Krystal (New York: International Universities Press, 1968), pp. 327–48.

2. H. Krystal and W. Niederland, eds., *Psychic Traumatization* (Boston: Little Brown, 1971), pp. 217–29. See also Ref. 1.

3. *Diagnostic and Statistical Manual of the American Psychiatric Association,* ed ed. 1980: 137–38.

4. P. Chordoff, "Effects of Extreme Coercive and Oppressive Forces: Brainwashing and Con-

centration Camps,'' in *American Handbook of Psychiatry,* vol. III, ed. S. Aristi (New York: Basic Books, 1966), pp. 384–405.

5. S.L. Rustin, ''The Legacy Is Loss,'' *Journal of Contemporary Psychotherapy* 3, no. 1, (Spring/Summer, 1980): 32–43.

6. S. Davidson, ''The Clinical Effects of Massive Psychic Trauma in Families of Holocaust Survivors,'' *Journal of Marital and Family Therapy,* January, 1980, pp. 11–21.

7. Y. Danieli, ''Families of Survivors of the Nazi Holocaust,'' in *Stress and Anxiety,* vol. 8, ed. C. Spielberger, I. Sarason, and N. Milgram (Washington: Hemisphere Publishing, 1982), pp. 405–21.

8. H. Klein, ''Families of the Holocaust Survivors in the Kibbutz: Psychological Studies,'' in *Psychic Traumatization,* ed. H. Krystal and W. Niederland (Boston: Little, Brown, 1971), pp. 67–92.

9. J. Sigal, ''Familial Consequences of Parental Preoccupation'' (Paper presented at the Annual Meeting of the American Psychiatric Association, Honolulu, Hawaii, May 1972); J. Sigal, ''Second Generation Effects of Massive Psychic Trauma,'' in *Psychic Traumatization,* ed. H. Krystal and W. Niederland; J.J. Sigal, D. Silver, V. Rakoff, and B. Ellin, Some Second Generation Effects of Survival of the Nazi Persecution, *American Journal of Orthopsychiatry* 43 (1973): 320–27.

10. J.N. Porter, ''Is There a Survivor Syndrome? Psychological and Socio-Political Implication,'' *Journal of Psychology and Judaism* 6, no. 1 (Fall/Winter 1981): 33–52.

11. H. Epstein, *Children of the Holocaust* (New York: G.P. Putnam, 1979).

12. Gloria R. Leon, J.N. Butcher, M. Klanmon, A. Goldberg, and M. Almager, ''Survivors of the Holocaust and Their Children: Current Status and Adjustment,'' *Journal of Personality and Social Psychology* 41, no. 3 (1982): 503–16.

13. P. Rosenthal and S. Rosenthal, ''Holocaust Effect in the Third Generation: Child of Another Time,'' *American Journal of Psychotherapy* 34, no. 4 (October 1980): 572–80.

4 CHRISTIAN ANTI-SEMITISM AND THE HOLOCAUST

Franklin H. Littell

For several years I have been working on a question put by a fellow inmate to Alexandre Donat, author of *The Holocaust Kingdom:*

> How can Christianity survive the discovery that after a thousand years of its being Europe's official religion, Europe remains pagan at heart?

In the same paragraph the author opened up the way in which the event of the Holocaust jeopardizes the direction of general history as well as confronts Christianity with the credibility question:

> And now all the nations have been shown that you can murder millions with impunity, the question will eventually be asked, "If Jews only yesterday, why not Americans, or Catholics, or Chinese tomorrow?"[1]

Actually, of course, the answer was "Indo-Chinese!" But the religious question, first put, remains: *Is Christianity still credible?*

As a professing Christian, I would like to affirm that it may be credible or perhaps better that it may become credible again. I am convinced, however, that this will never happen as long as Christian teachers continue to avoid dealing with the two most important events in recent Christian history — the Holocaust and a restored Israel — as long as they continue to draw their supplies through long tunnels reaching back to John Wesley or Martin Luther or Thomas Aquinas or even

Augustine without noticing whether outside the tunnel it is raining or snowing, 50 degrees below or 110 above, and sweltering in the shade.

My Temple University colleague Paul van Buren caused a sensation a few years ago by asking in a major theological meeting what would happen to certain traditional Christian doctrines if the Holocaust and a restored Israel were taken seriously.[2] My own question is somewhat different, though related: How is it that Christians, especially liberal Protestants, have such a hard time understanding the biblical dialectic of universalism and particularism? Why are they so determined to find in Jewish peoplehood, and especially as expressed in the survival of Israel, a threat to general human values — while keeping, of course, their own passports and denominational affiliations? Why are they so naive in respect to the Marxist and Muslim exercises in psychological projection that identify Zionism with racism? Why do good people like the American Quakers find it easy, in talking about refugees in the Near East, to forget that there are Jewish refugees was well as refugees recently trying to create a "Palestinian" identity?

My hypothesis: The rage for abstract "truths" — good for all times and places — has launched them out of history. If their self-contained spaceship lands at all, it is somewhere on an unearthly planet inhabited perhaps by specters but uninhabited by real human persons of flesh and blood. They remain untouched by the issues raised by Emil Fackenheim's discussion of Judaism after Auschwitz, *The Jewish Return into History*. This "return" has not yet been made by the Christian establishment, still dominated either by a baptized form of the perennial philosophy or, at vulgar level, by sundry forms of *Kulturreligion*.

The Rage for Abstract "Truths"

A popular but mistaken notion, sometimes cultivated by the protagonists, polarizes American Protestantism between "Fundamentalists" and "Liberals." In fact, however, these supposedly opposed religious positions are but two sides to the same coin: One specializes in propositions, the other in abstractions. Neither, nor, both together, can do justice to the rich metaphorical language of the Scriptures.[3] Neither, nor, both together, can preach and teach the parables and paradigmatic events of holy history. Unique, "epoch-making" events, which bind together personal history and the history of the people, remain outside the two styles of discourse. The story is not told, let alone reenacted.

The aesthetic poverty of the world of generalizations and abstractions can be documented in many ways, all of them working to make the inhabitants blind and deaf to the language of events. For example, I received recently a letter, answering a crisis appeal, from the senior minister of one of the larger churches of my own denomination:

> I receive letters from both sides, and they all sound quite convincing! With all the causes, I marvel that a general practioner like the Church can continue to make headway. But perhaps that is its purpose, to bring an overview to all the particularist interests of our day.[4]

What shall I write him? I know personally the two professors with whom he studied theology: Neither of them paid any attention to either the German Church struggle or the Nazi Holocaust. Both of them thought the chief challenges to Christianity to be "secularism" and "fundamentalism." Shall I write my old friend and tell him that his seminary shortchanged him 40 years ago? Shall I point out that today, after 40 years "in the wilderness," his seminary is still avoiding the world of real events and teaching timeless "truths?"

Those in flight from history and from the concrete events that give it color and transmit meaning to us are poorly equipped to understand the meaning(s) of "alpine" events like the Holocaust and a restored Israel. Indeed, they resent the particularism of a peculiar people, the Jews, and condemn the scriptural teaching about the nature of the church as "sectarianism."

The flight from history produces spiritual cripples, persons as handicapped as the color-blind and the tone-deaf. Among many beautiful parables and meditations in Elie Wiesel's *Souls on Fire* is a relevant passage:

> Any man who loves God while hating or despising His creation, will in the end hate God. A Jew who rejects his origins, his brothers, to make a so-called contribution to mankind, will in the end betray mankind.[4]

That is true also for Christians, especially those who have enjoyed a university and seminary education since the Enlightenment let loose among us a rage for universals. The rejection of history, the passionate embrace of a dream world of universal truths uncontaminated by the finitude and ambiguities of real life, has become the most subtle enemy of the Jewish people — and also the most insidious corrupter of any Christian church that seeks to be true to its calling as a counterculture.

The widespread apostasy of the baptized during the Holocaust, combined with the manifest irrelevance of the religious establishments, has opened the doors to the age of the Aquarius. Many youth and students do not want to hear of "history;" they think they are rejecting the burdens of the past, when as a matter of fact they are giving final and consequential expression to a mood that has dominated the West since university professors and political activists rejected the lessons of the past for dreams of the future.

History is not, of course, past events. Still less is it to be equated with "facts" about the past. The ocean of facts is infinite, and writers select from that ocean according to their response to present challenges. To live in history involves an intense awareness of this present moment of decision and choice, illuminated by an awareness of what has already transpired and a vision of what is yet to be. An escape from history can follow one of two routes, both of which blind us to present responsibilities: *either* a purblind devotion to a past reconstructed in mythical form and footnoted with antiquarian zeal *or* a devotion to some vision of the last things (''futurology''), which simply erases distinctions in the present age. One is the way of reactionaries, such as those in the United States who constantly refer to their mythical construct of a ''Christian America,'' which is supposed to have once existed. The other is the way of revolutionaries, so bemused by visions of the coming age that they have lost contact with the real life in which most of humankind must live. Reactionaries and revolutionaries of this type are but two sides of the same coin: They are in flight from the life we are assigned to live — ambiguous, earthy, human in measure.

History, as the Jewish and Christian Scriptures understand it, is lived in a *Zwischenstadion* — an arena that is ours *for the time being*. That is to say, any worthy understanding of the past, perception of present possibilities, vision of ultimate purpose, is carried in the here and now by a concrete community. The problem we face, particularly in dealing with liberal anti-Semitism, whether ''Christian'' or ''humanist'' or ''Marxist,'' is that this system of being has broken the essential dialectic of particularism and universalism. Enamored of a dream of universal humanity, it has leapt with abandon into rejection of all peculiar and special historical missions. It rejects the concept of ''chosenness'' as an offense against humanity, and in doing so it rejects the particular mission of the Jewish people and *also* of any Christian people that lives a peculiar counterculture. If its assumptions were correct, we should all be speaking Esperanto and worshipping with the Cao Dai. But, as I remember the lessons of my own faith, the tower of Babel is to be superseded by an age of the spirit of another kind, when each speaks his own tongue, and insight is given to the rest to understand (Acts 2:6). Neither Jews nor Christians are allowed to flee from a particular history.

Christian Anti-Semitism

In a recent address analyzing in detail Martin Luther's hostility to the Jews, Professor Gordon Rupp of Cambridge has made the striking suggestion that the medieval caricature of the synagogue as a blinded, broken captive might now be applied to the Christian church. For while the Jewish people have in this half century come through crucifixion (Auschwitz) to resurrection (Israel), Christianity has yet to master the meaning of the Church Struggle and the Holocaust — and is, in fact, caught in the most serious credibility crisis in two millennia. Christianity has repeatedly accommodated to paganism, while the Jewish counterculture reminded the ''Christian Israel'' of its own disobedience and accommodation. From the Synod of Elvira and the Council of Nicaea to the modern age, Christian anti-Semitism has been a function of the churches' consciousness of guilt and apostasy toward the One who is God. And added intensity of embarrassment and resentment at Christian failure to respond to the claims of the *Lex Christi* has substantially augmented hatred of the people of the *Torah*.

Now, in the rupture of history that was the Holocaust, Christendom stands exposed in rebellion and betrayal of the most awful measure. For the Holocaust is not another illustration of "man's inhumanity to man," as popular as this generalization has become. Golo Mann expressed the typical but quite wrong-headed view when he generalizes:

> But let us not think either that inhuman cruelty is a specifically German characteristic. The French under Napoleon did similar things in Spain — one need only look at Goya's drawings. If the leaders make a system out of bestiality there will always be a minority willing to obey. This has been so everywhere at all times.[6]

This amiable generalization is another flight from the specificity and concreteness of historic event. Of course inhuman cruelty is not "a specifically German characteristic," and neither is "inhuman cruelty" the appropriate rubric for the Holocaust. The Holocaust, in its uniqueness, was (*and is*) a *caesura* in Western civilization, a credibility crisis in Christianity, a credibility crisis in the modern university and its world of discourse. In Christendom it stands as a sign of the final blasphemy of the baptized Gentiles, an open revolt agaisnt the God of Abraham, Isaac, and Jacob — coupled with bitter resentment of the Jewish people, still a sign to the covenant by which they entered history (whether individual Jewish martyrs were "believers" or not).

Three major thought constructs have led the Christians astray. One, at the more vulgar and superstitious level, is represented in the calumny of deicide and blood guilt. The Greek and Latin fathers, as they magnified Greek philosophy and Roman administration, built a high wall against the Jewish heritage. Let Cyprian (258 C.E.) speak for the pack:

> There is a New Dispensation and a New Law, with abrogation of the Law of Moses and the old temple [#15]; The Man of Righteousness was put to death by the Jews [#14]; they fastened Him to the cross [#20]; Now the peoplehood of the Jews has been cancelled; the destruction of Jerusalem was a judgment upon them [#6]; the Gentiles rather than the Jews will inherit the Kingdom [#23];

Finally,

> by this alone the Jews could obtain pardon of their sins, if they wash away the blood of Christ slain in His baptism, and, passing over into the Church, should obey His precepts [#24][7]

This form of propositional teaching is not without influence even in the twentieth century. When a compassionate Russian officer wrote a critical report on the sufferings of the Jews under the pogroms, the czar — an ignorant and superstitious little man, to be sure — scratched a marginal note: "But we must never forget that the Jews sacrificed our saviour and shed his precious blood."[8] And

Monsignor John Oesterreicher has given us a detailed account of the extraordinary political pressures applied by Arab governments and their "Christian" anti-Semitic allies to prevent Vatican II from striking the deicide calumny from the table of Roman Catholic teaching.[9]

The second concept is more influential and still binds the minds of perhaps most Christian preachers and teachers. This is the idea that blends in Cyprian with the deicide charge: that with the New Dispensation the historic mission of the Jewish people is ended. They are to scatter, wither away and disappear from history. The "New Israel" has superseded the old.

That which Marcion, condemned as a heretic for his bold excision of the Jewish element, failed to accomplish by frontal assault was nevertheless accomplished by another, more subtle method: the propagation of the superseding or displacement myth.

Portions of the Jewish Scriptures are taken over, to be interpreted Christologically:

> And I will make my abode among you, and my soul shall not abhor you. And I will walk among you and will be your God, and you shall be my people. I am the Lord your God, who brought your fathers out of the land of Egypt, that you should not be their slaves; and I have broken the bars of your yoke and made you walk freed. [Lev. 26:11-13]

Even the word at Sinai is expropriated: "All that the Lord has spoken we will do and we will be obedient" (Exod. 24:7). So also the renewal of covenant with Joshua: "The Lord our God we will serve, and his voice we will obey" (Joshua 24:24). The promise in Leviticus, that even though tried, he keeps his promises —

> Yet for all that, when they are in the land of their enemies, I will not spurn them, neither will I abhor them utterly and break my covenant with them, for I am the Lord their God . . . [Lev. 26:14]

— is transferred from the Jewish people to the Christian church. In the process Christianity became a speculative philosophy, and finally an ideology of which a substantial component was theological anti-Semitism.

Early church historians discern a radical break between the age of the Jews and the age of the church, the latter the penultimate age of human history. But the superseding theory has manifest limitations. When Islam was launched, it claimed to supersede both Jewish faith and Christianity. A century ago Marxism appeared, claiming to supersede all prescientific religious systems with a modern and scientific *Weltanschauung*.

Moreover, such periodization creates an essentially meaningless space in church history: Between the Ascension and the Second Coming, nothing important can happen. A gray plain stretches out, with inclines and downward slopes — but no mountain ranges, no watershed events. To the supercessionist, both the Holocaust and a restored Israel are unintelligible. For that matter, the sixteenth century too is parenthetical.

As for the needed rectification of Christian teaching, Professor Jaroslaw Pelikan of Yale stated it well in his presidential address at the Fourth International Luther Congress. Addressing himself to the bad tradition left by Martin Luther vis-a-vis the Jewish people, he said:

> I cannot escape the conviction that the time has come for those who study Luther and admire him to acknowledge, more unequivocally and less pugnaciously than they have, that on this issue Luther's thought and language are simply beyond defense. But any such acknowledgment must be based theologically on a much more fundamental conviction, namely, that Judaism is not, as Luther and the centuries before him maintained, a "shadow" destined to disappear with the coming of Christianity even though it stubbornly held on to the existence, but a permanent part of the wondrous dispensation of God in human history.[10]

Such openness to interaction between a vital and ongoing Jewish people and a corrected and renewed Christian people not only affirms the importance of present Jewry to Christians but also implies that events are presently occurring that are of fundamental importance to the shape and direction of Christianity — which may, in fact, determine whether Christianity makes it or not.

In effect, by dropping Jewish history circa 100 A.D. — at the high intensity of the family quarrel — and picking it up again circa 1928, with the founding of the National Conference of Christians and Jews, our liberal Christian seminaries and graduate schools of religion help to popularize a false view of Holy History. This practice creates the same false concept that some Fundamentalists have reasserted bluntly, reaffirming an intellectual triumphalism that was once very common in Christendom:

> We want to say most emphatically that when Christ died on Calvery, the old Mosaic order died, never to be revived. . . . Judaism is a thing of the past. It is a glorious memory despite its limitations and ifs failings. . . . It may seem harsh to say that "God is through with the Jews." . . . Nothing has been taken from the Jews as individuals. . . . But the fact of the matter is that He is through with them as a unified national group. . . . The Old Testament was the time of the Jews. The New Testament era is the time of the Gentiles. . . . The Christian Church is the legitimate heir and successor of Old Testament Israel.[11]

If the language of the quotation is harsh, appropriate to a certain kind of sectarian Protestantism, the superseding concept here expressed is no different from that which lies behind of Arnold J. Toynbee's persistent reference to the Jews as "a semitic fossil."[12] Esteemed as a man of vast learning, Toynbee shows here one of the most commonplace misconceptions in Christendom — one that is inaccurate in fact, pseudoscientific in form, and anti-Semitic in content. Given that conceptualization, his political hostility to Israel — proof positive that the Jews are not a fossil — is predictable. We have mission boards, in fact, as little able to accept the fact that a living Israel refutes the old myth of Jewish decline and disappearance as the ideologically tainted historians who cannot fit Israel into their theories.

Toynbee was a layman of some importance in the early decades of the twentieth century ecumenical movement. His rubric for the Jews deserves analysis. "Fossil" is a word of rejection, reflecting an Anglican gentleman's repudiation of a counterculture that didn't fit his scheme of meaningful history. Significantly, Toynbee's essentially Greek philosophical incapacity to deal with Jewish survival conflicts head-on with Emil Fackenheim's Jewish philosophical affirmation of Jewish survival as a matter of ultimate meaning in a post-Holocaust world, for Christians and other Gentiles as well as for Jews.[13] "Semitic fossil" is a pseudo-scientific term, belonging to the same mythic construct as "Aryan race" and "Aryan" peoples.

About 1780, in the beginnings of modern anthropology, a German professor attempted to delineate the races of man by applying to tribes and peoples some of the theoretical constructs of his colleagues in early language theory.[14] There appeared to be an Indo-European or Aryan language group; hence there were "Aryans" — a conceptualization that has lost considerable attractiveness in the years since Houston Stewart Chamberlain and Alfred Rosenberg. There seemed to be a Semitic language group; hence there were "Semites" — a conceptualization still widespread. How many "Letters to the Editor" explain that the Arabs, unlike the Christians, cannot be guilty of anti-Semitism because they are also "Semites"! Even the word "anti-Semitism" shows how common the misunderstanding still is. If there is no "Semitism," how can there be, in the racial sense, "anti-Semitism"?

What we are speaking about is *Judenfeindschaft* (hostility to Jews) and *Judenhass* (hatred of Jews), and the *Kulturantisemitismus* of Christendom is so all-pervading that even the common language carries it. Using the materials of theological anti-Semitism and cultural anti-Semitism, the prophets of the twentieth century totalitarian creeds have shaped one of the most potent political weapons of all: political anti-Semitism, anti-Semitism as an ideological weapon.

The terrorist weapon, political anti-Semitism, rests upon a broad foundation of centuries of theological and cultural anti-Semitism. The Old Testament dispensation is finished. The "Old Israel" wanders on the margins of history, to disappear unnoticed by God or man. In the words of another nineteenth century man of Enlightenment: "Honor Jerusalem as you would the great dead, but do not disturb its peace."[15] From the superseding theory to "the final solution" is but an easy step. To adapt General Sherman's statement about the American Indians, in this view of history "the only good Jew is a dead Jew."

The third abstraction, which is a potent source of anti-Semitism and the most subtle, is a false universalism. False universalism would dissolve both Christian and Jewish counterculture. This is the major source of liberal anti-Semitism — the kind that has made *The Christian Century,* for example, across many years a predictable center of gentlemanly anti-Semitism. It is the intellectual corner from whence comes John Nicholls Booth, Unitarian clergyman and featured anti-

Jewish writer for *The American Mercury, The Cross and the Flag*, the magazine of the Christian Nationalist Crusade, and the *United Church Observer* of Canada. *The Christian Century* is the leading journal of liberal Protestantism in the United States. *The United Church Observer*, until recently controlled by an anti-Semitic editor, is the most widely circulated denominational journal in North America.

False universalism is the dogma exposed by Bernhard Olsen's brilliant study *Faith and Prejudice* — the book that is still the best study of the religious roots of prejudice, although unfortunately overshadowed by the much inferior Glock and Stark series. In his study of the curricula of four theological groupings, Dr. Olsen discovered that the most anti-Semitic was the "liberal" curriculum. That Sunday school curriculum was anti-Semitic for the same reason it was also anti-Roman Catholic and anti-Fundamentalist — that is, because of a "predisposition toward abstraction,"[16] which repudiated particularity and rejected the peculiar history of any discrete community.

Such "liberal" groups are promiscuous in their membership, their ranks blending readily into the patterns and values and prejudices of the dominant society. "There are no obligations imposed on members toward their own group which are not also considered obligations toward members of other groups."[17] In short, they have abandoned any pretense to counterculture, to going against the stream of the popular mind and mores. Fleeing from the earthiness of human history, with its concreteness of experience, they oppose the dream world of "humanity" to all particularity. Dr. Olsen pointed out the breakdown in their logic: "All history is particular — the history of my group, my church, my nation. Unsharable symbols, ideas, customs, and observances arise within these specific histories."[18]

Beyond that such emancipated Christianity has had predictable difficulty with the Hebrew Scriptures ("Old Testament"). The not-yet-laid ghost of Marcion, that "enlightened" laymen of old who published a "Christian" Bible purged of all Jewishness, haunts the pages of the second edition of *Die Religion in Geschichte und Gegenwart*. In Nazi time Marcion was virtually the patron saint of the collaborating *Deutsche Christen*, who sought to define an "Aryan Christianity" capable of fulfilling the requirements of Article 24 of the Nazi party platform (1920):

> We demand liberty for all religious denominations in the State, so far as they are not a danger to it and do not militate against the morality and moral sense of the German race. The Party, as such, stands for positive Christianity but does not bind itself in the matter of creed to any particular confession. It combats the Jewish materialist spirit within and without us, and is convinced that our nation can achieve permanent health from within only on the principle: "The Common Interest Before Self-Interest."[19]

"Self-interest" is the term the totalitarian mind applies to any counterculture. As for the rest, a resisting churchman said boldly, "The Protestant Church has to start every discussion with the avowal that its doctrine is a permanent affront to the morality and ethical feeling of the German race."[20] The specifics of such ideology were made explicit by Professor Cajus Fabricius of the University of Berlin:

> Every singling out of human individuals, every separation of interests, confusion of opinions, every irregular appearance of selfish interests, everything that calls forth and emphasizes differences between individuals and between various groups is repellent to the spirit of National Socialism, since it disturbs the unity of the *Volk*, breaks up the team spirit and menaces the powerful solidarity of the nation.[21]

But where, in such circumstances, are the Christian countercultures? That Nazism and Communism cannot tolerate a pluralism of value systems is a truism; either in the name of *Gleichschaltung* or under the pressure of the new Great Russian imperialism, countercultures in the German Third Reich and in the USSR suffer oppression and liquidation.

Significant is the fact that Professor Adolf von Harnack, the greatest of the "liberal" Protestant church historians and theologians, embraced Marcion's message — and flunked his exams on Nazism. But the Jews who suffered and perished in Hitler's *Festung Europa* suffered and perished for what the baptized Gentiles would have testified had they remained Christian: for being a counterculture, a sign to the One who is the True God, the Judge of history. A few thousand Christian martyrs cannot cover the fact that millions of Christians apostatized, betrayed the Name. The Holocaust is the major event in recent centuries of Christian history precisely because it exposed the thinness of the veneer that covered the sham of Christianity, the actual devotion of the European tribes to other gods. The six million perished because of the spiritual treason of Christendom.

Christian preaching and teaching had for centuries condemned the Jews to disappear from the pages of history: Finally a political *guru* appeared who was *Konsequent*. Nevertheless, it is important to note that the actual destruction of the Jews was a scientific achievement, planned and rationalized by technicians of euthanasia. Christianity taught that the Jews who survived, preferably in miserable condition, were there for exemplary reasons, and conversion was always a survival option until Hitler's professors took over.

Resentment of History

Clearly, the speculative bent of organized Christian thought did not begin with the Enlightenment, although the peculiar aberrations evident in "Fundamentalism" and liberal Protestantism can be located in the modern period. The devotion of Christian teachers to mythic anti-Semitic constructs that have little base in either Jewish or Christian Scriptures, and none in the language with which the encounter with the Divine is conveyed to us in the Apostolic Writings, was a product of Greek philosophical forms compounded by gentile envy.

The flight from the historical and earthy began with the gentile church fathers, the language of speculation replacing the language of events. The early Christian philosophers drew back from the earthy, fleshly, concrete, particular — and their influence persists today, in spite of the radical *caesura* that was the Holocaust. André Lacocque has written of the finicky taste of those modern Christians who have sought timeless truths and high spirituality and wished to divorce themselves from the paradoxes and concreteness of the Jewish foundations. Even the Scriptures do not escape the tampering of the befuddled, Gnostic mind:

> Within such a perspective, it was not without frowning that pious and moral Christians read the records of men, too "human" for their taste. Jacob the liar, Moses the murderer, David the adulterer, Solomon the idolatrous, the wars waged by Israel are not the most edifying models for readers looking for comforting ethical narratives. Besides, "Church" and state are so mixed up here, the concept of God's intervention in human history so desperately materialistic, and the people's feeling of being elected and chosen so particularistic, that it is really hard to "spiritualize" this Jewish book in order to match it with a truly Christian religiosity.[22]

Not only liberal Christians have fled from history and the God of history. Professor Y. Harkabi of Hebrew University has shown in his study, *Arab Attitudes to Israel,* how a Sunnite rationalist of modern type also rejects the Jewish people in the name of a false universalism:

> Judaism is not a monotheistic religion but a tribal creed. . . . The "God of Israel". . . is obsessed with his people, with the nethermost details of their daily chores. He watches their daily obscenities and their sins without moving a hair. After a few pretentious overtures in the first pages of Genesis, he has spent all his time, energy and intelligence, while the rest of the cosmos rotted, to dispossess a wretched little people of their land, put them to the sword and enter "his people" into possession of land and whatever tree, beast or child who escaped his "wrath." The truth is that this god has never travelled, has never seen the world not to speak of making it. He is a "country" man whose world ended with his tribe, beyond which everything and everybody is equally foreign and equally an enemy. In short, he is a regional, tribal, separatist god, with whom monotheism has absolutely nothing to do.[23]

Neither can Marxism, with its false universalism, handle the truth of Jewish counterculture. Most of us recall, I am sure, Malik's obscene tirade at the UN assembly in October 1973, which heralded the joint Communist and Arab League assault of the anti-Zionist resolution two years later: "Fascism and Zionism are racist creeds. The Zionists have come forward with the theory of the chosen people, an absurd ideology . . . that is religious racism." Malik had evidently repressed the fact that Lenin taught the Communist party to be "chosen" in precisely that sense, the party and its "professional revolutionaries" being the carriers of history. And he had also repressed the fact that the doctrine of divine election anteceded Zionism by three millennia.

The rage for universal truths, accompanied by abandonment of holy events and the Scriptures that record them, came to dominate university-educated thinking following the Enlightenment. It is this style of thinking, symbolized by Kant's principle of universalizability (but preferably in mathematical formulae), that is the single most influential source of liberal anti-Semitism — whether religious or secular. This conceptualization cannot handle the truth of unique events, and neither can it manage the biblical dialectic of particularism and universalism.

Religion in Life, a liberal Methodist journal now defunct, published some time ago a savage attack on Jewish particularism. The professor criticized the Jews of biblical event as conspirators, saboteurs, subversives, a fifth column in Egypt and Babylon. Charging "the Jews" with the same offense in the modern period, the author judges: "It is not surprising that Hitler retaliated against the chosen race by decreeing that it was not the Jewish but the Arian [sic!] race that was chosen.[24] This must be said in the writer's favor: He attacks the early Christians in the Roman Empire for the same perverse devotion to the covenant as the Jews. He would have a hard time showing, however, that in the modern period this has been a major fault of the Christians! Christian devotion to the covenant and obedience in counterculture, in opposition to the spirit of the times, is rare today as a living force — although some fossilized Christian communities can be found that are loyally maintaining the culture-religion of some past age.

Another illustration, in a book called *The Crime of Christendom: The Theological Sources of Anti-Semitism,* is a liberal churchman who manages 11 reasonable chapters. And then in the twelfth, on "The Jewish Dilemma," he demands that American Jews give up their existence — "assimilation or segregation, religion or nationalism, humanism or tribalism, in short, Judaism or Israel?" He praises the spirituality of the American Council for Judaism and concludes that "ethnic and cultural anti-Semitism . . . was originally provoked and continuously nourished by the orthodox Jewish dogma of uniqueness."

> Is God a tribal deity or a universal reality? Is he interested in revealing himself only at a certain point in time, at a certain place, through a certain man, to a certain people?
>
> Only a cosmic universal faith can raise man above the particularisms of the cult.
>
> The Spirit of the Space Age may help men to grow up metaphysically, to abandon our ethnocentric and geocentric theology and to substitute a spiritual religion for a physical one.[25]

To the believing Jew or Christian this flood of enlightened spirituality does not speak to the human condition. It lacks the appeal of a unique, remembered, and relived event. And if believers stop to think, too, they will have some misgivings about this celebrated "Spirit of the Space Age." They will think of six million who died in the Holocaust and three million lovely and simple little Vietnamese slaughtered by ruthless machines controlled by men who thought in abstractions. A red thread runs from Auschwitz to Mylai, but it is not defined by logic: It is defined by the truth that a civilization's attitude to Jewish history and treatment of the Jewish people are the litmus test of how it will act on all critical decisions affecting the powerless.

The Choice: Involvement or Flight

My mind keeps turning back to the spectators, to those whose abstract interest in universalism has made it impossible for them to relate to concrete particulars. All of us who circulate in religious and academic circles frequently run into a familiar type: highly vocal champions of "humanity" who obviously hate the human person. Another type is at least as common: individuals who think that their academic degrees entitle them to moral objectivity, which they confuse with fair play in methodology and reporting.

Scholars of the Holocaust divide people, apart from the Jewish victims and a few Christian martyrs, into the perpetrators and the spectators. The spectators are in a way more difficult to interpret. Satan and his angels, the perpetrators, have a classic place in Jewish and Christian mythology. The victims also are intelligible, although pat, traditional religious explanations cannot easily be applied to the martyrs of the *Shoah*.

What of the spectators? A long interview published 7 July 1975 in *The New York Times* gave me a useful key to unlock the psychology of the spectators. The interview, taken in secret behind curtained windows in a distant city, reported on the break of one Peter Diapoulos from the Mafia. As the story unfolds, we learn that after 15 years in the Gallo faction of the Colombo family of the Mafia, Diapoulos became disenchanted. A new leadership, nicknamed "the Blast," had taken over. "'The Blast,'" said Diapoulos, "is a high bleacher." It seems that the man supposed to be a leader, when "the boys" were down on the streets fighting, was way up in the bleachers looking on.

This gives us help in understanding people like Pius XII, the counterpart Protestant church leaders, or, for that matter, such American churchmen as the editors of *The Christian Century* and *America*. The diversionary question is, What could they have done? The real question is, What were they doing way up there in the bleachers — when an epic battle was joined, a battle of life and death for Jewry, a battle affecting the basic credibility of the faith they had taken vows to serve selflessly?

The first question affecting Christian credibility is not, as frequently asked, Why did the Christians abandon the Jews? The key question is, By what accommodating stance "above politics," by what perverted idealism, by what flight from real confrontations and choices, did the shepherds abandon their "sheep" — to be corralled into other pens, indeed to demonstrate in due season that they were not sheep at all, but wolves? The worst set of crimes in the history of humankind were designed by professors, engineered by Ph.D.s, and operated by baptized

Christians who had turned their faith into a speculative ideology of genocidal potential. Until the churches have come clean on that massive event, and stop trying to hide behind the skirts of an occasional Bonhoeffer or von Moltke — of whom they were not worthy then and are not worthy now — no amount of abstract reference to "humanity" or "universalism" will save them from the very specific and particular end the Bible reserves for betrayers and apostates: descent into the pit.

It is time for the Christians to go up to Jerusalem again — not for some vulgar triumphalist missions or patronizing political schemes, but to go back to school. When that happens, when Christians remember again the quarry from whence they were dug, the rock from which they were hewn (Isa. 51:1), the "cup of trembling" may perhaps be taken from their hands. That cup was taken out of the hands of the Jewish people with a reborn Israel and put into the hands of those who afflicted them (Isa. 51:22–23).

The metaphor of "the cup of trembling" is perhaps too mild, too indicative of a predictable recovery of Christianity from its self-inflicted wounds. A few months ago I received a letter from one of the great contemporary Old Testament Christian scholars. He was responding to the language of my book, *The Crucifixion of the Jews,* in which the question of the credibility of Christianity after Auschwitz is raised so sharply that some so-called "liberal" Protestant journals would not even allow it to be reviewed. The language of his letter was more terrible than mine:

> In Exodus we find in all three records, J, E and P, that first Pharaoh hardened his own heart, and only then did God harden it for him, giving him, could we say, the final coup de grace. This process God took up into his plan of grace. For there would have been no exodus of Israel if Pharaoh's heart had not grown hard. . . . It was part of the plan God had for Israel.
>
> Now, before our very eyes we see "Christendom," Europe and America, hardening its heart against the gospel which it rejected in the days of Hitler. The ordinary man is abandoning the Church in droves. I can only see this as God's giving the coup the grace again. . . .
>
> Western man, because of the Holocaust, has destroyed the credibility of the Gospel. . . .[26]

The writer went on to prophesy the appearance of a new and vital Christianity in Asia, Africa south of the Sahara, and other emerging nations — although the Christendom that committed and/or permitted the Holocaust and has refused to repent of it will be written off.

Perhaps the Christian churches, infused with new blood, may find their way back into history. Even in America some significant articles and books are now appearing, and since 1973 there has been a significant rise in the number of Christian congregations observing *Yom Hashoah*. Since 1970 the number of courses on the Holocaust in institutions of higher education, including Christian seminaries, has swelled from no more than a dozen to nearly one thousand. It is the issue of the Holocaust, which no person of conscience can avoid, that is forcing Christians to take a radical look at what the churches have traditionally taught about the Jewish people.

The most important official action of a Christian church, as distinct from individual theological writing, has come however not from America but from the German Federal Republic. I refer to the position paper adopted in the Synod of the Evangelische Kirche des Rheinlands in January 1980. Among those who played key roles in preparing the way for adoption of this important break with Christian triumphalism were men who have over the years wrestled with the lessons of the *Kirchenkampf* and *Shoah* — especially Professor Heinz Kremers of Duisburg and Dr. Eberhard Bethge of Bonn.

The Rheinland Synod's declaration goes right to the heart of the matter, and it deserves to rank with the Barmen Declaration that opened the confrontation of faithful Christians with Nazism in 1934. The high points are as follows:

> The provincial Synod accepts the historical necessity of attaining a new relationship of the church to the Jewish people. The church is brought to this by four factors:
> a. The recognition of Christian co-responsibility and guilt for the Holocaust. . . .
> b. The new biblical insights concerning the continuing significance of the Jewish people for salvation history (e.g., Rom. 9–11), which have been attained in connection with the Church Struggle.
> c. The insight that the continuing existence of the Jewish people, its return to the Land of Promise, and also the creation of the State of Israel are signs of the faithfulness of God toward God's people. . . .
> d. The readiness of Jews, in spite of the Holocaust, to [engage in] encounter, common study, and cooperation. . . .[27]

The concreteness with which the issue of the state of Israel is handled indicates the quality of the Synod's findings, turning back in the flight from history.

An affirmative attitude toward Israel is essential to the healing of the churches' misery: "Even-handedness" is the style of abstract religion and Gnostic politics, both of which are engines for Jewish death and Christian suicide. It is Israel that has brought the Jewish people out of accommodation and assimilation into self-respect; it is Israel that can bring the Christians, if anything can, out of wandering in an empty space, out of hardening of heart, into a real encounter with real people in real history.

Now let Christians and Jews unite in recitation:

"Many a time have they afflicted me from my youth:
  Yet they have not prevailed against me.
The plowers plowed upon my back:
  They made long their furrows.
Yet the Lord is righteous:
  he hath cut asunder the cords of the wicked.

Let all them be confounded and turned back
that hate Zion!'' (Is. 129:2–5)

Am Israel Chai!

Notes

1. Alexandre Donat, *The Holocaust Kingdom* (New York: Hold, Rinehart and Winston, 1965), pp. 230–31.

2. Cf. *CCI Notebook* 24 (November 1975), *passim.*

3. Cf. Sallie Te Selle, *Speaking in Parables* (Philadelphia: Fortress Press, 1975), *passim.*

4. Letter from TRP, 3 January 1976.

5. Elie Wiesel, *Souls on Fire* (New York: Random House, 1972), p. 32.

6. Golo Mann, *The History of Germany Since 1789* (New York: Praeger, 1965), p. 452.

7. Cyprian, ''Three Books of Testimonies Against the Jews,'' Treatise XII in volume XIII of *The Ante-Nicene Christian Library,* ed. Roberts and Donaldson (Edinburgh: T. & T. Clark, 1869), pp. 78–198.

8. Cited in Amos Elon, *The Israelis: Founders and Sons* (New York: Holt, Rinehart and Winston, 1971), p. 51.

9. ''Declaration on the Relationship of the Church to Non-Christian Religions,'' in *Commentary on the Documents of Vatican II,* ed. Herbert Vorgrimler (New York: Herder & Herder, 1969), III, pp. 1–136.

10. Cited in *CCI Notebook* 4 (October 1971), p. 2.

11. Loraine Boettner, *The Millenium* (Philadelphia: Presbyterian and Reformed Publishing Co., 1958), p. 311f.

12. Arnold J. Toynbee, *A Study of History,* abridged by D.E. Somervel (New York & London: Oxford University Press, 1947), I, pp. 22, 135, 388–89.

13. Emil Fackenheim, *To Mend the World* (New York: Schocken Books, 1982).

14. S.D. Goitein, *Jews and Arabs* (New York: Schocken Books, 1964), p. 19.

15. Abraham Geiger, quoted in H.G. Adler, *The Jews in Germany: From the Enlightenment to National Socialism* (Notre Dame & London: University of Notre Dame Press, 1969), p. 101.

16. Bernhard Olsen, *Faith and Prejudice* (New Haven: Yale University Press, 1963), p. 80.

17. Ibid., p. 49.

18. Ibid., p. 52.

19. Paul B. Means, *Things That Are Caesar's* (New York: Roundtable Press, 1935), p. 269.

20. Cited in Joachim Beckmann, ed., *Kirchliches Jahrbuch: 1933–1944,* (Gütersloh: Gütersloh Verlagshaus, 1948), p. 3.

21. Cajus Fabricius, *Positive Christianity in the Third Reich* (Dresden: Püschel, 1937), p. 13.

22. André Lacocque, ''Encounter with the Old Testament,'' *The Chicago Theological Seminary Register* 112, no. 2 (1972): 1.

23. Y. Harkabi, *Arab Attitudes to Israel* (Jerusalem: Israel Universities Press, 1971), pp. 261, 263.

24. George Wesley Buchanan, ''Jewish and Christian Relationships,'' *Religion in Life,* Summer 1971, p. 279.

25. Fred Gladstone Bratton, *The Crime of Christendom* (Boston: Beacon Press, 1969), pp. 204, 223, 224.

26. Personal letter from GAFK, 2 April 1976.

27. Published in *Journal of Ecumenical Studies* 12, 1 (1980): 211–12.

5 GERMAN PROTESTANT RESPONSES TO NAZI PERSECUTION OF THE JEWS

Ruth Zerner

In Nazi Germany no issue revealed more about the moral climate and sensitivity of traditionally humane institutions in German society than Christian churches' attitudes toward Jews and toward systematic governmental persecution of the Jews, first within Germany and then throughout Nazi-occupied Europe. In exploring the responses of Protestant leaders to the various stages of Nazi tormenting, transporting, and terminating of Jewish life in the Third Reich, we gain perspective on the degree of commitment of Protestants, both as individuals and as leaders of church institutions, to opposing injustices, inequities, and abuses of power in their society. In times of crisis church leaders face the dilemma of choosing between a focus on conserving traditional customs, doctrines, and organizational structures or the priority of working actively to alter glaring evils, particularly symptoms of group pathology and massive societal trauma. In this continual challenge of choosing between continuity and change, continuity has usually triumphed among contemporary Christian leaders and thinkers, unless cataclysmic events have called for rethinking and major changes.

During the last decade, for example, numerous German Protestant leaders have been working toward a reorientation of German Protestant attitudes toward Jews and Judaism. In this endeavor they have been impelled by knowledge of the facts of the Holocaust and awareness of the role that theological anti-Judaism played in preparing many Germans to accept without protest Nazi discriminatory measures aimed against Jews. Current German Protestant concern for dialogue and reconciliation with Jews represents the most significant development in post-World War II Protestant church life in West Germany.

During the 1930s, however, a common concern for persecuted Jews and for their religious traditions and rights was not characteristic of most of the statements issued by German Protestant church leaders. In these decisive early years of Hitler's regime the pattern for German Protestant responses to Nazism was set for the duration of Nazi rule. Therefore, Protestant pronouncements from 1933 to 1938 deserve special scrutiny. Unfortunately, even among the non-Nazi protesting, "confessing," Christian Church leaders, institutional self-preservation and ultimately survival became the primary concerns. From 1933 on a battle (*Kirchenkampf*) emerged in the German Evangelical (Protestant) Church to preserve the continuity of church doctrine against the increasing inroads of the Nazi state, which was transgressing traditional boundaries by attempting to interfere with church practices. But even the vanguard of German Protestant opposition to Hitler's tactics — leaders of the Confessing Church who emerged from the Pastors' Emergency League (numbering 7,036 clergy in January 1934 out of a total of 18,000 pastors)[1] and who criticized the German Evangelical Church because of its capitulation to or compromise with the Nazis — did not focus on the plight of Jews as Jews. Instead public statements of these protesting Protestant spokesmen concentrated on the plight of baptized Jews, who were members of Christian church communities throughout Germany.

Yet one young Confessing Church leader stands out for his foresight in being one of the first to focus on the Jewish issue as the crucial one in the church struggle. Although this precocious Lutheran pastor-scholar, Dietrich Bonhoeffer, concentrated his attention on the special tragedy of baptized Jews, he early recognized the injustices done to all Jews, when he proposed in April 1933 that the Christian Church should aid the victims of state action "even if they do not belong to the Christian community." In what Bonhoeffer termed "the Jewish problem" at that time, he saw such action as the compelling demand of the hour; but Bonhoeffer also anticipated that a time might come when direct political action might be necessary "not just to bandage the victims under the wheel," but to jam the spokes of the wheel itself.[2] This comment foreshadowed Bonhoeffer's later involvement (in the 1940s) in the conspiracy against Hitler, an activity for which he was executed by the Nazis in April 1945.

During 1933 the 26-year-old Bonhoeffer (who had received his doctorate in theology at the age of 21) revealed in personal letters the depth of his concern about "the cultural barbarization" of his nation, which would soon necessitate the creation of a civil liberties union in Germany.[3] He also lamented the fact that some of "the most sensible people" in the church had "completely lost their heads and their Bibles" in dealing with "the Jewish question."[4] The most dramatic statement Bonhoeffer uttered on the persecution of Jews was a sentence spoken to his students after the horror of Crystal Night in 1938: "Only he who cries out for the Jews may sing Gregorian chants."[5] One of Bonhoeffer's students in an underground seminary of the Confessing Church recalls that after observing the effects of Crystal Night in Berlin, Bonhoeffer "utterly refused to see in destruction of the synagogues by the Nazis a fulfillment of the curse on the Jews. This, he said was a case of sheer violence. 'If the synagogues burn today, the churches will be on fire tomorrow.'"[6]

In deeds as well as words Bonhoeffer expressed his concern for the plight of German Jews; in 1943 his arrest by the Gestapo was linked to his involvement in the illegal smuggling of 14 Jews into Switzerland. As an agent in the intelligence service run by Admiral Canaris and as a person committed to the conspiracy against Hitler's life, Bonhoeffer clearly recognized, in his writings of the early 1940s (later compiled in a volume titled *Ethics*), his personal guilt, along with the collective guilt of the Christian Church: "She [the Church] was silent when she should have cried out because the blood of the innocent was crying to heaven. She has failed to speak the right word in the right time and at the right place. . . . She is guilty of the deaths of the weakest and most defenseless brothers of Jesus Christ."[7] Although far-sighted and finally aware of the guilt of his church, some of Bonhoeffer's statements in the 1930s (to be indicated later in this paper) show that he was bound by certain Christian theological presuppositions, such as the cursed Jews tradition.

The legacy of Christian anti-Judaism had been intensified in Germany by Martin Luther's vituperative comments during his last years about Jews (especially two 1543 tracts: *On the Jews and their Lies* and *Vom Schem Hamphoras*). While calling Jews ignorant, stupid asses, blasphemers, thieves, and devils incarnate, he urged the burning of their synagogues and schools, destroying their homes, burning their sacred books, banning teachings by their rabbis, curtailing their movements, depriving them of money obtained through usury, and then ejecting them "forever from the country."[8] Such name calling and intemperate use of language against Jews represent a tragic legacy within the German Lutheran tradition. Just as many American Evangelicals have dissociated themselves from the anti-Semitic statement made by Bailey Smith — that God does not hear the prayers of Jews[9] — so one wishes that German Protestants in the pre-Nazi and Nazi eras had clearly denounced and repudiated Luther's legacy of anti-Judaism. In fact in 1977 Eberhard Bethge, student, friend, and biographer of Dietrich Bonhoeffer, lamented the fact that the most important study of Jewish-Christian relations to be issued by his German Evangelical Church is the post-World War II era (*Christen und Juden,* Gütersloh, 1975) made no mention "of the fatal influence of Luther's theological and social anti-Semitism."[10]

Contemporary Christian theologians, who have become particularly sensitive to the inherent dangers of a philosophical emphasis on a mind-body duality, should recognize that words and actions cannot be simplistically separated. Conceptual frameworks, words selected, infuse power, which may build or destroy communities. The failure to speak out is also a form of action, basically a support of the status quo or the political institutions in power. The Protestant lack of protest against blatant anti-Semitic measures of the Nazi state was admitted immediately after the Second World War in *Kirchliches Jahrbuch,* which conceded that at least the Confessing Church (representing about one-third of the German Protestant clergy) had protested discrimination against Jewish-Christians, "but against anti-Semitism they uttered no word, and even at the time of the Jewish persecutions and of their extermination it could not bring itself to stand up against these acts of terrorism in the Third Reich. The official church in general approved openly or secretly Jewish policy and accepted the measures of the National Socialist regime both in and without the church."[11] One of the most perceptive scholars of the dilemmas the Christian churches faced under Hitler's persecution, the Canadian John Conway, has aptly summarized the responsibility of the churches:

> The German Churches were trapped in a situation which exposed their every weakness and encouraged every temptation. Humanly speaking, their leaders, by collaborating with the Nazis, were no more and no less guilty than the rest of their fellow countrymen. But, as custodians of the Christian Gospel, their conduct must be judged by different standards. Their readiness to allow the truths of the Christian faith to be distorted for the purposes of political expediency, and their failure to denounce the crimes so openly committed in their society, place a heavy burden of guilt upon them.[12]

Although leaders of the Evangelical Church had done nothing before 1933 to prepare their parishoners to resist the flood of anti-Semitic propaganda or to warn against the dangers of Christian wallowing in anti-Jewish feelings, the most obvious examples of virulent anti-Semitism in the church itself were found among the "German Christians," supporters of Hitler, who wanted to link Nazism and Christianity. They repeatedly condemned Jewish influence in Germany as corrupting, quoted from Luther's anti-Semitic tracts, and warned against marriage with Jews, even converted Jewish-Christians. When the German Christian leader Ludwig Müller won election as reich bishop of the Evangelical Church in July 1933, the church struggle began in earnest. Shrewdly, Müller attempted to focus clergy concern purely on pastoral duties (while he and his cohorts tried to nazify the Church). Thus he wrote in 1934 to his ministers:

> I beg you, for the sake of the church, for the sake of the people, direct your whole attention for the time being to your parishes, to the duty that lies plain before your feet. Visitation of the sick is a better medicine than wranglings over church politics![13]

But moral equivocation and paralysis were also evident in 1933 among the intellectual leaders of the church who did not become "German Christians." For example, a group of theologians at Erlangen University, including the distinguished scholars Paul Althaus and Werner Elert, defended, in certain instances, the notorious "Aryan paragraph," which called for dismissal of non-Aryan clergy from office. Althaus, however, had already revealed his anti-Judaism in the pre-Hitler period; in 1927 he had declared publicly that the church was threatened by a "demoralized and demoralizing, urban intellectual class which is represented primarily by the Jewish race."[14]

On the other hand, the Protestant clergy who joined in the Confessing Church included courageous pastors who were willing to risk their own lives to help save persecuted Jews, regardless of whether they were Jews who had converted to Christianity or who had remained Jews. Immediately after Crystal Night in 1938, Pastor Karl Immer in Barmen-Gemarke held a moving service in which he reminded his congregation that within a few hundred yards of the church building the Word of God had been burned. Then he read the Ten Commandments and the story of the good Samaritan. He invited those in the congregation who understood the meaning of these texts to join him after the service, and between 40 and 50 persons joined him afterward to plan how they could help Jewish neighbors emigrate from Germany with false passports.[15] In a more systematic, organized way Pastor Heinrich Grüber of Berlin set up, on his own initiative, an Evangelical Welfare Office for Jews, in September of 1936; this Grüber bureau was an effective center for the assistance and guidance of Jews who sought to emigrate, until Grüber himself was arrested by the Gestapo in December 1940 and sent to the concentration camps of Sachsenhausen and Dachau. Grüber's bureau, and its subsidiaries in at least 20 other German cities, became "welfare service, consulate, legal aid bureau, school headquarters, health department, clothing store and spiritual power-house all rolled into one."[16] Although Grüber survived his term in the concentration camps, few of his 35 co-workers in the Berlin Grüber bureau survived the end of the war. Numerous other individuals secretly saved the lives of Jews by helping them to escape Germany.

Yet after the war was over, the leaders of the German Evangelical Church recognized the need for confessions of guilt, beginning with the vague generalizations of the Stuttgart guilt statement of 1945, which did not deal specifically with the Holocaust. By 1950, in the Weissensee Synod, the German Evangelical Church admitted: "We must say that by omission and silence we have become guilty as well before the merciful God for the evil deed, which has been performed by the people of our nation towards the Jews."[17]

When we focus on the segment of the Evangelical Church that formed the Confessing Church, we observe that their preoccupation in the early years of Nazi rule was with the issue of non-Aryans in their churches — concern for baptized Jews, not for all Jews. Since elsewhere I have analyzed in detail the comments of Confessing Church leaders concerning Jews,[18] I shall now briefly survey their stance toward Nazi persecution of the Jews in the 1930s.

The first Protestant church leader who reacted in writing to the initial Nazi measures against the Jews was Dr. Walter Künneth, who later became a member of the Confessing Church and a strident critic of Nazi ideology. On 11 April 1933 at a church administrators' conference, Künneth presented a paper on "The Jewish Problem and the Church," a response to the promulgation on 7 April 1933 of the "Law for the Re-establishment of the Professional Civil Service," with its famous "Aryan clause." Article 3 of this law called for the retirement of all civil service officials of "non-Aryan descent," with the exception of those "who were already in service on 1 August 1914, or who fought in the world war at the front for the German Reich, or who fought for its allies, or whose fathers or sons were killed in the world war."[19] Discussing this qualifying clause, Künneth commented condescendingly that there could be "valuable Jews," ready to sacrifice their lives for the nation.[20] Arguing that the expulsion of Jews from the Christian Church would be a debasing of the sacrament of baptism, he concluded that there was no reason to deny Jews the opportunity for church membership or office holding as pastor or church administrator.[21] On the other hand, he undermined this position by considering it a "foregone conclusion" that the "post of Bishop and other positions of leadership in the Church should be reserved for those of the German race."[22]

Even the title of Künneth's essay revealed his willingness to accept the Nazi designation of a "Jewish problem." Accepting the fundamental right of the state to regulate the "Jewish question" and reflecting traditional Lutheran teaching on church-state relations, Künneth declared that the church did not want to interfere with the state's functions: "The church knows that the state must wield the sword. This office implies harshness and severity."[23] Although Künneth spoke of the importance of exercising Christian love, he was willing to accept the concept of "the elimination of Jewish influence" in Germany. Throughout his essay, Künneth's descriptions of Jews were telling indications of his judgmental, negative attitude toward Jews:

–a "foreign body" in Germany
–Jewish influence which threatened to overrun German intellectual life and to allow foreign control of German public life
–the disproportionate number of Jews in important posts and professions (civil servants, doctors, lawyers)
–the need to protect Germany by law from this Jewish monopoly
–necessity of erecting dams against the Jewish overflow.[24]

In addition to reinforcing these popular stereotypes of Jews, Künneth emphasized the Christian tradition that the rejection of Jesus, the Messiah, led to a curse resting on all Jews, a burden also borne by Jewish Christians: "The cross of Christ meant the collapse of Jewry as a people."[25] In a 1935 anti-Nazi publication Künneth reiterated his negative characterization of Jewish influence:

> The people of salvation became the people of the curse; the people of God became germ carriers for the poisoning of nationalities. The Christian revelation does not blind one to the destructiveness of Jewry, but rather makes one more sharp sighted than the heathen,

> nationality-oriented person. To equate today's Jewry with the people of Israel of the Old Testament means to turn the course of history upside down.[26]

Moreover, Martin Niemöller, the most outspoken leader of the Confessing Church, also expounded publicly on the theological tradition of the cursed Jews. He proclaimed in a 1935 sermon:

> What then is the real reason for this manifest penal judgment which continues in force century after century? Dearly beloved, the answer is evident, the Jews have caused the crucifixion of God's Christ. . . . They bear the curse, and because they rejected the forgiveness, they drag about with them as a fearsome burden the unforgiven blood-guilt of their fathers.[27]

While upholding the rights of Jewish Christians to hold office within the German Protestant Church, Niemöller interjected that Germans "as a people have suffered much under the influence of the Jewish people."[28] Despite such personal prejudices, Niemöller staunchly opposed the application of the Aryan clause to the church; in October 1933 he drafted the vow to be taken by the members of the Pastors' Emergency League: "Under this vow I testify that a violation of the Confessional position is perpetrated by the application of the Aryan paragraph within the Church of Christ."[29]

Because of his opposition to Nazi inroads in church life and because of his role in presenting a May 1936 Confessing Church memorandum to Hitler, Niemöller was imprisoned by the Nazis in 1937 and remained Hitler's personal prisoner until the end of the war. This 1936 memorandum firmly rejected hatred of the Jews: "When within the framework of the National Socialist *Weltanschauung* an anti-Semitism is forced on the Christian, which demands hatred of the Jews, opposed to this concept stands the Christian command to love one's neighbor."[30] After 1945 Niemöller emerged as the most vigorous postwar proponent of the guilt of the Christian Church in Germany: "The guilt exists, there is no doubt about it. Even if there were no other guilt than that of the six million clay urns, containing the ashes of burnt Jews from all over Europe."[31]

Another Confessing Church leader who revealed a tragically judgmental attitude toward Jews was the Bavarian Protestant bishop, Hans Meiser. On the eve of the promulgation of the 15 September 1935 Nuremberg Laws (which deprived Jews of German citizenship and of other civil rights), Meiser, at a 13 September 1935 Berlin meeting, warned the Confessing Church leaders against any public moves regarding the Jewish question, since the Jews were only undergoing "a self-incurred martyrdom."[32]

In 1967 Karl Barth, the distinquished theological mentor of the Confessing Church, also confessed his failure to focus on the issue of the persecution of the Jews in the two Barmen Declarations he authored in 1934.[33] Earlier, in September 1933, Barth had indicated in a private letter to Dietrich Bonhoeffer that instead of a possible church split over the non-Aryan issue, "the clash could occur on an even more central issue."[34]

During the first months of Nazi rule Bonhoeffer recognized the crucial character of the Jewish question, and, like Künneth, he rapidly responded to the 7 April 1933 Nazi law depriving Jews of their civil service positions. Recognizing the danger this legislation posed for baptized Jews, Bonhoeffer opposed the application of the Aryan clause within the German Protestant Church. In his 15 April 1933 essay, "The Church and the Jewish Question," Bonhoeffer separated the Christian Church's attitude toward the new political problems of Jews in general from the special problem of baptized Jews. Maintaining that the Church of the Reformation had no right "to praise or to censure the laws of the state," Bonhoeffer argued that the right to accuse the state of offenses against morality was reserved to individuals and to "humanitarian organizations," a grouping in which the church was not included.[35] Unfortunately, Bonhoeffer, like Künneth, acknowledged the right of the state to deal with "the Jewish problem":

> Without doubt the Jewish question is one of the historical problems which our state must deal with, and without doubt the state is justified in adopting new methods here. . . . The Church cannot in the first place exert direct political action, for the Church does not pretend to have any knowledge of the necessary course of history. Thus even today in the Jewish question, it cannot address the state directly and demand of it some definite action of a different nature. . . . It is not the Church, but the state, which makes and changes the law.[36]

In this April 1933 essay Bonhoeffer also accepted and expounded on the Christian teaching concerning the "cursed" Jews: "The Church of Christ has never lost sight of the thought that the 'chosen people,' who nailed the redeemer of the world to the cross, must bear the curse for its action through a long history of suffering."[37] Later in 1933, however, Bonhoeffer focused on restraining popular attitudes of revenge and contempt toward Jews. He participated in framing resolutions at two church conferences, both revealing unwillingness to capitalize on traditional Christian condemnation of Jews: "No nation can ever be commissioned to avenge on the Jews the murder at Golgatha."[38] "We especially deplore the fact that the State measures against the Jews in Germany have had such an effect on public opinion that in some circles the Jewish race is considered a race of inferior status."[39] Despite the anti-Judaic biases of centuries of Christian teachings, Bonhoeffer continued to actively help Jews, both in Germany and in England (where he lived from the end of 1933 until 1935). By the end of 1933 it was evident that Bonhoeffer would not permit such theological ideas (even when reinforced by the doctrine about the "cursed Jews") to paralyze his actions on behalf of Jews.[40]

Although Dietrich Bonhoeffer, executed by the Nazis, did not survive the Second World War, his students and theological heirs in postwar Germany have taken the lead in rethinking the Christian legacy of anti-Judaism and its historical consequences. Outstanding among these pastors and theologians are Eberhard

Bethge, student and biographer of Bonhoeffer,[41] Wolfgang Gerlach,[42] and Bertold Klappert.[43] In the Federal Republic of Germany the serious scholarly explorations of these men have recently been accompanied by official church studies and statements on Jewish-Christian relations. In 1975 the executive council of the German Protestant Church issued an informative study of Christian-Jewish relations titled *Christians and Jews*.[44] Originally intending to give this memorandum a more decisive, authoritative character, the Rhineland Synod of the German Protestant Church in 1976 set up a commission to study Jewish-Christian relations. After four years of deliberations this commission, made up of twenty-two members, four of whom were Jews, moved beyond the original 1975 study and proposed their own set of theses, which was adopted overwhelmingly by the General Synod of the Rhineland Church on 11 January 1980, the "Resolution on the Renewal of the Relationship Between Christians and Jews."[45] This document stands out as the most progressive and pointed statement to be adopted by a Protestant church body in Germany on issues of common concern to Jews and Christians today. It also represents the first time that Jews participated actively in the formulation of an official Christian Church statement in Germany. Leading Christian scholars of Jewish-Christian traditions participated in the commission, including Bethge, Klappert, and Heinz Kremers.[46] Their final declaration lists the Holocaust as the first motivating factor impelling the Rhineland Synod "to achieve a new relationship between the Church and the Jewish people." The document recognizes "Christian co-responsibility and guilt in the Holocaust, the defamation, persecution and murder of Jews in the Third Reich."[47]

The Christian leaders and Jewish scholars who formulated this statement recognize the power of language, an inescapable lesson drawn from the record of Protestant responses to Nazi policies. Words and silence are both responses that empower the community in constructive or destructive ways. How we label, categorize, and characterize those outside our immediate grouping can ultimately have fatal consequences, as many Christians have learned in Germany.

Moreover, the changing, dynamic qualities of institutional life call for continuing reexamination of institutional goals, priorities, and activities. In times of crisis individuals are faced with the basic alternatives of supporting or unmasking the institutions in which they participate, including church and state. In the Nazi era the German Evangelical Church, even in its more outspoken and courageous manifestation — the Confessing Church — appears in retrospect primarily self-protective, not prophetic. The church leaders failed to show themselves as "men for others" (Bonhoeffer's capsule description of Christians).[48] Observing their behavior, we can conclude that in Nazi Germany ambivalence, the inability to take a clear position, or silence lent support to the persons in control of the state.

Finally, a challenge to the leaders of all Christian churches emerges from the German record, not just to the German Protestants. After the Holocaust, all

Christians must ask themselves whether anti-Judaism is basically intrinsic to Christian churches or extrinsic. If it is intrinsic to Christianity, as at least two leading female scholars have argued (Charlotte Klein and Rosemary Radford Ruether),[49] then it is incumbent upon Christians to eliminate its poison from their language, attitudes, and action.

A postwar, self-reflective analysis by Martin Niemöller fittingly summarizes the lessons that German Protestants have learned from their own responses to Nazi persecution policies:

> First the Nazis went after the Jews, but I was not a Jew, so I did not object. Then they went after the Catholics, but I was not a Catholic, so I did not object. Then they went after the Trade-Unionists, but I was not a Trade-Unionist, so I did not object. Then they came after me, and there was no one left to object.[50]

Notes

1. Ernst Christian Helmreich, *The German Churches under Hitler: Background, Struggle, and Epilogue* (Detroit: Wayne State University Press, 1979), pp. 156, 495. After January 1934 the withdrawal of large numbers of Protestant pastors from Bavaria, Hanover, and Württemberg "left a membership of 5,256, which remained relatively unchanged in the following years." Ibid., p. 156.

2. Dietrich Bonhoeffer, "Die Kirche vor der Judenfrage" (Vortrag April 1933), *Gesammelte Schriften* [hereafter cited as *GS*] (Munich: Christian Kaiser Verlag, 1965), II, pp. 44–53. For the English translation, see Dietrich Bonhoeffer, *No Rusty Swords: Letters, Lectures and Notes, 1928–1936* [hereafter cited as *NRS*], ed. Edwin H. Robertson (London: Collins, 1965, 1970, 1971), p. 221.

3. *GS* (1974), VI, p. 260. Letter of Dietrich Bonhoeffer to Professor Reinhold Niebuhr, 6 February 1933.

4. *GS* (1965), I, p. 37. Letter of Dietrich Bonhoeffer to Erwin Sutz, 14 April 1933.

5. Eberhard Bethge, *Dietrich Bonhoeffer: Man of Vision, Man of Courage,* translated from the German by Eric Mosbacher, Peter and Betty Ross, Frank Clarke, William Glen-Doepel, under the editorship of Edwin Robertson (New York and Evanston: Harper & Row, 1970), p. 512.

6. Gottfried Maltusch, "When the Synagogues Burnt," in *I Knew Dietrich Bonhoeffer,* ed. Wolf-Dieter Zimmermann and Ronald Gregor Smith, translated from the German by Käthe Gregor Smith (London: Collins, 1966, 1973), p. 150.

7. Dietrich Bonhoeffer, *Ethics,* ed. Eberhard Bethge (New York: Macmillan, 1955, 1965), pp. 113–14, 116.

8. Martin Luther, "On the Jews and their Lies," in *Luther's Works,* ed. Franklin Sherman, trans. Martin H. Bertram (Philadelphia: Fortress Press, 1971), vol. 47, pp. 190, 213–14, 216–17, 227, 268–72.

9. *Christianity Today,* 24 April 1981, p. 12.

10. Eberhard Bethge, "The Holocaust and Christian Anti-Semitism: Perspectives of a Survivor," *Union Seminary Quarterly Review* 32, nos. 3 & 4 (Spring & Summer, 1977): 152.

11. Quoted in Helmreich, *The German Churches under Hitler,* p. 332.

12. John S. Conway, *The Nazi Persecution of the Churches, 1933–45* (New York: Basic Books, 1968), p. 46.

13. Quoted in F. Burton Nelson, "The Holocaust and the American Future," *Radix,* January/February 1981, p. 5.

14. Quoted in J.R.C. Wright, *"Above Parties": The Political Attitudes of the German Protestant Church Leadership, 1918–1933* (Oxford: Oxford University Press, 1974), p. 54.

15. Heinrich Albertz, "Erinnerung eines Augenzeugen: Der Gottesdienst nach dem Judenpogrom in Barmen-Gemarke am 13.11.1938," in *Umkehr und Erneuerung,* ed. Bertold Klappert and Helmut Starck (Neukirchen-Vluyn: Neukirchener Verlag, 1980), p. 282.

16. Richard Gutteridge, *Open Thy Mouth for the Dumb!: The German Evangelical Church and the Jews, 1879–1950* (Oxford: Basil Blackwell, 1976), p. 208.

17. Quoted in Bethge, "The Holocaust and Christian Anti-Semitism: Perspectives of a Christian Survivor," pp. 149–50.

18. Ruth Zerner, "Germany's Confessing Church Leaders and the Jews in the 1930s: A Comment," *Centerpoint: A Journal of Interdisciplinary Studies,* special issue on *The Holocaust* 4, no. 1 (Fall 1980): 101–12.

19. Jeremy Noakes and Geoffrey Pridham, eds., *Documents on Nazism, 1919–1945* (New York: Viking Press, 1975), pp. 229–30.

20. Walter Künneth, "Das Judenproblem und die Kirche," in *Die Nation vor Gott: Zur Botschaft der Kirche im Dritten Reich,* ed. Walter Künneth and Helmuth Schreiner (Berlin: Im Wichern Verlag, 1934), p. 118.

21. Ibid., p. 124.

22. Ibid., p. 126.

23. Ibid., p. 135.

24. Ibid., pp. 117, 119, 120, 130.

25. Ibid., p. 129.

26. Walter Künneth, *Antwort auf den Mythus: Die Entscheidung zwischen dem nordischen Mythus und dem biblischen Christus* (Berlin: Im Wichern Verlag, 1935), p. 69.

27. Martin Niemöller, *First Commandment* (London: William Hodge and Company, 1937), pp. 246–47. Quoted in Gutteridge, *Open Thy Mouth,* p. 104.

28. Martin Niemöller, "Sätze zur Arierfrage in der Kirche," 2 November 1933, in *Die Bekenntnisse und grundsätzlichen Äusserungen zur Kirchenfrage des Jahres 1933,* ed. Kurt Dietrich Schmidt (Göttingen: Vandenhoech & Ruprecht, 1938), p. 97.

29. Arthur Frey, *Cross and Swastika: The Ordeal of the German Church* (London: Student Christian Movement Press, 1938), p. 144.

30. *Die Evangelische Kirche in Deutschland und die Judenfrage: Ausgewählte Dokumente aus den Jahren 1933 bis 1943* (Geneva: Verlag Oikumene, 1945), p. 152. Also to be found in Karl Kupisch, *Quellen zur Geschichte des deutschen Protestantismus (1871–1945)* (Göttingen, Berlin, Frankfurt: Musterschmidt Verlag, 1960), p. 295.

31. Martin Niemöller, *Of Guilt and Hope* (New York: Philosophical Library, 1947), pp. 13–14.

32. Kupisch, *Quellen zur Geschichte des deutschen Protestantismus,* p. 398.

33. Eberhard Bethge, *Bonhoeffer: Exile and Martyr* (New York: Seabury Press, 1975), pp. 65–66.

34. *GS* (1965), II, p. 128.

35. *NRS,* p. 219.

36. Ibid., pp. 219–20.

37. Ibid., p. 222.

38. Ibid., p. 237. The first draft of the Bethel Confession, 26 August 1933.

39. Resolution of the Sofia Conference of September 1931, in Eberhard Bethge, *Dietrich Bonhoeffer: Man of Vision, Man of Courage,* p. 201.

40. See Ruth Zerner, "Dietrich Bonhoeffer and the Jews: Thoughts and Actions, 1933–1945," *Jewish Social Studies* (Summer/Fall 1975) 37, nos. 3–4, pp. 235–50.

41. Eberhard Bethge, "The Holocaust and Christian Anti-Semitism: Perspectives of a Christian Survivor," pp. 141–55. This 1977 article, which has been cited above, was written while Professor Bethge was teaching at Union Theological Seminary in New York City in the fall of 1976. For a reflection on the effects of Bethge's American experiences on his understanding of the Holocaust and of Jewish-Christian relations, see Ruth Zerner, "Begegnungen mit Juden: Eine neue Ära in Bethges geistlichem Amt" [Encounters with Jews: A New Era in Bethge's Ministry], in *Wie eine Flaschenpost:*

Oekumenische Briefe und Beiträge für Eberhard Bethge, ed. Heinz Eduard Tödt, translated from the English by Ilse Tödt (Munich: Christian Kaiser Verlag, 1979), pp. 322–327. Included among Bethge's writings on Jewish-Christian relations are: "Geschichtliche Schuld der Kirche" in *Christliche Freiheit im Dienst am Menschen,* ed. Karl Herbert (Frankfurt am Main: Verlag Otto Lembeck, 1972); "Dietrich Bonhoeffer und die Juden" in *Konsequenzen: Dietrich Bonhoeffers Kirchenverständnis heute,* ed. Ernst Feil and Ilse Tödt (Munich: Christian Kaiser Verlag, 1980), pp. 171–214; "Der Holocaust als Wendepunkt" in *Umkehr und Erneuerung,* ed. Bertold Klappert and Helmut Starck, pp. 89–100.

42. Wolfgang Gerlach, *Zwischen Kreuz und Davidstern: Bekennende Kirche in ihrer Stellung zun Judentum im Dritten Reich* (Hamburg: Dissertion zur Erlangung der Doktorwürde der Evangel-Theologischen Fakultät der Universität Hamburg, 1972). Unfortunately, this important dissertation has never been published.

43. Bertold Klappert, *Israel und die Kirche* (Munich: Christian Kaiser Verlag, 1980). See also Klappert's contributions in *Umkehr und Erneuerung,* ed. Bertold Klappert and Helmut Starck; "Die Wurzel trägt dich," pp. 23–54; "Jesus Christus zwischen Juden und Christen," pp. 138–66.

44. *Christen und Juden: Eine Studie des Rates der Evangelischen Kirche in Deutschland* (Gütersloh: Verlag Gerd Mohn, 1975). An expanded "workbook" appeared a few years later: *Arbeitsbuch Christen und Juden: Zur Studie des Rates der Evangelischen Kirche in Deutschland* (Gütersloh: Gütersloher Verlagshaus Mohn, 1979).

45. "Synod Resolution on the Renewal of the Relationship of Christians and Jews" in *Umkehr und Erneuerung,* ed. Bertold Klappert and Helmut Starck, pp. 264–66. See also "Theses on the Renewal of the Relationship between Christians and Jews," pp. 267–81. For the professorial debate concerning these statements, see *Dokumentation* Nr. 42/80, *Kritische Stellungnahmen zu einem Bonner Theologen-Papier über das Verhältnis von Christen und Juden.* A publication of the Evangelische Pressedienst (Frankfurt am Main: 29 September 1980). An analysis of this debate may be found in David Cairns, "Towards a New Relationship between Christians and Jews," *Scottish Journal of Theology* 34 (1981): 357–67.

46. Heinz Kremers, *Judenmission heute? Von der Judenmission zur brüderlichen Solidarität und zum ökumenischen Dialog* (Neukirchen-Vluyn: Neukirchener Verlag, 1979).

47. "Synod Resolution on the Renewal of the Relationship of Christians and Jews," in *Umkehr und Erneuerung,* p. 264.

48. Dietrich Bonhoeffer, *Letters and Papers from Prison: The Enlarged Edition,* ed. Eberhard Bethge (New York: Macmillan, 1953, 1967, 1971), pp. 381–83.

49. Charlotte Klein, *Theologie und Anti-Judaismus* (Munich: Christian Kaiser Verlag, 1975). For the English translation see Charlotte Klein, *Anti-Judaism in Christian Theology,* trans. Edward Quinn (Philadelphia: Fortress Press, 1978). Rosemary Radford Ruether, *Faith and Fratricide: The Theological Roots of Anti-Semitism* (New York: Seabury Press, 1974).

50. Quoted in *Time,* 2 March 1981, p. 91.

FROM WITHIN:
A Variety of Responses

6 THE IRGUN AND THE DESTRUCTION OF EUROPEAN JEWRY

Yitshaq Ben-Ami

Though the monstrous roots of the twentieth century anti-Semitism reach back to the origins of the Jewish Diaspora over 2000 years ago, commencing with the last century will suffice for our study.

Enough warning signals were sounded in the nineteenth century. In 1881–1882 Richard Wagner gloated over the Russian pogroms against the Jews and called on the West to emulate and pursue the physical elimination of the Jews from Europe. Nietzsche, the German philosopher, predicted; "In the 20th century, in a fit of nihilistic frenzy, they [pious Christians] will turn all of Europe into a butcher's slaughter house and wash their sins white in the blood of Israel." Nietzsche quoted Heine as prophesying: "The coming debacle of Christian civilization . . . when the Germans dust off their old Pagan gods and plunge the West into a terrible blood bath."

In 1882 Dr. Leon Pinsker seems to have heard the warning. In his *Auto-Emancipation* he called for an end to Jews living like ghostlike beggars amongst the nations of the world. He said they must establish a home and remember that relations between people are ruled by respect, not love.

By 1896 Theodor Hertzl had obviously read the warning. The poet Uri Zvi Greenberg disturbed us in 1923 when he wrote:

> "One-tenth shall remain, ten Jews bleeding,
> This the saved remnant.
>
> Testimony that there once was a nation on
> the sorrowful soil of Christianity.
>
> One-tenth shall remain, with necks as lambs.
> . . . But I will relate a prophecy to you, a black prophecy.
>
> From our depths here will rise up a pillar of smoke. . . .
>
> You will continue to prattle while your tongues wag in burnt mouths.
> Jews! Jews!
>
> When the poison gas will make its way into your sacrosanct halls
> Even the Icons will shudderingly shriek in Yiddish.[1]

Later some of us, as youngsters, read Zeev Jabotinsky's writing about the realities of nationhood and about the use of power and physical strength in international affairs. At the same time, we were puzzled by Chaim Weizmann's agreement with the first high commissioner of Palestine on the need to limit Jewish immigration because of the elusive concept of the "absorptive capacity" of the country.

Middle class immigrants were escaping the Grabsky regime of Poland, bringing their small savings to *Eretz Israel* to invest, sometimes, to our chagrin, in land speculation. We knew that since 1919 the Zionist organization had rejected Louis Brandeis's concepts of promoting private enterprise in Palestine and emphasized instead pioneering socialism-Zionism. These were the early twenties: the Jews in Palestine building an exemplary society of the few. In time, some of us, even in Palestine, began to discern the warning signs.

We witnessed Britain's contempt for the Jews of Palestine and of the world. We saw Pan-Arabism fanned by the British and, later, the embers of anti-Semitism by Hitler. During the Arab riots of 1929 we were shocked by the lack of preparedness of the *Haganah* (self-defense organization) and outraged that our hard-won Jewish settlements and *Kibbutzim* had to be given up under Arab attack. As if that were not enough, we were punished by anti-Zionist edicts of the British Colonial Office.

Many of us were brought up on socialist-Zionist tenets. We were pacifists, antimilitarists, and humanists and believed in the universal solidarity of socialism. Suddenly, we felt orphaned and betrayed — especially by a British socialist government in London that rewarded Arab pogroms and punished the law-abiding *Yishuv* (Jewish community of Palestine). Something had gone wrong. The leaders of Labor Zionism — Berl Katznelson and David Ben-Gurion — had displayed the dream to us: We were to join ranks with the exploited Arab workers and peasants to create a happy and just society of Arabs and Jews in *Eretz Israel*. But it did not work out that way. Jews were attacked by these very Arab workers and peasants, who were not impressed by our historic link or our claims to the land.

Nor did it matter that we raised their standard of living or improved their health. Thus, we were forced not only to part ways with universal socialism, but to look for new ways to realize our national survival and renaissance.

It was Jabotinsky who defined our priorities. He told the Jewish leaders and the Jewish youth that the time had long passed to agonize over the morality of Zionism, that the time had come to speak in concrete terms. Notice had to be served to the world that (1) the Arabs had more land and countries than they could develop and rule effectively; (2) the tiny sliver of land on the shore of the eastern Mediterranean, known as Palestine, was the only home the Jewish nation ever had or ever would have; and (3) we in Palestine were not going to acquiesce to being slaughtered in ghettos; we would answer force with force and do our utmost to bring desperate Jews, whatever their ideologies, to Palestine.

In 1931, the disappointed Jewish youth of Palestine formed the *Irgun Z'vai L'eumi* (National military organization). Within its ranks a small core that adopted Jabotinsky's concepts was forming. This core realized the Jews would soon have to resort to revolutionary force, to armed resistance, to breaking British laws, and to eventually forcing Britain out of Palestine.

The evolution toward revolution was brought about by events in Palestine and Europe. The more Jewish distress increased in Europe, the more the British cut off immigration to Palestine. Alone among all Jewish and Zionist leaders, Jabotinsky now called for mass evacuation from what he called the "Zone of Jewish Danger." And as immigration from Germany and Central Europe to Palestine increased in the mid-thirties, so did Arab resentment, and so did British determination to strangle *Aliyah* (immigration to Palestine).

In 1936 Arab riots were followed by another British commission of inquiry, and once again, Jewish leaders pleaded with Britain. In the *Irgun* the feeling of frustration grew as we read in 1937 the account of Weizmann's report to the Zionist Congress on his appearance before the Peel Commission. He said that his familiarity with the laws of physics made it plain to him that the 6 million Jews who hoped to leave Europe would have to be disappointed since a small country like Palestine could not absorb them. This leader of the Zionist movement — who 18 years before had rejected Nordau's appeal to quickly move half a million Jews to Palestine and establish control of the land, who had accepted Britain's restrictions on immigration based on the economic absorptive capacity of the country *as determined by Britain,* this leader and future president of the State of Israel — told the Congress that all he wanted now was to save the youth, two million young people who had all of life before them and had lost the most elementary of their rights — the right to work. He said, "The old will go; they will adjust or not adjust; today they are dust, the economic and moral dust of a cruel world. . . . Two million people and perhaps less, the *Sheerith Hapleita* (remnant of survivors) will survive. . . ."

New Judea reported that, upon hearing Weizmann's tragic and defeatist admission of the failure of the basic dream of Zionism, the delegates rose to applaud Weizmann and burst into spontaneous singing of the *Hatikva*. It was probably at that moment that we in the *Irgun* gave up all of our already tenuous links with "Establishment Zionism."

By mid-1937 we were moving on two parallel courses of action. The first was armed resistance in Palestine; we retaliated to Arab terror and prepared for eventual action against the mandatory power. In Europe the foundation for Hebrew military action already existed. In 1937 the *Irgun* command sent Abraham Stern to Poland to establish contacts with the Polish government. A year later the *Irgun* expanded its military training in Poland, Lithuania, and Czechoslovakia, and *Irgun* officers were ordered to Europe to build the organization's reserve in the Diaspora.

The second parallel course of action was our *Ha 'apalah* work ("illegal" *Aliyah*). In the Diaspora, heeding Jabotinsky's repeated call for evacuating the Jewish masses trapped in Europe, we began an attempt to break the British immigration restrictions and the Jewish Agency's acquiescence to them. In July 1937 I was sent to Europe to represent the *Irgun* in this activity, in which we joined with the *Betar* and the New Zionist Organization (NZO) — the organization Jabotinsky had founded in 1935 when we finally parted with the Zionism of Ahad Ha 'am, Weizmann, and Ben-Gurion.

We started by recruiting members from our own youth and small groups from nonsocialist youth movements. The socialist and left-of-center organizations would not talk to *Irgun* or *Betar* people, let alone cooperate with them. The youngsters we enlisted were ready to go to Palestine on our rickety boats, but often their parents objected. We lacked funds to help the *Olim* (immigrants), especially those from Eastern Europe who were penniless. As I traveled from town to village in Poland enlisting candidates, I found antagonism not only to *Ha 'apalah* but to the basic Jabotinsky concept: *evacuation*. Every Jewish leader and intellectual (Zionists, Yiddishists, socialists, and others) opposed evacuation. Sholem Asch in Europe, Stephen Wise in New York, Zionist labor in Palestine, united against the concept of evacuation as promulgated by Jabotinsky. Only the faceless Jewish masses and nonsocialist felt differently. While the intellectuals debated, this people, given up for dust by their leaders, gathered on the street corners of the Jewish ghetto, on Nalewki and Djika in Warsaw, and elsewhere, with nothing to do and nowhere to go. They were the proletariat of Jewish misery.

Slowly, we built a skeleton *Ha 'apalah* organization in Warsaw, Bucharest, Prague, Paris, and other Jewish centers. In Palestine we developed a small, tight cadre of men who became experienced in receiving the *Ma'apilim* ("illegal" immigrants). Always, we were hampered by a lack of funds. Nevertheless, from very modest beginnings — using small, motorized sailboats — we gradually evolved into a substantial operation. Events accelerated our growth. Hitler was increasing his pressure in Central Europe; virulent anti-Semitism was flourishing. The NZO, of which Jabotinsky was president at the time, met for a conference in Prague in February 1938. We *Irgun* men appeared to argue for increased training, intensified military preparedness, and greater *Ha 'apalah* efforts.

Jabotinsky outlined a ten-year plan to resettle one and a half million Jews in Palestine, with British approval and cooperation. To the *Irgun* this sounded like a program that should have been presented to the British by the Zionist leadership in 1917; it now appeared that Jabotinsky's political Zionism and our emerging revolutionary concepts might go their different ways. However, this did not happen. Hitler marched into Austria in March 1938, and Europe was bent upon an irreversible course of disaster. We in the *Irgun* — I was then stationed in Vienna — knew that grave events were rushing upon us, and though we could not foresee with what intensity darkness would engulf us, we knew that our impatience was vindicated. The behavior of the Nazis in Austria, British intransigence in blocking Jewish immigration to Palestine, and the barren Evian Conference were the final developments that carried Jabotinsky from political Zionism to our side, to what was then considered unthinkable — armed resistance and eventual rebellion against Britain.

The conversion was not an overnight one. It evolved gradually. Jabotinsky was subjected to intense pressure from the *Irgun* leadership, from the rank and file of the Jabotinsky movement, from the younger generation of *Betar* in the Diaspora. In the spring of 1938 I met with Jabotinsky to report on our work under the Nazis in Austria. He questioned the extent they were willing to permit Jews out of the territories under their control and my impressions of their longer-range intentions. I told him that I believed that Adolf Eichmann meant what he said in Vienna when he told us that, above all, the Nazis wanted the Jews out. I said that we had to take advantage of it before they changed their minds.

By late 1938 new *Irgun* goals were set. We embarked on building a military force in the Diaspora that, at a given moment, could reach the shores of Palestine and, together with the *Irgun* there, would attempt to occupy the seat of government in Jerusalem. Then, if we could hold out long enough, we would seek to mobilize world support and force Britain to meet its obligations under the Balfour Declaration and the League of Nations Mandate.

The weapons and training facilities we had in Poland would enable us to mobilize between 30 and 40 thousand men. The *Irgun* in Palestine would mobilize up to 10 thousand members. Poland, although not as vicious as Nazi Germany, was anxious to get rid of a million or two Jews. *Irgun* officers traveled from Palestine to be trained by Polish army instructors. The first course was scheduled for early 1939 in the Carpathian Mountains. The Polish government supplied us with 25,000 rifles and additional materiel and weapons. By the summer of 1939, we had 5,000 rifles, 1,000 machine guns, and other supplies stored in our Warsaw warehouse and hundreds of weapons were already in Palestine. *Irgun* cells were functioning and training in Poland, Lithuania, and, prior to the German invasion, Czechoslovakia.

Our immigration work continued unabated. Any Jews willing to risk running the British blockade could do so if they could raise the fare and especially if they were able to contribute to the fare of other penniless youngsters — and if they were healthy enough to withstand the rigors of the voyage. Our success in landing *Ma-apilim* triggered off countermeasures by Britain, which sent its emissaries to the Adriatic and Balkan governments — from whose territories chartered ships sailed — insisting that they halt this activity. While Europe was cowering before Hitler's aggression, King George VI found the time, in April 1939, to send a special message through his private secretary to the British Foreign Office to make sure that "steps have been taken to prevent these people [Jews] leaving their country of origin. . . ."

After Munich and the Sudetenland capitulation, we had less difficulty convincing parents that their children should leave Europe. Thousands of people of all ages began flocking to our offices in Central and Eastern Europe, hoping to get out. Limited by lack of funds, we were not equipped to deal with such numbers. There were large boats that had to be purchased, vessels that could carry thousands of *olim* (immigrants). We chartered some and planned to acquire others. We also purchased sailboats, which picked up the *olim* outside the territorial waters of Palestine and were used to run the British blockade. Thus, if the small boats were caught, the loss was minimal.

We dispatched a dozen *Irgun* men, most of whom had seafaring experience, to Europe to pilot the ships. Our ships now carried groups of five to eight hundred *olim*. By early 1939 hardly a month passed that we did not have a transport underway. Still, we could not even remotely cope with the impending emergency.

Jabotinsky now concentrated on two parallel courses of action. First, he intensified his diplomatic activities. Having given up hope that Britain would voluntarily change its anti-Jewish policies, he attempted to persuade the United States to effect a change in British policy. His meeting with the U.S. ambassadors to Poland and Britain led him to believe that constructive intervention by Roosevelt with Britain was a possibility. Jabotinsky selected Robert Briscoe, a member of the Irish Parliament, for this mission. Briscoe was to present to the White House a plan by which, as Jabotinsky stated in a letter to Briscoe, "one million Jews were to be transferred to Palestine within a couple of years, it being understood that this should be considered . . . as the first phase of the Exodus." Jabotinsky also wrote to Bricoe: "We frankly doubt whether it would be worth your while . . . to spend any special effort at this stage in gaining Jewish circles. . . . Their support . . . can be had if Washington is for it." Jabotinsky certainly knew the American Jewish leadership.

Second, Jabotinsky expanded the *Ha'apalah* work. In cooperation with David Raziel, the newly appointed commander of the *Irgun,* a mission was sent to the United States to raise funds for *Ha'apalah*. It was headed by our old friend, Col. John H. Patterson, who commanded the Zion Mule Corps in the Gallipoli campaign and the (Jewish) 38th Royal Fusiliers in the 1917–1918 liberation of Palestine. Haim Lubinsky of the *Irgun* was to accompany Patterson. I was to leave Europe to join them in March 1939, after transferring my *Ha'apalah* duties to a replacement from Palestine. Robert Briscoe, who arrived in the United States in February 1939, devoted himself partly to helping the mission raise funds.

Despite assurances of American ambassadors Joseph P. Kennedy and Anthony D. Biddle, Briscoe was never able to reach the White House. Briscoe told me that Stephen Wise saw to it that he was not received at the White House or at the State Department. Briscoe did meet with Justices Louis Brandeis and Felix Frankfurter, Governor Herbert Lehman, and some others, but he failed in his mission. American Jews seemed not to understand the need for, or to be willing to sponsor, an emergency campaign to move millions of threatened Jews from Europe to Palestine, to the United States, or to Timbuktu. And non-Jews simply were not interested. For similar reasons, we failed in our fund-raising efforts. Wise, Paul Baerwald, Maurice Wertheim, and the rest of the Jewish establishment saw us as threatening their relationship with Washington and their images as leaders of the Jews of America and their control of Jewish charity funds. Their violent negative reaction to the *Irgun*'s entry into the American Jewish scene persisted for the next nine years.

In Europe "Crystal Night" came and went. The Nazis pushed thousands of Polish Jews across the Polish border and marched into Prague. The British intensified their campaign against "illegal immigration" to Palestine: Their 1939 White Paper limited "legal" immigration to 15,000 annually for the coming five years. Thus, the *Irgun* declared war on the British administration and its infamous White Paper and attacked government installations and communications throughout Palestine. European Jewry was then at its "Neilah" hour (the final repentance).

But all this did not have much impact on the Jews of America. Our mission had failed. Briscoe went back to Ireland, Patterson back to London. Lubinsky returned to Palestine, and I remained in the United States, attempting to hold the small circle of friends we had enlisted together.

Despite the ominous events in Europe, the Jews of America felt no sense of urgency or emergency. At the 21st Zionist Congress (August 1939) Rabbi Abba Hillel Silver said, "The White Paper is a document of passing value. . . . I call upon you to avoid resistance, civil disobedience, etc. There is no vision we can offer our youth except the actual building of our home in Eretz Israel. No military heroics except the heroism of rebuilding from the ruins. . . ."

In spite of our diplomatic and financial failures in the United States, we moved ahead with our activities in Europe. Further military plans were developed. In

Palestine David Raziel, the commander of the *Irgun,* was apprehended and jailed, but the high command continued to function.

On Jabotinsky's initiative, a special bank was formed — *Bank Aliyah* — and plans were made to send emissaries to the United States and South Africa to raise the basic capital. The bank would involve itself in the purchase of vessels, foreign exchange transactions, loans to *olim,* and so forth. Robert Briscoe agreed to go to South Africa, where Jews were more responsive to the needs of European Jewry: They seemed to retain a closer link to the "old country," were less taken with leftist ideologies, and were prouder of their heritage and identity.

It is devastating to recall May and June of 1939 and the letter written by Arthur Lurie, political secretary of the Jewish Agency, to Herbert Morrison, an Englishman acting as League of Nations high commissioner for refugees, in which he informed on us. Lurie submitted the names of the vessels we were using to transport *Ma 'apilim* from Greece to Palestine, as well as a list of the countries of origin of their passengers. Morrison immediately forwarded this information to the British foreign and colonial offices.

In August 1939, as tensions mounted in Europe, the *Irgun* and allied organizations had six groups moving to embarkation ports or sailing toward Palestine — a total of 3,800 people. In New York we had actually managed to get a contribution of 500 dollars from Young Israel. And at the 21st Zionist Congress in Zurich, Rabbi Silver inveighed against breaking British laws.

At that very moment Jabotinsky presented to the *Irgun* Command in Tel Aviv a detailed plan for an armed landing in Palestine to take place later in the year. At no time was there a greater conceptual split within the Zionist-Jewish leadership. But within a few days, that gap was to become academic. For early on the morning of September 1 the German *Wehrmacht* crossed the Polish border, and the darkest chapter in blood-soaked Jewish history began. Even those who had predicted the cataclysm could not foresee the extent of the tragedy that would be.

The war had an immediate effect. Jabotinsky declared the defeat of Hitler to be the primary goal of the nationalist movement. David Raziel, still in British detention, announced a cease fire in the battle against the British administration in Palestine. With Poland's fall, our organization there was shattered. We returned the weapons we had accumulated, enough to equip about 5,000 men, to the Polish army.

The *Irgun* network in the Diaspora was in shambles; the *Ha 'apalah* network functioned only spasmodically. Our top European coordinator, Joseph Katznelson, who had come from Jerusalem, became ill and died in Warsaw, as did hundreds of thousands of Jews, forced to live in the cramped urban quarters assigned to them by the Germans.

Yitshak Zarzewsky, who had replaced me as the *Irgun's Ha 'apalah* coordinator in Europe, remained in Warsaw until February 1940. Our sole success occurred when Zarzewsky managed to buy a sackful of old Polish passports, which enabled several hundred Jews to reach as yet neutral Italy and eventually Palestine. NZO and the *Irgun* assigned other men to France (Eliahu Glaser and Abraham Stawski) and to Bucharest (Eri Jabotinsky, Rudi Hecht, and others).

But our *Ha-apalah* work was winding down. Vessels became scarce and expensive. We had no money. We could barely support our men in Italy, Romania, Switzerland. By mid-1940 we sent our last ships to Palestine. Some of our most devoted Romanian *Aliyah* activists went down with the *Struma* in February 1942.

We had launched our *Ha'apalah* effort too late. We had achieved too little and had done it in the face of the opposition of almost every Jewish leader in Europe, Palestine, and the United States. Except for Jabotinsky, there was hardly a Jewish leader who would face reality.

Let me return to our military activities. In the summer of 1939 Abraham Stern instructed Zarzewski to concentrate on the creation of *Irgun* battalions to fight alongside the Polish army in case of war; within a matter of weeks, however, there was no Polish army. Nevertheless, a nucleus of armed Jewish resistance was formed in Poland and Lithuania from the remnants of the *Betar* and *Irgun* organizations. At the same time former officers of the Polish army and other veterans gathered in Warsaw around David Apelbojm to form *SWIT* (Dawn), which fought with Polish units in the September 1939 siege of Warsaw and which later established contact with a Polish leader of the Resistance who supplied them with weapons over the years. In December 1939 in Warsaw 39 men and women took the oath of loyalty to Dawn. The close-knit, five-men units under David Apelbojm numbered about 320 members by the spring of 1942. At that time the final negotiations and merger with the *Irgun-Betar* units, headed by Paul Frankel, resulted in the formation of the Warsaw Ghetto's Jewish Military Organization (JMO).

There was no chance of opposing the large-scale Nazi actions of July 1942. The emerging JMO — *Zydowski Zwigzek Wojskowy* (ZZW) — comprised of cells of four members each plus a commander. The leadership was divided into eight departments, including medical and legal; the latter ruled on the liquidation of Gestapo agents — Jewish and Polish. The military leadership consisted of Frankel, Apelbojm, and Arieh Rudel. A tunnel 50 meters in length, dug between the main base of the JMO and the Aryan side of the Warsaw Ghetto wall, was used for obtaining weapons and supplies and would be used in the last phase of the final battle.

Details of the JMO's organization, its scope and activities up to the April 1943 revolt appear in Emanuel Ringelblum's *Diaries,* in David Wdowinski's *Memoirs,* in Ber Mark's work, in testimonies of non-Jewish resistance leaders, but they are totally ignored in the well-known Jewish publications in English in the United States and by Labor in *Eretz Israel*. Unlike the common resistance front that was formed in Vilna, Bialystok, as well as with Marxist partisan groups in the Polish forests, the Jewish Socialists of Warsaw could not see their way clear to dying under a common Jewish banner. While the JMO asked its adherents for a commitment to Jewish survival and honor, the Socialist Jewish Fighting Forces (JFO) were seeking a pro-Soviet, so-called "anti-Fascist" ideology. The pupils of Jabotinsky did not see why Jewish survival and honor needed additional distinctions or provisos.

We are also able to draw on the descriptions of Nazi General Stroop, who commanded the troops assaulting the Warsaw Ghetto. He reported on the fight the JMO put up, especially at its Muranowska base, where the Blue-and-White and the Polish Red-and-White flags continued to flutter for two days beginning 27 April 1943, despite tank and artillery fire. David Apelbojm commanded the action at Muranawska.

In that battle, according to General Stroop, about "120 armed gang members were defeated by about 630 German and Polish police, Waffen SS and Ukranian and Latvian auxiliaries." The Nazis used armored vehicles and half-trucks. When the fight was over, 24 fighters were dead and 54 were captured, most of them wounded. David Apelbojm, who since 1939 had worked and organized the youth for this battle, was wounded and died a few days later. Paul Frankel and a handful of comrades who managed to cross into the Aryan sector were reportedly the group that was surrounded in June 1943 at Gazibowska II and went down fighting. The fighting career and life of a young student, who joined an *Irgun* cell in Warsaw in 1939 and carried his loyalty to the Jabotinsky-*Betar-Irgun* tradition to the ultimate point, was thus ended.

The remnants of the JMO went into action with the partisans around Otwock. Some eventually participated in the Warsaw uprising of 1944. A handful of the JMO fighters survived, among them my friend David Wdowinski, who was in the Warsaw Ghetto, eight camps, and the 1943 uprising, and lived to tell the story.

The records of the earlier armed resistance in the forest of Narobishov, in March 1942, with the survivors returning to the Warsaw Ghetto; accounts of the heroic acts of Joseph Glassman, head of the *Betar* and *Irgun* in Lithuania, who headed the underground in the Vilna Ghetto and led the first group of combatants out of the ghetto on 25 July 1943 to the forests of Narocz — all can be found in David Niv's chronicle, *History of the Irgun*. In the context of the global struggle then going on, the sacrifice of this tiny band of *Irgun-Betar* soldiers may appear insignificant; it does not, however, make it less heroic.

While the remaining *Irgun-Betar* fighters of the Warsaw Ghetto joined the Warsaw revolt in 1944 and the non-Jewish partisans in the forests, their comrades in Palestine raised the banner of revolt. By the end of 1942 even the confused leadership of the *Yishuv* and the Jews of Palestine had to face the scope of the tragedy that befell the Jewish people. Early in 1943 the *Irgun* in Palestine attempted to ascertain the possibility of reestablishing contact with the ghettos that still existed. The NZO and *Irgun* command sent Itzhak Zarzewski to Istanbul. There, together with Itzhak Berman and Dr. F. Haffner, who served in the British and American intelligence, they contacted our people in the Balkans and incredibly, by direct phone, spoke with our comrade, Samuel Ariel, in Bucharest. Zarzewski returned to Jerusalem and reported to Yitzhak Gruenbaum, head of the Rescue Committee of the Jewish Agency, that it was possible, through our contacts, including the Polish underground, to deliver food and weapons inside and outside the ghettos, and even to plan for resistance. Gruenbaum was excited by these reports and promised to come back within a few days with Ben-Gurion's reaction to the news. Zarzewski never heard anything further from Gruenbaum. However, the *Haganah* did later proceed with the mission of the parachutists to occupied Europe.

The reports coming out of Europe in 1943 convinced the *Irgun* in Palestine that the time for action against the British was overdue. The mainly symbolic 1943 ghetto revolt was the last prod the *Irgun* in Palestine and in the United States needed to cancel the truce that Jabotinsky and Raziel had unilaterally declared with Britain.

The *Irgun* command in Palestine would be reorganized. We sent Arieh Ben Eliezer from the States to Palestine. Several months later he succeeded in obtaining Menachem Begin's release from the Polish army. On February 1 1944 the *Irgun* launched its revolt whose goal was the ousting of Great Britain from Palestine. The *Irgun* declared: "There is no longer an armistice in the land of Israel between the Jewish people and the British administration, which is literally handing over our brethren to Hitler."

The *Irgun*'s battle for independence ended only with the establishment of the homeland that had been denied to the massacred Jewish millions.

During these soul-trying and heartbreaking years, the *Irgun* delegation in the United States continued to search for workable rescue activities. Between September 1939 and June 1948, our work went through four phases. The first lasted until our people in Europe could no longer accomplish physical rescue. In that phase, which continued until mid-1940, we in the United States were able to play only a small role. We helped move 2,300 *olim* out of the Danube Delta. Eri Jabotinsky, Eliahu Glaser, and others of the *Irgun-Betar* organizations in Central Europe led this group to Palestine, where they were interned briefly by the British. We did not contribute directly to the movements of the last groups of 1940, on the vessels *Pentcho* and *Rudnitschar*. Our fund-raising efforts in the United States were continuously frustrated. The United Palestine Appeal campaign against us (see Henry Montor's letter dated 1 February 1940) urged the Jews of America to withhold support for us. They accused us of bringing to Palestine "prostitutes and criminals," the same statements and accusations that Robert Briscoe faced in the

South African Zionist Review. This opposition seriously hampered our rescue efforts. The campaign against our *Ha 'apalah* work continued to the bitter end, to mid-1940. We were able to send small sums to the *Irgun* in Palestine, which helped keep our emissaries going in Romania, the Balkans, and Italy. But our *Ha 'apalah* work, which was launched with the high hopes of Eri Jabotinsky, Moshe Galili, David Raziel, and others, was ending.

We had transported about 12 thousand people to Palestine; and thousands more — about 16 thousand — were moved by private individuals, with whom we cooperated in landing operations. These numbers pale into insignificance in the face of six million lost; nevertheless, a life saved is a world saved. For us, who from July 1937 to mid-1940 devoted our lives to *Ha 'apalah,* even the tiniest success was always a triumph.

We now entered the second phase of our work — in the United States. Zeev Jabotinsky arrived in the United States in March 1940 to launch a campaign for a Jewish army. We put at his disposal our small organization and the handful of connections we had established. In August 1940 Jabotinsky died. Gradually, we assumed the burden and responsibility for his campaign. We believed that the one people, chosen by Hitler for total destruction, should be given the status of combatant and national ally. We believed that only a national identity, backed by military force — air squadrons, commando units, and, if need be, suicide units — would save Jews from the status Hitler was imposing upon them — a nonpeople, a valueless flotsam. We saw a repetition of the events in Palestine, where the British military and colonials discounted the Jewish ability to react to the imperialistic machination and Pan-Arab terror tactics. Hitler was reaching the same conclusion about Jewish impotence — not to mention non-Jewish indifference.

By the summer of 1941 the Jabotinsky movement and the *Irgun* were scattered and shattered. David Raziel had been killed in Iraq while on a mission for the Allies. The best of the *Irgun* were in British uniforms or, following Abraham Stern, had split to eventually form the *Lehi* or else had become disaffected. A few individuals continued to function on their own in Switzerland and in Romania. The *Irgun* delegation in the United States, however, was still functioning.

The 1941–1942 period tried not only our hearts but our basic ideological premises. The essence of our commitment to the *Irgun* was a rejection of historical fatalism and passivity in Jewish life. As the war engulfed all of Europe, Russia, and finally the United States, we centered our activity more and more on the creation of a national army — which we felt was the most effective way to halt the dangers facing the Jews of Europe.

Our campaign for a Jewish army of Palestinian and stateless volunteers as well as volunteers from any country — remember that America did not enter the war until December 1941 — lasted about two and a half years. Although our campaign basically ended in failure, it aroused sympathy among the non-Jews in the United

States and even in Britain where our colleague, Irma Halpren, had organized the British Committee for a Jewish Army. We also succeeded in embarrassing the British, both in the United States and in the British Parliament, and so even in defeat left our message in the annals of history. Josiah Wedgwood, our old friend in the House of Commons, in June 1941 sent a message to one of our rallies in the United States:

> We should have today in Palestine four fully equipped divisions of Jewish troops. We should have got them, we should have got the equipment from America, the men from Palestine, from America. We might have had them fighting beside us today. . . . As I saw it, the goal of Zionism [is] to create among the Jewish people a national self-respect which would see them through their troubles and give them an anchorage in the world.

As the ominous news kept issuing out of Europe, the need for radical action was absolutely clear. The pupils of Jabotinsky and Herzl watched uncomprehendingly as the leaders of world Zionism gathered in May 1942 at the Biltmore Hotel in New York and declared at long last that the goal of Zionism was a Jewish Commonwealth in *Eretz Israel*. While we urged and campaigned intensely for an army and a national status to impress upon Germany that the disenfranchised Jews had taken their place among the nations of the world and that a day of reckoning awaited them, Zionist leadership embarked on postwar planning.

We were alone in our campaign — Weizmann downgraded our objective to a demand for Jewish units, and the Labor Zionists attacked us with ridicule. As late as February 1943 Haim Greenberg wrote in the *Yiddisher Kempfer* that there was no way in the world that 250,000 Jewish men could be found to join a Jewish Army! Once the United States entered the war, plans for American Jewish volunteers were dropped. The assimilated bourgeoisie and the Marxist intellectuals were then, as always, aghast at the concept of a Jewish nationalism expressing itself through physical and military avenues.

Throughout 1942 the news from Europe grew more and more gruesome. By the second half of 1942 we realized that whatever the allied victory would bring and whatever plans we might have for the future of our people, a Jewish people might not be left in Europe to plan for.

As the war turned in favor of the Allies, Britain hardened its opposition. In Washington Cordell Hull declared that the goal of our campaign for a Jewish army was only to "divide the Allies." By early 1943 it was almost too late to hope that Britain and the United States would change their policy toward creating a Jewish army. A Jewish army would have achieved recognition of the Jews of Palestine and the stateless Jews of Europe as combatants, enabling us to confront the attack on our people both on the battlefield and in the councils of the emerging United Nations.

In September 1942 we laid the basis of the third phase of our work in the United States: a campaign to save the Jews of Europe. Its roots went back to May 1940 when, shaken by the news from Central and Eastern Europe, Jabotinsky appealed to the established leaders of Jewry — Rabbi Wise, Paul Baerwald, Justice Brandeis, Weizmann, Ben-Gurion in Palestine, and others — to form a world Jewish committee to coordinate information and plan action. Scarcely one of the recipients even deigned to acknowledge the message. World Jewish leadership remained in the hands of the World Jewish Congress; the Zionist Weizmann-Ben-Gurion alliance; Wise-Goldmann; the Joint Distribution Committee, the American Jewish Committee; and somewhat more on the fringe, the Yiddishist Socialist–American Jewish Labor Committee. This combination "led" the doomed Jews of the East and the frightened ones of the West through years of war and extermination. Tragically, we were compelled to face their unrelenting opposition to our activities over and above that of the real enemy — Germany — the callous British and the indifferent, aloof U.S. State Department.

The news we gathered came mostly from the general press and the JTA bulletins. Jews, and all who cared, read the same papers. But amazingly, the Jewish leadership seemed to draw, at least officially, different conclusions. We saw destruction sweeping over the millions of Jews in Europe; I do not know what the Jewish leadership read into the privileged reports that reached it from Russia, Slovakia, Romania, and, via Switzerland, from Poland. It was incredible that a man like Isaiah Berlin, a British Jew and second secretary of the British Embassy, who was stationed in wartime Washington and "continuously met with Weizmann, Ben-Gurion, Sharett and others," could claim that "very little was reported to the press" on the calamities wiping out millions of Jews. And the Jews of the West accepted almost totally the Allies' position that only an Allied victory would save the Jews of Nazi-occupied Europe.

By the end of the summer in 1942 we could no longer delay the review of our activities in the United States. At the time that our comrades in Eastern Europe were intensifying their preparation for armed resistance and escape from the ghettos, we in New York were laying the foundations for an all-out campaign to awaken America to the annihilation and follow through in an attempt to penetrate the hostility of the State Department and the indifference of the White House.

Gradually, our path became clear: awaken sympathy among the public at large; go on to enlist support in Congress, and then pressure the White House and Department of State to change their policies. Rescue would have to be undertaken by governmental bodies with or without the cooperation of the British. We could count on little or no support from the Jewish establishment: Nothing in our experience of the past decade in regard to their policies in Palestine or the Diaspora indicated that they would join us in an aggressive, uninhibited, perservering, all-out campaign to attempt to rescue those who were still alive.

At the time we knew nothing of the appeals that the World Jewish Congress had been receiving from Slovakia since early 1942; or of the *Europa Plan* conceived by Rabbi Michael Dov Weissmandel of Bratislavia; or, in November 1942, of the

Romanian offer to ransom 70 thousand Jews from Transnistria; or, later, of the desperate message from the Jewish National Committee in Poland (13 January 1943) confirming that three million Jews were dead and pleading for funds, weapons, communications — imploring Wise, Goldmann, and the JDC to try to arrange for the exchange of 10 thousand Jewish children. To this day, I do not know what the above gentlemen and the Jewish Agency in Jerusalem *did* about these heartbreaking appeals. By June 1942 we knew that the information received by the Polish government in London was of utmost gravity. We knew about the activities of the Bund's leaders and Josiah Wedgwood of London. We knew the worst was upon us. We began to doubt that our campaign for a Jewish army would ever bear fruit in time to affect the fate of the Jews of Europe.

By the fall of 1942 our organization had grown not only in numbers but in composition. We enlisted the aid of a number of prominent Gentiles — Congressman Andrew Sommers, Louis Bromfield, Senator Guy Gillette, labor leader Dean Alfange, members of the departments of the Interior and Treasury, and others. We were joined by some old-time Socialist-Zionists like Isaac Zaar and Haim Lieberman of the Yiddish press. We broke through to non-Zionist, often assimilated Jews such as Ben Hecht, Frances Gunther, Konrad Bercovivi, and others who were free of the inhibitions carried by the four Jewish apocalyptical horsemen: fear, fatalism, passivity, and defeatism. The coalition became ever more odd when we received the help of the Union of Orthodox Rabbis and the Union of the Grand Rabbis of the United States. Then we produced the stirring pageant, written by Ben Hecht, "We Will Never Die," and filled the largest U.S. halls with tens of thousands of viewers. Our supporters ranged from Jews like Kurt Weil and Moss Hart to the venerated Orthodox Rabbi Eliezer Silver. However, our relentless opposition was also broad-based. We disturbed almost everyone in the American Jewish establishment. The opposing front was not united since the umbrella of the American Jewish Conference (formed in August 1943) proved to be short-lived. Now, Jewish leaders like Morris Waldman of the American Jewish Committee were denouncing the "alien Nahum Goldmann" and the "East European" types like Isaiah Berlin to the officials of the State Department but were nevertheless in agreement on one subject: the need to rid the United States of the "Fascist renegades — Bergson and his colleagues."

Our campaign had three goals:

1. To ask the Allies to appoint a commission of military experts to formulate policy concerning the wholesale slaughter of European Jewry;
2. To create a Jewish army of Palestinian and other Jews, including commando squads that would strike deep into Germany and air squadrons for retaliatory bombings of the Nazis;
3. To transfer, via existing neutral ships, Jews from Hitler-dominated countries to Palestine or any temporary refuge.

We worked feverishly. Our Jewish critics then — and established historians today — still refer to our campaign as "hysterical." We knew, early in 1943, that several million Jews had already been murdered and that the annihilation process had been accelerated. Our campaign became more aggressive. We formed the Emergency Committee to Save the Jewish People of Europe and continued to publish our potent advertisements throughout the United States. We formed chapters of the Emergency Committee in Washington and in other major cities. Months were passing and nothing concrete was being done by the Allies to stop the annihilation. Whatever we learned from friends in government was grim. The State Department adamantly continued to sabotage any opportunities for rescue in the Nazi satellite countries. The American military in North Africa proved as anti-Jewish as the British under their colonial secretary, Lord Moyne. The time was ripe for involving Spain and Portugal in serious rescue efforts, but these nations wanted the refugees already there moved to camps in North Africa. Nothing of the kind happened. And the more agitated we became, the harsher were the attacks on us from the Zionist establishment — Wise, Goldmann, and Arthur Lurie.

The opposition of the Jewish establishment was not, however, the major obstacle we faced. Although the U.S. Justice Department, the U.S. State Department, and the FBI wanted to deport or arrest us, or turn us over to the British authorities in Canada — steps advocated by the Jewish and Zionist leadership and enthusiastically endorsed by various officials in Washington — these government agencies could not find legally defensible means of taking such action.

Our problems were primarily with the policymakers in the State Department, who, with the full concurrence of FDR and Cordell Hull and given the passivity of such Jewish leaders as Sam Rosenman, Congressman Sol Bloom, and a discreet Justice Felix Frankfurter, continuously sabotaged even the smallest chances for the rescue of Jews. On 6 October 1943 Wise and Goldmann went to see Breckenridge Long at the State Department, who, together with his British counterpart, seemed obsessed by the specter of millions of Jews dumped on the Allies by a mischievous Hitler. The major complaint of Wise and Goldmann was, in the words of Long, with "the Emergency Committee to Save the Jewish People of Europe. . . . They said it was a body composed of a lot of persons who were not Jews . . . that their program of advertisements and demonstrations was severely criticized by the other Jewish organizations."

The establishment's shock was even greater when we organized the March of Rabbis, the only wartime American Jewish demonstration in Washington, to appeal to the President and Congress to act on behalf of European Jewry. The event was described as recently as 1973 by Sir Isaiah Berlin as the "Notorious March" and at that time was ridiculed by the establishment press, though warmly applauded by the Yiddish press.

As mentioned before, as early as the fall of 1942 we realized that nothing could be achieved in the United States unless it was through Congress, which was susceptible to the pressures of its constituents — Jews and non-Jews. Only public opinion could change the position of the administration and the President and move them from indifference to action. Gradually, we were also helped by progress in the war. Our committee members Senator Gillette and Congressman Rogers offered a joint resolution in Congress in November 1943. The text, drafted by our friend Professor Fowler Harper, solicitor-general in the Department of the Interior, called for the establishment by the executive of a commission to effect the rescue of the Jewish people of Europe. The resolution, unanimously approved by the Foreign Affairs Committee of the Senate, became bogged down under Sol Bloom's chairmanship in the House. Gillette was subject to enormous pressure to withdraw his sponsorship, including a personal visit by Rabbi Wise, who believed "that the action as proposed by the resolution was not a wise step to take." In Palestine one voice disagreed with the establishment: Rabbi Meir Berlin reported that Sol Bloom had asked his opinion on our (Gillette-Rogers) resolution, telling Berlin that "the Zionists were against it." Berlin answered that he was definitely in favor of it.

From September 1942, when the "secret" of Jewish annihilation was exposed, to November 1943, more than a million additional Jews were murdered. No sign of a letup in the annihilation process was seen, but neither the Jewish leadership nor the American Jew was stirred to aggressive action, nor was FDR or Secretary Hull moved to do more than reconfirm that the Jews of Europe were being annihilated on a serious scale. The non-Jewish leaders relied on a simple alibi: We have to defeat Hitler — then the Jews will be safe. No one questioned how many Jews would be left. Even to this day, apologists for the Jewish leadership claim that nothing more could have been done.

While Sol Bloom pigeonholed the Gillette-Rogers Resolution in the House, it was about to go to a vote in the Senate. A few days prior to the Senate vote, FDR, prodded by Henry Morgenthau, Jr., created by Executive Order the War Refugee Board (WRB).

The record of the WRB has still not been properly evaluated. One fact is clear: It saved from 100 to 200 thousand or more Jewish lives. Certainly, had the State Department alone remained in charge of rescue work, the number of people rescued would have been minute or nil. At the same time we sought places of temporary shelter for Jews in Allied and in neutral countries. Because it was important to evoke at least a symbolic gesture from the United States, we launched a petition campaign that resulted in the passage of a Senate resolution that led to the establishment of the Oswego Shelter in upstate New York.

In March 1944, as the Nazis took over full control of Hungary, the last large Jewish community of Europe faced impending catastrophe. We called an emergency meeting of Hungarian Jewish leaders to which we invited members of the Hungarian clergy and community leaders. In addition, in large national ads, we called the attention of the American public to the impending tragedy. We sent a delegation to Washington on April 19, which through Senator Gillette's good offices met with John Pehle, executive director of the WRB. At the same time Senator Gillette raised the subject on the Senate floor. On May 15 a telegram was sent to Stalin — signed by, among others, Louis Bromfield, Claudio Arrau, Dmitri Mitroupolis, Erwin Piscator, Arthur Szyk, Sigrid Undset — asking Stalin "to warn the Hungarian puppet-government to desist from executing its diabolic intention." We urged FDR, Churchill, and Stalin to warn the Hungarians not to carry out the Nazi plans of extermination. During June we further involved the Hungarian churches in the United States in this campaign. We sent a delegation to the apostolic delegate to the United States. We called upon Pope Pius XII to "condemn the action of the Hungarian Government and all of those who are now torturing and murdering the Jewish people" and "to request the active cooperation of all pious Catholics in Hungary in the work of rescuing the Hebrew people of Europe."

By now, with the Allies winning the war, inhibitions about mentioning Jews began at last to disappear. The Office of War Information, and even the BBC, reported about Jews in their broadcasts to the Continent. During July we once again appealed to FDR for help. The Hungarian churches in the United States held special nationwide services on 9 July 1944 as a gesture of solidarity with Hungary's Jews. We elicited responses from the International Red Cross and the apostolic delegate in Washington, which led us to believe that our campaign had influenced the Hungarian government to temporarily halt the deportation of Jews to concentration camps. We did what we could from here. The rest is on the record: Most of the Jews of Hungary eventually went to their deaths, with the full knowledge and within plain view of the entire world.

We dispatched Eri Jabotinsky to Istanbul, with the blessing of the WRB and against the opposition of the State Department and the British. From Istanbul, Eri managed to speak frequently to Budapest. There was no way to save large numbers of Jews because Lord Moyne would not permit any leniency in the British immigration policies regarding Palestine or anywhere else in the vast British empire. Actually, nobody really cared. It was then that Eri had his first heart attack. His independent attempts to circumvent British adamancy had earned him the enmity of the Jewish Agency people in Istanbul, of Wise and Goldmann, who incessantly complained to the State Department in Washington, as well as that of the State Department itself.

I will not dwell on the bickering and backbiting that went on between the delegates from Palestine and the JDC people stationed in Istanbul. It is a sad and depressing episode. One thing alone, however, united the organizations there: the decision to expel Eri from Istanbul. We suspected that, under pressure, the Americans also had a part in it. The American attitude was a forewarning of an aggressive stand against "*Aliyah* B" (illegal immigration to Palestine), which they pursued in the following years.

By the end of 1944 tens of thousands of Jews would have safely reached Turkey from Balkan countries, had Turkey been assured that they would not remain in the country but would proceed farther. The British issued only 1,500 immigration certificates monthly for Palestine; the Jewish organizations obediently apportioned this pitiful handful of permits according to internal Zionist party affiliations. Eri concluded that the time had come to shatter this arrangement and expose British hypocrisy to the free world. He also wanted to jar the many Jewish representatives in Istanbul from their hand-wringing and impotent stance. As soon as the Zionist establishment became aware of Eri's activities and plans, it tried to isolate him from the U.S. Embassy and from Ira Hirschmann, the WRB representative, whom we had originally recommended to the Board.

When Eri became involved in negotiating for a Turkish vessel to carry about 2,500 people weekly to Palestine — to sail from Constanta to Haifa without British permission — and we in New York authorized him to make a financial commitment of up to $250,000, the British decided they had had enough. They told the Turkish authorities that Eri had been involved in the assassination of Lord Moyne, and since he was carrying a British passport, they wanted to extradite him. Eri later told me that he suspected that Ehud Avriel, one of the leading men of the Jewish Agency in Istanbul, took part in the campaign that resulted in his expulsion. Eventually, the Turks apologized to Eri and put him on the train to Palestine where the British jailed him.

We could not achieve much against such formidable opposition. One must remember that the WRB was functioning by Executive Order, was without a meaningful budget, and depended on Jewish funds to carry out any substantial rescue activities. We could not assure Mr. Pehle that we would be able to provide funds. So Eri was handed over to the British, and *Aliyah B*, in which the *Haganah* and the Jewish Agency became so deeply and enthusiastically involved in 1946, was unnecessarily delayed.

The story on Eri Jabotinsky's activities in Istanbul has never been told. Documentation is available in the files of the WRB in Hyde Park and in the files of our Emergency Committee at Yale University.

One more chapter on our rescue role deserves mention. When the Nazis entered Zagreb, Yugoslavia, in April 1941, Reuben Hecht, then in town for meetings on matters of *Aliyah*, managed to slip back to Switzerland, his native country. For several years, he was kept outside the circle of Jewish activities: The Jewish Swiss and other respectable leaders did not forgive him for establishing our Zurich office for *Ha'apalah* in 1939 and for his attempts to raise funds for it. However, during the following years, Hecht established a close relationship with the U.S. consul in Zurich, Sam Edison Woods, a key man in the U.S.-European intelligence network. Woods introduced Hecht to Yitshak and Rachel Sternbruch of the Orthodox Rescue Committee. As happened elsewhere — for example, the relationship between the *Irgun* and the Hebrew Committee of National Liberation (HCNL) men, and my experience in Vienna in 1938 when I worked with the Orthodox generations — Hecht and the orthodox Sternbruch were harmonious.

I will avoid the chapter on disagreements between the Orthodox Rescue Committee and the Jewish Agency people — the Joint's representative, Saly Mayer, Rudolph (''Rezso'') Kasztner, and the British-Jewish Agency connection. The matter I wish to touch on is the Musy-Himmler attempt to save Hungarian Jews and other camp inmates between October 1944 and April 1945.

Sternbruch and Hecht were convinced that high-level efforts could help crack the Nazi obsession with the Jewish extermination. The Orthodox Rescue Committee learned that a former president of Switzerland, Jean-Marie Musy, had managed through his personal friendship with Himmler to rescue two Jewish friends from an extermination camp. Two Jews were better than no Jews. Sternbruch and Hecht approached Musy, and a meeting resulted between Musy and Himmler in October in Berlin. At the meeting, according to Hecht, when Musy raised the matter of sparing Jewish lives, saying that it was an issue about which the Allies felt strongly, Himmler reacted with disbelief and rejected Musy's statement. At this and following meetings Musy kept pressing one point: Given the fact that the war was going badly for Germany, certain concessions might be obtained for the SS personnel of the concentration camps, such as considering them prisoners of war instead of war criminals. The negotiations were protracted and complicated. Finally, Himmler agreed to let a train with up to 1,200 Jews leave the camps weekly for Switzerland and to halt the extermination process in the camps.

One of the ugliest inter-Jewish rivalries followed, involving Saly Mayer, the impulsive JDC representative in Zurich, and Kasztner, who were negotiating with Nazis Kurt Becher, Adolf Eichmann, Ernst Kaltenbrunner (a close confidant of Hitler) on ransoming Jews. When Becher learned about Himmler's activities and the departure of the first train, he denounced the plan to Hitler, who overrode Himmler's order — and so a second train never left. In spite of opposition to the activities of Sternbruch and Hecht, of the Jewish Agency's Nathan Schwalb, Kasztner, and the JDC's Saly Mayer, Musy managed at the last minute to have Himmler countermand Hitler's order to push survivors into forced marches. According to Sternbruch, this was effective at Bergen-Belsen and Mauthausen. The Musy rescue effort was the last one in which *Irgun* people participated.

In Switzerland, as in the United States, the establishment leaders acted as supreme authorities, having no communitywide nonideological body to which they had to report or account. They fought each other and they fought any rescue effort independent of their own jurisdiction, inexcusably damaging rescue opportunities.

In May 1945 our Emergency Committee in New York issued its final communique:

> We feel that it is our duty to tell the surviving Jews of Europe a story not of achievements but of endeavors on their behalf. . . . They have the bitter feeling that in this great

> country, nobody — literally nobody — cared about their disaster. One group did not rest. . . . It hammered away through every channel, employed every conceivable method to impress the fact of Jewish suffering and death, and their heroic, hopeless fight.
>
> In hundreds of newspapers, the message of Jewish torture was brought to the breakfast table of millions of Americans. . . . Radio stations . . . leaders of the nation in Congress . . . were urged to take action. It declared the Bermuda Conference a mockery. . . . The WRB was created. This group made itself a nuisance to all government agencies and departments.
>
> It organized manifestations of tribute to Sweden and Denmark. . . . We tried with all the powers conceivable to disentangle the demand for rescue from any political complications. . . . Our radio messages asked "how well are you sleeping when a whole people is being put to death?"

We did the best we could, certainly, we disrupted Jewish passivity. But obviously it was not enough.

In 1947, in Palestine, Moshe Feinstein was sentenced by the British to hang because he was a soldier of the Hebrew revolution. Moshe cheated the hangman by pressing a grenade to his chest and dying a free man. Before his death he told his British judges what our youth had learned from the fate of its people:

> You officers of the invading army, hear me! Do you mean to scare us, we who have for years been hearing the clickety-clack of wheels carrying our brothers and parents and our finest people to the chambers of death? Us — who have been repeatedly asking ourselves, why did fate treat us differently than the millions of our brothers? How come we did not share their agony?
>
> And to this we have only one reply: We have remained alive not in order to live in slavery and repression and await a new Treblinka. We have remained alive in order to make certain that life, freedom and honor will be our lot, and of our nation and of our generations unborn. We have remained alive in order to make impossible a recurrence of what happened there. . . . We have learned our lesson and paid for it dearly.
>
> We have learned that there is a mode of life which is worse than death, and there is death that is a prerequisite to life.[2]

Notes

1. *Albatros,* Berlin, no. 3/4, 1923. The poem, which originally appeared in Yiddish, was translated into English by Yisrael Medad.

2. Itzhak Gurion, *Triumph on the Gallows.* (New York: The American Memorial Committee, 1950), p. 116.

7 *HALAKHAH* AND THE HOLOCAUST: *Historical Perspectives*

Jonathan I. Helfand

Jewish Law — *halakhah* — has been in continuous use for two, if not three thousand years. As such, it has been applied in countless situations and employed to adjudicate numerous conflicts.[1] The multitude of legal decisions rendered by scholars and courts over the past two millennia regulate all areas of human activity — religious, as well as what today would be called civil — and lie at the very core of Jewish life and vitality through the ages. Jewish law maintained communal order, promoted economic welfare, guided development, and contributed to the sense of peoplehood and unity that insured Jewish survival.

In modern times historians have recognized the importance of the body of Jewish legal literature for the writing and interpreting of Jewish history. In particular, scholars have come to utilize responsa literature — collections of legal opinions on specific cases written by the most distinguished rabbinic authorities of each generation — as an important primary source in the writing of Jewish history.[2] The questions, sometimes even more than the answers, shed important light on the state of Jewish social, economic, communal, as well as religious, affairs in different ages. For example, medieval responsa that discuss letters of credit, contracts, monopolies, and marketing practices reveal much about economic conditions of that period, just as the eighteenth century responsa on hunting, frequenting coffee houses, raising dogs, reading newspapers on the Sabbath, and attending medical school tell us about the social and cultural changes of that age.[3]

During the period 1933–1945 hundreds of legal questions were addressed to rabbis and answered under the shadow of Nazi rule and persecution. Still more were raised in the postwar years as a consequence of the Holocaust. Scattered in numerous legal tomes, these responsa offer a unique perspective on Jewish life and attitudes during those tragic years.[4] Many of these texts contain poignant, heart-rending accounts of suffering and sacrifice endured by the condemned Jews of Europe. To consign these documents to the category of the lachrymose history of the Holocaust would be as much a mistake as to reserve them for homiletics, fund raising, political rhetoric, or self-indulgent breast-beating on auspicious public occasions. Despite the unusual circumstances surrounding their composition, or perhaps because of it, they should be viewed as an integral part of the ongoing Jewish legal tradition and as a valuable source for legalist and historian alike.

This paper presents some of these sources to illustrate the nature of the material available to us today and to indicate the kind of insights that can be gleaned from them. However, a word of caution is in order. Not all the sources are equally reliable for the historian and even the legalist. Some, perhaps most, responsa were written down after the war, and the authors may have confused what they wished had happened with the reality.[5] The legalist too must read these responsa critically, for the solutions or opinions offered are frequently in the category of *hora'at sha'ah,* or exceptional rulings, and were not intended to be used as a precedent in normal, peaceful times.

The responsa literature of the Holocaust era can be divided into three categories or periods: the prewar years (1933–1939), the war years (1939–1945), and the postwar period (1945 to the early 1950s).[6] The responsa of each of these periods reflect the unique historic circumstances that prevailed beginning with the onset of the persecution in the early years of the Nazi regime, to the destruction and devastation that dominated the second stage, and, finally, to the repercussions and shock of the postwar years.

Prewar Years, 1933–1939

In the first period, the responsa generally, but not exclusively, emanated from Germany and later from Austria. Some involve correspondence between German and foreign scholars, while several involve questioners and respondents who both reside outside the Nazi sphere but discuss issues related to the Nazi threat. The questions, on the whole, deal with the deteriorating conditions in Germany — economic and social problems, emigration, and religious observance under difficult circumstances. By the latter part of the period, as the noose tightened around the doomed communities, the nature of the questions and the tone of the answers reveal the increasingly desperate situation and reflect changing priorities.

The rise of the Nazis to power in 1933 brought about a number of *halakhic* inquiries. Some of these questions reflect the increasing hostility between the Jews and their erstwhile countrymen and the growing isolation of the Jewish community. For example, in the early 1930s the refusal of non-Jewish neighbors to cooperate with Jewish dairy farmers raised a serious legal problem. Since Jewish law forbids the milking of cows on the Sabbath, neighboring Gentiles were asked to perform the task. In two recorded instances the non-Jews who normally performed this service refused to continue, leading the dairy farmers of Würzburg and Fulda to ask their respective rabbinic authorities for permission to milk the cows themselves. In both cases either personal prejudice or pressure from other Gentiles clearly appear to have brought about this break in established practice.[7] In January 1936 the great Lithuanian scholar, Rabbi Chaim Ozer Grodzinski, adopted a lenient view on this question because he considered the situation in Germany a "time of great emergency."[8]

The exclusion of the Jews from German society through the Nuremberg laws was particularly painful to those Jews who had always participated in German cultural life. The desire to fill the void created by this segregation is evident in the following question posed to Rabbi Jacob J. Weinberg: Is it permissible, he was asked, to hold concerts or public lectures on secular topics in a synagogue since such surroundings were normally reserved for sacred purposes? The questioner points out the need to give moral support to Jews in "this hour of distress" and adds that such activities were already being held in non-Orthodox synagogues and might attract and influence Orthodox Jews if no alternative was offered in their own congregations. Rabbi Weinberg's responsum gives approval for a very limited cultural program and then only under the dire circumstances prevailing in Germany.[9] The question and answer make it quite clear that German Jewry was under growing psychological pressure as a result of legal disabilities and social ostracism. Equally obvious is their unwillingness to accept cultural deprivation; perhaps in an effort to demonstrate that they were not inferior beings, they sought to continue their intellectual and cultural activities in the one realm left to them — the synagogue.

The economic strains created by Nazi legislation and boycotts have left their traces in responsa literature as well. Many Jews applied to their rabbis for permission to keep stores open on the Sabbath or for other exceptional rulings because of great financial need.[10] In one decision relating to such a question Rabbi Weinberg notes that the earning of a livelihood under the present conditions is "more difficult than the splitting of the Red Sea."[11]

The Nazi boycott of Jewish stores on 1 April 1933 occasioned important correspondence between rabbinic authorities outside Germany. At issue was the question of a counterboycott.[12] While some rabbinic authorities strongly endorsed the counterboycott as a means of discouraging further persecution of the Jews of

Germany, others were more cautious. Rabbi Chaim Ozer Grodzinski, for example, wrote to Rabbi Eliezer Silver of Cincinnati in the fall of 1933 that the imposition of such a boycott was having adverse effects on German Jewry and that German Jews feared that it would lead to bloody retaliations there.[13]

The pattern and pace of Jewish emigration from Germany is also reflected in a variety of responsa. In May 1933, shortly after the Nazis came to power, a question was raised about the existence of a religious ban *(herem)* on living in or traveling to Spain. A popular tradition existed that the exiles of the Spanish expulsion of 1492 had placed a ban on that country that still remained in effect. In an exchange of letters between Rabbi Menahem Mendel Landa and Rabbi Weinberg, the authenticity of this tradition was questioned, as it was in a responsum of Rabbi Chaim Eliezer Spira.[14] The posing of such questions in 1933 indicates that while emigration was indeed on the minds of many, and some 25 thousand Jews did leave Germany in the first half of 1933, after the initial panic the situation was not viewed as desperate.[15] The majority of German Jews were not convinced of the danger that lay ahead, and even those who were alarmed still had other geographic options. Had it been viewed otherwise, the ban, real or imaginary, would not have served as a religious barrier, as indeed was the case in later years.

The increasing pressure on the Jews after the legislation of 1935 and the hardening of Nazi emigration policy after Munich, not to mention the restrictive immigration policies of the Western powers, shocked many Jews into the realization that they must flee at any cost. The existence of bans, or even the absence of religious amenities, no longer concerned the many who sought to escape the Nazi Reich. As a consequence a number of questions arose when Jews found themselves in havens lacking proper religious facilities for burial and circumcision. For example, one couple fled Germany for Africa, where the husband died. The wife gave birth to a son after his death and, in the absence of a *mohel* (ritual circumcisor), arranged for the operation to be performed by a non-Jewish doctor while she recited the appropriate blessing. A question was later raised whether this had been the proper procedure.[16] In another case, an emigrant asked Rabbi Jacob Breisch what procedure to follow in his place of refuge that did not have a proper Jewish cemetery.[17]

Various attempts were made to circumvent the economic restrictions placed by the Nazi authorities on emigrants. A question regarding ritual immersion (*tevilah*) sheds light on one such practice. A woman had a precious stone implanted in her tooth to avoid its confiscation by the Nazis. Since ritual immersion cannot take place if there is a *hazizah* (obstruction) anywhere on the body, Rabbi Isaac Weiss was asked whether the gem inside the tooth would render the woman's immersion invalid.[18]

The decline of German Jewry reflected in these responsa was accelerated by the tragic events of 1938. The violence of *Kristallnacht* produced questions that prefigure the tragedy about to befall German and European Jewry. Of the thousands of Jews rounded up, many did not return home alive. In some cases the families were only notified of death; in others the cremated remains of the deceased were returned. In January 1939 Rabbi Menachem Mendel Kirschbaum issued regulations for dealing with the legal problems that these circumstances presented. They included directives on how the ashes should be treated and when the mourning period should begin — issues that would return to the legal agenda in the wake of the violence yet to come.[19]

War Years, 1939–1945

As German military advances placed even greater numbers of Jews under Nazi domination, new measures of oppression and new forms of persecution were implemented against them. Tens of thousands of Jews were eventually crowded into ghettos, segregated from society, drafted into forced labor details, and placed under unbearable economic and physical restraint. Ultimately they were transported to concentration camps, where the process of degradation continued and culminated in their extermination. Through all this nightmare the stream of questions continued on religious practice as it applied to the hellish conditions that prevailed in the ghettos and camps. These responsa demonstrate the perseverence and tenacity of the victims and their desire to preserve their religious life and traditions even in the midst of chaos and bloodshed. The topics dealt with in this literature cover all aspects of Jewish law, from intricate questions on the baking of *matzah* to awesome discussions on life and death situations.

The pattern of violence and degradation to which the Jew was subjected is typified by a recurring question on shaving off one's beard. According to Jewish law, shaving the face with a blade is forbidden. Furthermore, a beard was considered a sign of religious distinction and piety. The Nazis chose this symbol as a target, frequently attacking Jews and cutting or tearing off their beards, leaving them disfigured and shamed. Since, under these conditions, the beard was an open invitation to violence, many Jews inquired if and how they could remove their beards. In each case the respondents allowed whatever was necessary to avoid assault and humiliation.[20]

Faced with starvation and death, many Jews took desperate chances to stay alive in the ghettos. One responsum tells of a Jew who, doing forced labor outside the ghetto, agreed to smuggle out a gem for a friend and exchange it for food. The plan failed and the laborer was caught and shot. His body was returned to the ghetto where, in accordance with Jewish law, he was promptly buried in his blood-stained clothes. When it was later learned that the stone was hidden in the victim's garment, the owner requested permission to exhume the body (a practice generally forbidden by Jewish law) in order to retrieve his property. In agreeing to this procedure, the respondent notes that the family to whom the gem belonged was near starvation.[21]

Many of the problems discussed in the responsa resulted from the general conditions of deprivation rather than from specific policies instituted by the Nazis to disrupt religious life. The observance of Passover, for example, was difficult because of the limited food supplies available. Thus, in Kovno, permission was given to eat black peas (traditionally not eaten by European Jews on Passover) and special instructions were given for making *matzah* with the addition of potato peelings.[22]

In another ghetto, reading the Scroll of Lamentations in the synagogue on the night of the Ninth of Av was impossible because of the curfew. The curfew, of course, was not instituted to disrupt the ritual observance. Ironically, in ruling that Lamentations should be read privately at night, rather than earlier in the day, the rabbi invoked the principle that "it is not proper to hasten the advent of tribulation."[23]

In many cases the local authorities deliberately harassed the Jews by disrupting or forbidding their religious activities. In Kovno, in 1941, the Nazis threatened Jewish laborers who stayed away from work on Yom Kippur. The rabbi therefore decreed that announcements be made in the synagogues on that day ordering the laborers to their jobs.[24] In that same city the Nazis later forbade public worship and study.[25]

Even under the adverse conditions in the death camps, heroic efforts were made to uphold Jewish law. Rabbi Zvi Hirsch Meisels, an inmate of Auschwitz, reported that the rituals of *shofar* and the four species *(Sukkot)* were observed in that camp.[26] Similar reports exist for other camps and include the observances of Yom Kippur, Hannukah, and Sukkot.[27]

In observing Jewish law in defiance of Nazi wishes, the Jew risked severe punishment and even death. A question was therefore posed whether Jews had a right or an obligation to thus endanger their life; if not, they would be guilty of violating the law that required the protection of human life. The answer to this question depended, to a large extent, on the way the rabbinic authorities viewed the Nazi oppression. If seen as primarily an assault on the person of the Jew, then technically it was not a time of religious persecution and heroic sacrifices were not only unnecessary but even contrary to Jewish law. On the other hand, if Judaism too was under attack, then it was a classic example of *yehareg ve'al ya'avor,* let him be killed and not violate the law.

In Kovno Rabbi Oshry broached this issue when the Nazis prohibited public worship and study classes. While not obligating the Jews to martyr themselves under these conditions, he clearly indicated that he considered the persecution to be directed against Judaism as well as against the Jew.[28] Similar sentiments were expressed in another context by Chaim Kaplan, diarist of the Warsaw ghetto:

> Judaism and Nazism are two world outlooks, neither of which is compatible with the other, and for this reason they cannot live together. For two thousand years Judaism has left its imprint, culturally and spiritually, on nations of the world. It stood like a rock,

> blocking the spread of German paganism whose teaching was different and whose culture was carved out of a different source. Two kings cannot use one crown. Either humanity would be Judaic, or it would be idolatrous-German. . . . The new world which Nazism will fashion is directed toward primitive idolatry. . . . It is therefore ready to fight Judaism to the finish.[29]

This perception of the nature of the Nazi onslaught was undoubtedly reinforced by the participation of local anti-Semites who aided and abetted the German occupiers and brought to their work the traditional animosities and religious prejudices that had long prevailed in Eastern Europe.

Apparently, from the slim evidence available, the same opinions did not prevail among German Jews and rabbinic authorities. In prewar Germany even the prohibition against *shehitah* (ritual slaughtering) of meat was not assumed to be a form of religious persecution. Thus, in a responsum dealing with this problem, Rabbi Weinberg declared that it was not a time of religious persecution and suggested therefore that certain changes might be made in the regulations of ritual slaughtering to comply with the Nazi regulation. Had he viewed the laws as an attack on Judaism, any changes would have been prohibited, as the principle of *yehareg ve'al ya'avor* would have been invoked.[30]

While there is a paucity of *halakhic* material from Germany during the war years, an interesting series of letters between the surviving communities of Hamburg and Berlin in 1942–1943 have been preserved.[31] These letters, which deal with ritual matters, shed further light on the difference between the persecution in the Polish territories and in the *Altreich*. In the fall of 1942, Jacob Katzenstein asked Dr. Michael Gescheit of Berlin if, under given conditions which he detailed, he could carry his food out of his *sukkah* in his courtyard on the Sabbath. *Inter alia* we learn that the *Jüdischer Religions Verband* had forbidden Jewish tenants to violate the Sabbath publicly by hanging out their wash or beating their rugs. Another letter reveals that the *Hevra kadisha* (burial society) of Hamburg still functioned and that regular prayer services were held in the community house. In the winter of 1943 Dr. Gescheit apparently guided his colleague in the rebuilding of a *mikvah* (ritual bath) and, in return, received a copy of a dedication poem that was placed in the wall of the new structure. Dr. Gescheit's response indicated that he too intended to build a new *mikvah* in Berlin to replace one that was located in a building that had been sold.

This exchange of letters began several months after the deportation from Berlin and Hamburg had begun. The near normal conduct of community functions and the absence of any indication of religious harassment in these letters, however, stand in stark contrast to the conditions described in the responsa from Eastern Europe. This contrast, the result of Nazi policy and other given circumstances as much as the ethnic differences between Polish and German Jews, accounts for the different perceptions of the persecution and, in reaction, the strong motivation to make great sacrifices to maintain Jewish law and rituals.

Many of the responsa from the war years show an astonishing sensitivity to issues of life and death in the face of overwhelming barbarity and bloodshed. In Kovno in June 1941 a group of Yeshiva students was seized by Lithuanian guards. Rabbi David Itzkowitz, fearing for their lives, wanted to intercede to save them, at the risk of his own life. At issue was the principle of "who says that your blood is redder?" — that is, no one has the right to take one innocent life to save another. After lengthy discussion the rabbi was permitted, though not obliged, to take the risk, on the grounds that it was only a possible danger that he faced and that it would be considered an act of great piety.[32]

This story is particularly striking when contrasted with the episode recounted by Henri Sauguet, which took place in Vichy, France. When the aged poet and artist Max Jacob, a converted Jew, was interned in Drancy, a group of his friends urged Picasso to intervene on his behalf with the Nazis who frequented his studio. Picasso, eating his lunch, heard out his colleagues and replied, "Max is an angel. He'll fly over the wall." Max Jacob perished in Drancy.[33]

In a world in which life was cheap and death cheaper, Jews agonized over moral issues of life and death. Did a man have the right to bribe his son out of internment if it meant that another boy would have to die in his place? Were birth control and abortions permissible when the Nazis threatened pregnant women with death? Could a Caesarean section be performed on a pregnant woman who had been shot by the Nazis? Under what circumstances could someone who threatened the survival of his comrades be killed? Was suicide or homicide justifiable in face of anguish and torture?[34]

As absurd as such discussions may appear in retrospect, for the doomed participants they represented a form of resistance. If, as they perceived it, this was a campaign against Judaism and not just the Jew, their actions denied the Nazis a desired victory. They cast themselves in the image of ancient Jewish martyrs whose heroic sacrifices and death had assured the survival and ultimate triumph of Judaism.

Postwar Years, 1945–1950

The Allied victory in Europe brought an end to the persecution, but legal problems related to the Holocaust persisted into the postwar years. Many of the questions posed dealt with family and marital status. For example, in Jewish law a wife cannot be released to remarry if her husband disappears with no evidence of death. Such a woman is called an *agunah,* and hundreds of *agunot* appealed to rabbinic authorities to review the circumstances of their cases and release them to marry. One of the most important factors in all the deliberations on these cases was what the rabbis considered to be the certainty of death and the near impossibility of survival in most circumstances.[35] As many of these respondents were themselves inmates of concentration camps, their opinions reflect their wartime perception of the utter hopelessness of their situation and the absence of any alternatives for survival.

Some questions offer details on how Jews did survive. They tell of Gentiles who hid Jews, of Jews who masqueraded as Christians, and of children whose Christian guardians refused to relinquish their charges after the war.[36]

The status and disposition of Jewish property also engaged rabbinic authorities after the war. How were deserted and desecrated synagogues and cemeteries to be treated? Did property confiscated by the Nazis have to be returned to the original owner? What should be done about sacred objects stolen and sometimes desecrated by Nazis or the local anti-Semitic population?[37]

There were questions, too, about how to care for the dead, the mass graves, and the ashes, and, finally, how to memorialize them.[38]

This brief survey of responsa written under the impact of the Holocaust is, of course, far from exhaustive. It demonstrates, however, that much remains to be learned about the history of this tragic period and about the nature of the Jewish response from this rich and varied literature.

Notes

1. For a brief survey of Jewish legal literatures, see David M. Feldman, "The Structure of Jewish Law," in his *Marital Relations, Birth Control, and Abortion in Jewish Law* (New York: Schocken Books, 1977), pp. 3–18.

2. Solomon B. Freehof, *The Responsa Literature* (Philadelphia: Jewish Publication Society, 1959), pp. 193–223; Bernard D. Weinryb, "Responsa as a Source for History: Methodological Problems," in *Essays Presented to Chief Rabbi Israel Brodie*, ed. H.J. Zimmels, J. Rabbinowitz, and I. Finestein (London: Soncino Press, 1967), pp. 399–417.

3. For the use of responsa as a source for Jewish history in the Middle Ages, see, for example, Irving A. Agus, *Urban Civilization in Pre-Crusade Europe*, 2 vols. (New York: Yeshiva University Press, 1965); and Isidore Epstein, *The "Responsa" of Rabbi Solomon Ben Adreth of Barcelona (1235–1310) as a Source of the History of Spain* (London: Kegan Paul, Trench, Trubner, 1925); for the modern period, see the frequent citations of such literature in Azriel Shohat, *Im Hilufei Tekufot* [With the Changing of Eras] (Jerusalem: Mosad Bialik, 1960).

4. Two of the major sources of such material are the collected responsa of Rabbi Jacob Jehiel Weinberg, *Seridei Esh* [Remnants of the Fire], 4 vols. (Jerusalem: Mosad Ha-Rav Kook, 1961–1969); and Rabbi Ephraim Oshry, *She'elot u-Teshubot mi-Ma'amakim* [Responsa from the Depths], 3 vols. (New York: p.p., 1959–1969).

Rabbi Weinberg (1885–1966) was a Lithuanian scholar who emigrated to Germany, received a doctorate from the University of Geissen, and joined the faculty of the Orthodox Hildesheimer Seminary in Berlin. He served as rector of the seminary and was considered one of the leading rabbinic authorities in Western Europe before the war. He was expelled from Germany before the outbreak of the war and lived in Switzerland until his death. His responsa deal with many of the prewar problems and issues that will be discussed below.

Rabbi Oshry (b. 1914) was one of the last rabbinic authorities in the Kovno Ghetto. From 1941 to 1944 he answered hundreds of questions for the inhabitants of the ghetto, keeping records on bits and scraps of paper. He survived the war and currently resides in New York City.

Much of the rabbinic literature dealing with the Holocaust has been summarized and made available to the English reader in the works of H.J. Zimmels, *The Echo of the Nazi Holocaust in Rabbinic Literature* (New York: Ktav, 1977), and Irving J. Rosenbaum, *The Holocaust and Halakhah* (New York: Ktav, 1976).

5. Cf. Weinryb, *Responsa as a Source for History,* pp. 404–06.

6. Zimmels, *The Echo of the Nazi Holocaust,* p. 1, proposes dividing the prewar period into two stages, reflecting the increased hostility and persecution that began with the expulsion of the Polish Jews and Crystal Night — from 1933 to October 1938 and from October 1938 to the outbreak of the war.

7. Weinberg, *Seridei Esh,* II, no. 24; responsum of Rabbi Barukh Kunstadt of Fulda, in *Sefer ha-Zikaron le-Kevod ha-Rav Ya 'akov Yehiel Weinberg* [Memorial Volume in Honor of Rabbi Jacob Jehiel Weinberg] (Jerusalem: P. Feldheim, 1969), pp. 41–50.

8. *She 'elot u-Teshuvot Ahiezer,* III (Vilna: F. Garber, 1939), no. 34.

9. Weinberg, *Seridei Esh,* II, no. 12.

10. Cf. Zimmels, *The Echo of the Nazi Holocaust,* pp. 7–9.

11. Weinberg, *Seridei Esh,* II, no. 21. The reference is to a Talmudic expression found in *Pesahim,* 116a.

12. For a general discussion of the boycott, see M. Gottlieb, ''The First of April Boycott and the Reaction of the American Jewish Community,'' *American Jewish Historical Quarterly* 57 (1968): 516–56. The article does not refer to the episode cited here.

13. *Ahiezer Kovetz Iggerot* [Collected Letters], vol. 1 (Bnei Brak: Netzah, 1970), pp. 296–97.

14. For a discussion of this and several other sources, see Zimmels, *The Echo of the Nazi Holocaust,* pp. 16–20 and 253–58.

15. Leon Poliakov, *Harvest of Hate* (Philadelphia: Jewish Publication Society, 1954), p. 12. See also Lucy Dawidowicz, *The War Against the Jews 1933–1945* (New York: Holt Rinehart and Winston, 1975), pp. 188–89.

16. Rabbi Isaac Jacob Weiss (Weisz), *Minhat Yitzhak,* III (London: n.p., 1962), no. 101.

17. Rabbi Mordekhai Ya 'akov Breisch, *Helkat Ya'akov,* II (London: Mahzikei ba-Dat, 1959), no. 4. The responsum is dated 5715 (1955), but see Zimmels, *The Echo of the Nazi Holocaust,* pp. 29–31.

18. Weiss, *Minhat Yitzhak,* I (London: n.p., 1955), no. 23.

19. *Tziyun le-Menahem,* ed. J. Rubenstein (New York: Makhon le-heker ba'ayot ha-yahadut ha-haredit, 1965), pp. 363–65.

20. Oshry, *Mi-Ma'amakim,* I, no. 19. Cf. Zimmels, *The Echo of the Nazi Holocaust,* pp. 39–40. In another recorded case the commandant of a labor camp forced the Jewish internees to remove their beards with a chemical on the Sabbath. See Joseph Safran, ''She'elot Halakhah be-Yemei Sho'ah ve-Hurban'' [Legal Questions in Days of Holocaust and Destruction] *Sinai* 64, no. 6 (1968–1969): 191.

21. Oshry, *Mi-Ma'amakim,* II, no. 12.

22. Ibid., I, no. 17. Cf. Rosenbaum, *The Holocaust and Halakhah,* pp. 101–08.

23. Rabbi Zvi Hirsch Meisels, *Mekadeshei ha-Shem,* I (Chicago: n.p., 1955), no. 70. Responsum no. 71 deals with a similar question involving the proper time for immersion in a ritual bath (*mikvah*).

24. Zimmels, *The Echo of the Nazi Holocaust,* p. 48. Rosenbaum, *The Holocaust and Halakhah,* p. 113, reports another case where the Nazis tempted Jews with food on the fast of Yom Kippur. While some of the starving prisoners succumbed, others resisted temptation and did not break their fast until nighttime.

25. Oshry, *Mi-Ma'amakim,* II, no. 11. Cf. Rosenbaum, *The Holocaust and Halakhah,* pp. 50–56.

26. Meisels, *Mekadeshei ha-Shem,* I, pp. 11–15.

27. Rosenbaum, *The Holocaust and Halakhah,* pp. 91–119.

28. Oshry, *Mi-Ma'amakim,* II, no. 12.

29. Chaim A. Kaplan, *Scroll of Agony,* trans, and ed. by Abraham I. Katsh (New York: Macmillan, 1965), p. 130.

30. Weinberg, *Seridei Esh,* I, no. 1.

31. "She'elot u-Teshuvot bein Hamburg le-Berlin" [Responsa between Hamburg and Berlin], *Beit Ya'akov* 22 (Adar, 5721/1961): 22–23.

32. Oshry, *Mi-Ma'amakim,* II, no. 1.

33. The anecdote is related by Mavis Gallant in a review of Herbert R. Lottman, *The Left Bank* (Boston, 1982) in *The New York Times Book Review,* 4 April 1982, p. 3.

34. Rosenbaum, *The Holocaust and Halakhah,* pp. 35–46. Cf. A. Guttman, "Humane Insights of the Rabbis, A Chapter in the History of the Halakhah," *Hebrew Union College Annual,* 46 (1975): 433–55.

35. Zimmels, *The Echo of the Nazi Holocaust,* pp. 215–43; Safran, "She'elot Halakhah," pp. 195–97.

36. Oshry, *Mi-Ma'amakim,* I, 31; Zimmels, *The Echo of the Nazi Holocaust,* pp. 160–69. The refusal of some Christians to return their Jewish charges after the war led to several famous cases, including that of the Finaly children in France (Zimmels, *The Echo of the Nazi Holocaust,* p. 167).

37. Rosenbaum, *The Holocaust and Halakhah,* pp. 143–55.

38. Zimmels, *The Echo of the Nazi Holocaust,* pp. 150–60, 169–75; Safran, "She'elot Halakhah," pp. 192–93.

8 THE SURVIVING VOICE: *Literature of the Holocaust*

Ellen S. Fine

In his foreword to a book entitled *La Fin de l'espoir* by Juan Hermanos, Jean-Paul Sartre describes an incident that took place one night in Paris during the German occupation.[1] He was working with a group of friends in a hotel room, when suddenly from the street below an anguished voice cried out for help. The group ran down to the dark, empty street. They looked around and saw no one. Finally, they returned to the hotel to resume work. But all night long the penetrating sound of the disembodied voice haunted them; they could not forget its strident plea.

This voice, Sartre tells us, has not been silenced. Under different forms and in different countries, it continues to echo in our ears, and will persist until no one is left to shout — or to listen. It is the outburst of the oppressed, the shriek of terror issued forth when no hope is left. It is what Primo Levi in his memoir, *Survival in Auschwitz,* depicts as "the cry of the doomed man" whose last call to his comrades from the gallows strikes the living core in each of them.[2]

The scream of one man or woman in the death camps may have dissolved into a "landscape of screams,"[3] often soundless, often unheard, and punctuated by the despair of silence. Yet this outcry, so powerful in its utterance, still reverberates today. It has been transformed into the collective voice of the survivor and has been translated into what we call the literature of the Holocaust.

What is Holocaust literature? Can we even begin to define this body of writing born of terror and of silence? Because of the nature of the event itself, the works that grew out of the Nazi mass murder and degradation of the Jewish people cannot truly be classified in conventional terms, nor are there yet critical methods to evaluate their artistic merit. After Auschwitz traditional categories are broken down. A thin, almost indistinguishable line often exists between testimony and fiction, between the facts and their representation. The dimensions of atrocity surpassed anything the human imagination could have possibly conceived. Reality itself became surreal. How then can appropriate language, narrative forms, and literary structures be found to portray the limits of human endurance? These are some of the perplexities with which writers, scholars, and the survivors themselves must grapple. These are also the troubling matters that confront the reader who comes face to face with material never before expressed on the printed page.

Writing about the Holocaust poses a basic problem, particularly for survivors: how to speak of the event, how not to speak of it? The imperative to testify conflicts with the impossibility of recapturing the experience. A wide gap often exists between the survivor's memory and its reflection in words. In retrospect, the survivor comes to doubt the reality of what took place. "I am no longer sure that what I have written is true but I am sure that it happened," states Charlotte Delbo at the conclusion of her book, *None of Us Will Return*.[4] And Elie Wiesel notes in *Legends of Our Time*, "Some events do take place but are not true; others are — although they never occurred."[5]

How can one who has lived through an unprecedented and systematic series of atrocities find a vocabulary adequate to record the darkness? "Auschwitz negates all literature as it negates all theories and doctrines. . . . To substitute words, any words for it is to distort it," Wiesel proclaims.[6] He points to the difficulty of transmitting the phenomenon to those who were not there. How, he asks, can you articulate the cries of children being thrown into flaming pits? "The language of night was not human," he states. "It was primitive, almost animal — hoarse shouting, screams, muffled moaning, savage howling, the sound of beating . . ."[7]

Surely these sounds are intranslatable. Attempts to reproduce them can only diminish the madness of a kingdom where men, women, and children were transformed into an unrecognizable species — dispossessed of their clothes, their hair, their names, and their identity. The Nazis degraded humanity as it poisoned its syntax. In *l'univers concentrationnaire* speech was dismembered. "Our language lacks words to express this offense, the demolition of a man," Primo Levi declares.[8] He indicates that expressions such as "hunger," "tiredness," "fear," and "pain" are "created and used by free men who lived in comfort and suffering in their homes," and no longer make sense in the concentrationary world. Had the camps lasted longer, Levi observes, "a new harsh language would have been born; and only this language could express what it means to toil the whole day in the wind, with the temperature below freezing, wearing only a shirt, underpants, cloth jacket and trousers, and in one's body nothing but weakness, hunger and knowledge of the end drawing nearer."[9]

However, if language was corrupted under the Nazi regime and ordinary terms lost their true meaning, a new linguistic code was not formulated in the aftermath of the event. Therein lies the predicament: how to transpose the experience of extremity into written testimony? One must fall back on old words, that is to say, pre-Holocaust terms and concepts, to signify the new reality that was Auschwitz. The other alternative is to say nothing. We need only recall photos taken by the Nazi slaughterers of their victims before they were shoved into the crematorium; or documentary films such as *Nuit et Brouillard* [Night and Fog], by Alain Resnais and Jean Cayrol, showing bulldozers pushing piles of dead bodies into pits. There are no words to describe what one feels when one gazes at these sights of twentieth century barbarity. "Before what we now know the mind stops," Lionel Trilling wrote in his essay, "Art and Fortune," after he had seen films of Bergen-Belsen and Buchenwald in 1948. "The activity of mind fails before the incommunicability of man's suffering," he acknowledged.[10]

A possible response to the images we behold is a shrill scream; or a prayer mutely uttered from the depths of our being. The logical response is paralysis, a retreat from the word, a closing off of speech, a holding of the breath — terminating in absolute and deafening silence.

The Mission to Bear Witness: The Diaries

And yet the paradox of the Holocaust is that while it imposes silence, it demands speech. In spite of the brutality that mutilated the human face and stifled the human voice, a large body of literature, international in scope and written in a multiplicity of European languages, has grown up around the subject. Immediately after the war and then for years to follow, many manuscripts were published, including diaries, eyewitness accounts, journals and memoirs. At the YIVO-Institute for Jewish Research alone, over 2,000 such titles are listed. Lucy Dawidowicz has pointed out in her introduction to *A Holocaust Reader* that the documentary sources of the Holocaust "surpass in quantity and comprehensiveness the records of any other historical era."[11] It took longer — from 15 to 20 years — for the Holocaust experience to be assimilated into the fictional realm. As Albert Camus has noted, "There is a stage in suffering, or in any emotion, or passion, when it belongs to what is most personal and inexpressible in man and there is a stage when it belongs to art."[12] Although many novels, plays, short stories, and poems deal extensively with the Holocaust, this paper will limit itself to the "most personal" stage of the literature of testimony: the diaries and memoirs.

Let us first consider the diaries, some of which were smuggled out of the ghettos or buried in the rubble and later found as relics of a vanished civilization. Two of the most articulate chroniclers were Emmanuel Ringelblum and Chaim Kaplan.

Emmanuel Ringelblum was a historian in Warsaw who dedicated himself to the mission of bearing witness for posterity. In May 1940, before the ghetto was set up, he organized an underground group of researchers who kept a collective record of Jewish experiences under the German occupation. After November 1940 the group continued to operate within the ghetto walls, using the code name *Oneg Shabbat* (The Joy of Sabbath) because it met on Saturdays. Volunteers not professionally trained as historians or journalists took upon themselves the systematic documentation of ghetto conditions. They wrote about ghetto folklore and cultural activity, as well as the arrival of Jews from various parts of Poland and Germany, the searches by the Jewish police, and the roundups and deportations. Other members of the organization had the task of packing and hiding the material. One 19-year-old boy describes his feelings about his job: "It was perhaps the riskiest, but it was worth doing. . . . We have bequeathed and safeguarded our rich heritage. I don't want any thanks. It will be enough for me if the coming generations will recall our times. . . . What we could not cry out to the world, we buried in the ground."[13]

Ringelblum himself was smuggled out of the ghetto in April 1943 just before the uprising. He could have escaped from Warsaw with the help of the Polish government in exile in London but chose, instead, to remain in hiding with his wife and 12-year-old son. He continued to write until March 1944, when they were discovered by the Gestapo and executed outside their bunker. Before his death, however, he managed to bury his notes in sealed rubberized milk cans. In 1946, the first section of his manuscript was found under the rubble of Jewish Warsaw, and four years later the second was located. Ringelblum's account, written in Yiddish, was edited and published in Poland in 1952. A second, more complete version appeared in 1963. The English translation, *Notes from the Warsaw Ghetto,* was based on the first edition of the journal.[14] Although often fragmentary, Ringelblum's observations presents us with a chapter of Jewish history that depicts the destruction of a people as well as its heroism in the most extreme of circumstances.

Chaim Kaplan, the founder and principal of a Hebrew elementary school in Warsaw for 40 years, also kept a journal that he wrote in Hebrew and copied into a series of children's notebooks. In 1941 he could have secured an exit visa but chose to stay in Poland for the purpose of recording history. Less matter of fact than Ringelblum, Kaplan is a diarist: He discloses his personal reactions to the political and social events. He tells us that his obsession to write down everything is a duty, "a sacred task," but not without pain. Often the misery of the ghetto distresses him to the point of making him want to throw his pen away. No words can describe the cruelty he sees and hears. Dante's Inferno seems mild compared to the inferno of the Warsaw streets, he says.[15] "We are so tired. There is no strength left to cry; steady and continual weeping finally leads to silence. At first, there is screaming; then wailing; and at last a bottomless sigh that does not leave an echo. We live broken and shattered lives" (pp. 85–86).

Kaplan's own doubts about his power to verbalize what is happening, especially during the massive expulsions from the ghetto in the summer of 1942, are reinforced by friends who urge him to stop writing. "Why? For what purpose?" they ask. "Will you live to see it published? Will these words of yours reach future generations? How?" (p. 383). Nevertheless, Kaplan persists:

> And yet in spite of it all I refuse to listen to them. I feel that continuing this diary to the very end of my physical and spiritual strength is a historical mission which must not be abandoned. My mind is still clear, my need to record unstilled, though it is now five days since any real food has passed my lips. Therefore, I will not silence my diary. [pp. 383–84]

Kaplan's diary becomes his friend and his ally; it spiritually sustains him as an instrument of survival and a weapon of defiance. When bitterness overcomes him he drags himself to the diary and is overcome by what he calls "a wave of creative inspiration," although he questions whether the act of chronicling deserves to be called "creative" (p. 278). Kaplan is aware of the importance to testify but suggests that an artist's pen is more appropriate to convey the lamentations of mass suffering than the notes of a scribe. He calls for a poet like Bialik who commemorated the Kishinev pogrom in his poem, "The City of Slaughter" (1905), and declares: "A poet who clothes adversity in poetic form immortalizes it in an everlasting monument. And this monument provides historic material from which future generations are nourished. Who will write of our troubles and who will immortalize them? . . . Poet of the people, where art thou?" (p. 79). Little did Chaim Kaplan know that his own diary would come to be a poetic pillar in the collective history of Holocaust darkness.

At the end of 1942 Kaplan gave his diary to a Jewish friend who worked at forced labor outside the ghetto and returned each evening. He, in turn, smuggled out the notebooks, one by one, to a Polish worker named Wladyslaw Wojcek who lived in Liw, a small village near Warsaw. Wojcek buried the notes in a kerosene can on his father's farm, and when he emigrated to the United States in 1962, he brought some of Kaplan's notebooks with him. They were translated from the Hebrew and published in English, first under the title *Scroll of Agony* in 1965 and later as *The Warsaw Diary of Chaim Kaplan* in 1973. Curiously, while Kaplan revealed his innermost thoughts in his writing, he never mentioned his own name — probably for reasons of security. It took Abraham Katsh, the editor and translator of his work, a year and a half to establish the author's identity. Kaplan and his wife are believed to have perished in the extermination camp of Treblinka in December 1942 or January 1943.

What is the role of the reader facing this kind of literature, dug up from the ruins and transmitted through milk and kerosene cans? First, we cannot help but feel reverence for testimonies by such spokesmen as Ringelblum, Kaplan, or Janus Korczak, the director of a Jewish orphanage in the Warsaw Ghetto. (At the last moment Korczak refused to be saved and instead accompanied the two hundred children of his institution to the gas chambers of Treblinka.) The diaries left us by children are particularly moving — Anne Frank in Holland, Moshe Flinker in

Belgium, Yitzkhok Rudashevski in the Vilna Ghetto, Eva Heyman in Hungary, all of whom were killed by the Nazis. Most extraordinary of all are the diaries transmitted by the *Sonderkommando,* the special work squad of Jewish prisoners who had to remove the dead from the gas chambers and cremate them. They too were doomed to die, but some wrote accounts and buried them under the ashes of Auschwitz, deep in the soil. After the war some of these diaries were uncovered and are now collected in the Jewish Historical Institute in Warsaw. These testaments take on "the aura of a holy text," as Alvin Rosenfeld observes in his book, *A Double Dying*. Surely, says Rosenfeld, we do not hold manuscripts such as these in our hands and read them as we do volumes that reach us through the normal channels of composition and publication.[16]

Along with the sense of the sacred for what has miraculously reached us from the other side, we may also experience a sense of the tragic. One no longer perceives the agony of individual victims who gain insight into their destiny as they become aware of what is happening to them. The anonymity and arbitrary nature of death during the Holocaust put an end to the traditional notion of the tragic hero. How could death take on meaning when not one person but an entire community was in its death throes? "The tragedy of the individual is neutralized and ignored," Chaim Kaplan says. "Before a companion opens his mouth to tell of his troubles, I can anticipate the details in advance" (p. 75). And Ringelblum, too, describes "the tragedy of persons who have lost some thirty members of their family — left all alone in the world — without a purpose in life" (p. 321).

Like tragic heroes, the authors of these documents are well aware of the collective fate of their people but cannot foresee their own: their works stop at the threshold of destruction. Because we, the readers, know what happened after their last line was written, the tragic spirit of the text is implicit, and we are obliged to complete the tale. On the one hand, the knowledge we bring to the work puts a special responsibility on us not encountered in other types of literature. On the other hand, the knowledge we gain from confronting this material makes us into new kinds of witnesses: those who live in the aftermath of the Holocaust and who bear the lasting burden of its anguish. Although the reader entering this sealed universe is "temporarily an insider and permanently an outsider" as Lawrence Langer notes in his book, *The Holocaust and the Literary Imagination,*[17] he or she must have the courage to listen to the collective scream and the reverberating silence — to hear that which is unspoken. We must remember that *we are posterity,* the future generation to whom this testimony was addressed under penalty of death.

Literature of Testimony: The Memoirs

Let us turn now from the diaries, which plunge us into the undiluted rawness of history itself and which in their own way are survivors or substitutes for those whose lives were cut off before their time, to the *témoignages* and memoirs written after the event. These testaments were recorded and published by survivors who emerged from the death camps, from forests where they had been hiding, or from bunkers where they had been buried alive. Some spoke out to provide judicial evidence in order to indict their oppressors. Others testified out of a sense of moral duty: They wanted to warn humankind how close it had been to its own annihilation. Still others, often the sole survivors of their families and communities, sought to commemorate the dead. Almost all who came back indicated that the will to bear witness had kept them alive and became the justification for survival in post-Holocaust times. As the Yiddish writer Mendel Mann affirmed, "I write to prove that I am alive, that I exist, that I too am still on this planet. The world condemned me to die. . . . I write because through my books, I bear witness to my existence."[18]

The literature of testimony that came into existence right after the war was for the most part produced by men and women who were not accomplished writers. The texts, overcome with detail, are often repetitive, fragmentary, and limited in scope. But do we read them for their literary quality or historical accuracy per se? Lucy Dawidowicz has been critical of these records because of what she calls "the egocentric predicament," or "the ability to see only through one's eyes and in the light of one's own experiences."[19] She points to the defects, discrepancies, and imperfect observations that test the credibility of historical truth. Similar conditions are represented in vastly different ways by eyewitnesses who based some of their evidence on hearsay and speculation. "With a few noteworthy exceptions," states Dawidowicz, "survivors are individuals who suffered and endured in obscurity, far from the seats of authority and decision."[20] Moreover, she speaks of their "feebleness of expression" and their flawed memories. With the passage of time, she says, the survivor consciously or unconsciously forgets certain things that can slant the perception of history and lead to its falsification if not carefully scrutinized by the historian.

In reaction to Dawidowicz's need to apply rigorous methods of critical scholarship to these texts, I would argue that the authority of history is less important than the authenticity of experience. These documents of consciousness contributed by survivors translate abstract statistics and figures into deeply felt human responses. Holocaust literature enables us to observe the impact of a catastrophe without parallel on the lives of ordinary men, women, and children. We read of their struggle to live in a world that condemned them to die. That we are granted access to this world and to the formulation of their struggle, be it "feebly" or artistically expressed, seems to take precedence over the verification of historical accuracy.

Perhaps in time new types of criteria will be developed to measure the factual credibility and literary expression of survivor literature. Old standards and traditional modes of judgment simply do not suffice, for how can the truth of the Holocaust be conveyed in its totality? Quoting the Polish Jewish historian Dr.

Isaac Shipper, Alexander Donat notes, "There is no such thing as historical truth. There is just interpretation. It depends on who writes the history of our time."[21] And Elie Wiesel has stated, "Every witness expresses only his truth in his own name."[22] Wiesel does not pretend to transmit the truth but rather his personal vision of history — *his story* — which, while valid in and of itself, is contained within a circumscribed perspective.

This leads me to a second objection to Dawidowicz's viewpoint. One listens to the unique utterance of the survivor and realizes that it is accumulative, part of the shared effort to engrave the experience of the Holocaust on the memory of humankind. All the narratives, in a sense, tell *one* story and must be glimpsed as different pieces that form a whole. "Almost all survivors say 'we' rather than 'I,'" Terrence Des Pres observes in his book, *The Survivor: An Anatomy of Life in the Death Camps,* stressing that their accounts are "invariably group portraits, in which the writer's personal experience is representative and used to provide a perspective on the common plight. Survival is a collective act and so is bearing witness."[23] Those who have been able to find words, however inadequate — and let us not forget that language itself was damaged by the Nazi reign of terror — speak not only for themselves but for the anonymous dead whose screams stopped in the gas chambers and who left behind solely their silence.

Along with those witnesses who chose to speak out in the first few years following World War II, many preferred to remain silent. Still others waited a decade or more before reconstructing their fragmented recollections into a coherent narrative. Even today, over 35 years after the event, memoirs continue to be written — *Blood and Hope* by Samuel Pisar, *When Memory Comes* by Saul Friedländer, *Elli: Coming of Age in the Holocaust* by Livia Bitton Jackson, and *The Survivor* by Jack P. Eisner, to name only a few.

We have pointed to the difficulty of matching words to the new order of reality ushered in by *l'univers concentrationnaire*. Yet if we look closely at some of the memoirs published in the aftermath of the Holocaust, we see survivor-writers capable of using language to evoke scenes that linger in our minds long after we have read the books. Distance from the event, combined with their particular sensibilities and literary talents, enabled these men and women to freeze the horror of the Holocaust onto the printed page. The splinters deeply embedded in their memories seem to have grown sharper with the passage of time, finally erupting into unforgettable cries, memorialized by the written word. I have selected from the following texts scenes and images that emit the soundless screams still resonating from the kingdom of the dead: *The Holocaust Kingdom* by Alexander Donat, *None of Us Will Return* by Charlotte Delbo, and *Night* by Elie Wiesel.

Alexander Donat was a journalist and publisher of a Warsaw daily newspaper when the war broke out. He survived the Warsaw Ghetto uprising and the Maidenek concentration camp. At the end of the war he was miraculously reunited with his wife and son in Poland. In 1946 they emigrated to the United States. Donat's first-hand account of his experiences, *The Holocaust Kingdom,* was not published until 1963. The chronicle offers a detailed analysis of the structure of the Warsaw Ghetto and its living conditions, but above all recalls deeply human scenes that illuminate the material and make it intensely personal.

A scene from *The Holocaust Kingdom:*[24] It takes place in July 1942 during the early stages of the roundups in the Warsaw Ghetto. The *Ausweis,* or work certificate, was still respected by the Germans as a guarantee of not being selected for "resettlement." Donat is witness to this incident.

Early one morning a young mother, still dressed in a bathrobe and slippers, ran down into the street with an empty milk bottle in her hand. She was headed for a shop where they sold milk under the counter, when the police spotted her and asked for her *Ausweis.* She said that it was upstairs and she would get it immediately. "We've heard that one before," the police shouted and started dragging her to a boarded wagon already jammed with victims. "But my baby is all alone. Milk . . .," the young woman stammered in disbelief. Realizing what was happening, she wrenched herself free. First two policemen, then four, fell on her, hitting her, throwing her to the ground, and picking her up again. Finally she was tossed into the wagon like a sack. "I can still hear her screaming in a half-crazed voice somewhere between a sob of utter human despair and the howl of an animal," Donat tells us.

The author forces us to behold the transformation of the human voice into a beastly roar issuing from the depths of a mother who is separated from her child under the most violent and senseless of conditions. Her agonized cry, the last means of protest at the zero moment when no hope is left, assaults us and echoes in our ears. It does not leave us quickly.

If we turn from the strident sounds of the ghetto to those of the camp itself, from one woman to many, we find in Charlotte Delbo's memoir, *None of Us Will Return,* a series of nightmarelike fragments depicting the collective experience of women in Auschwitz. Charlotte Delbo was secretary to theater director Louis Jouvet before she and her husband joined the French Resistance movement at the beginning of the Nazi occupation. Both were arrested in March 1942. Two months later her husband was shot, and she was sent to Auschwitz with a convoy of French political prisoners in 1943. A year after liberation she wrote down her impressions but kept the manuscript in a drawer for nearly 20 years before she was ready to share it with the world. Her book, *Aucun de nous ne reviendra,* was published in Paris in 1965 and translated into English as *None of Us Will Return* in 1968.

Delbo's work is rendered in a poetic, condensed, somewhat surrealistic style. Phrases with the subject "we" or "they" and rarely "I" are repeated in rhythmical incantation. Stark images of cold, light, and silence are solidified into the barren landscape of Auschwitz. Time and movement are suspended, gestures abolished, sensations no longer exist. In the anonymity of this vast whiteness, women scream out, but their mournful cries are frozen fast into the ice.

Delbo describes the trucks loaded with women outlined against the blue sky, women whose shaven heads make them look like little boys. Headed for the gas chambers, they cry out. "They cry out and we hear nothing," says Delbo. "They cry out to us but no sound reaches us. Their mouths cry out, their outstretched arms cry out, and every bit of them cries out. Each body is a cry. . . . Each woman is a materialized cry, a scream that is not heard." The truck silently carries off the unheard pleas of the women, and Delbo is left with "eyes that cry out, that do not believe," but that can do nothing. "The screams remain inscribed on the blue of the sky."[25]

From the muted voices that disappear in the motionless plain, a chorus of terror bursts forth from the yard of Block 25, where women, condemned to die, huddle together to keep warm. Stripped of their coats, dressed in rags, they sit shivering on the ground crusted with snow. This is how Delbo transfixes the moment:

> Suddenly, as if at a signal, they all began to scream. A scream that swelled, mounted and spilled over the walls. Now they were only mouths that screamed, screamed at the sky. A flower bed of twisted mouths.[26]

The image of a flower bed is a tragic reminder of the once-blossoming women, full of life and beauty, and now mutilated in body and in spirit. The frenzy of revolt gives way to the resignation of silence, punctuated by isolated sobs. But once again, as it coming from another realm, a wilder scream rises higher and higher, reaching a fierce crescendo — only to be followed by an even more absolute stillness.

This shared song of death — and of its refusal — swells and falls for hours before being drowned out by the rumbling of trucks that come to seize their victims. But the symphony of disembodied screams reaches far beyond the walls of Block 25. We continue to hear the voices of the dying because Charlotte Delbo has had the courage to preserve the agony of the victims. She has chiseled these reverberating echoes into word monuments. Her language does not mitigate the suffering but heightens it. And how are we to classify such a piece of writing? Is this a personal testimony or documentary art? Surely it is a poetics of pain, crystallized into images all the more intense because they grow out of a real, not imaginary vision. The splintered memories of Delbo's inner voice create an artistic whole that brings us closer to the edge of the abyss.

Elie Wiesel, too, initiates us into Holocaust terror in his book, *Night*. Described as an autobiographical narrative, a fictionalized autobiography, a nonfictional novel, the work defies all categories. Essentially it is a personal memoir of the concentration camp experience written over 10 years after the event, and told from the point of view of the young narrator, Eliezer. Elie Wiesel grew up in the town of Sighet (Máramarossziget) on the Hungarian-Romanian border. At the age of 15 he was deported to Auschwitz along with his parents and three sisters. Only he and his survived. After the war he lived in Paris, studying at the Sorbonne and also working as a journalist. For 10 years he vowed not to speak of the Holocaust, "long enough," he discloses, "to learn to listen to the voices crying inside my own. Long enough to regain posession of my memory. Long enough to unite the language of man with the silence of the dead."[27] In 1954 he had an interview with the French Catholic writer Francois Mauriac who encouraged him to bear witness. Two years later his long *témoignage* was published in Yiddish under the title, *Un di velt hot geshvign* (And The World Has Remained Silent), and in 1958 the work was condensed and translated into French as *La Nuit*. The English edition, *Night* (1960), was translated from the French.

The long journey into Holocaust blackness is presented in *Night* in a straightforward manner. Eliezer, the narrator, does not attempt to interpret the facts but lets them speak for themselves. Yet *Night* is more than an eyewitness account, and the 15-year-old youth is more than a witness. From another level of consciousness we hear a voice that reveals how a young religious boy lost his faith in God and in man. We see how a child is forced to watch the gradual death of his father, and the spiritual death of himself.

Throughout the text the sounding of the voice is a sign of life, a counterforce to the darkness. The act of speaking is synonymous with survival; the stifled voice signifies paralysis and death. In the polluted atmosphere of *Night* the camp inmates can barely whisper because of "the thick smoke which poisoned the air and took one by the throat," Wiesel writes.[28] The collapse into silence by suffocation, or the cutting off of breath, is most dramatically exposed in the scene describing the hanging of the young boy with the eyes of a sad angel.

The youth had aided in an attempt to blow up an electric power station at Buna, the industrial camp that was part of Auschwitz. After days of torture he is condemned to be hanged along with two other men. The entire camp is summoned to witness the execution. The two adults die quickly, but the child, because his body is so light, suffers a slow agonizing death. As the camp prisoners march past the gallows in total silence and look the child in the face, Eliezer hears a man behind him ask, "'Where is God now?' And I heard a voice within me answer him, 'Where is He? Here He is — He is hanging here on this gallows. . . .'"[29]

The scene of the hanged child is probably the central incident of *Night*. Through Eliezer's eyes we gaze at the innocent face desperately struggling for life, and we see on the gallows of Auschwitz the literal death of God. The drama unfolding before our eyes makes us *feel* the tragedy of the Holocaust. The six million are embodied in this one angelic figure whose young voice is permanently stilled by the powers of evil.

What the 15-year-old narrator contemplates lies beyond speech. Yet he hears *a voice within,* which becomes the generative principle of the will to bear witness and the source of survival. It is this inner voice that compels Elie Wiesel 10 years later to mobilize words and memory in the fight against forgetfulness. By speaking out he transforms his voice into a life-giving force so as to infuse his dead father, the hanged child, and other victims of the Holocaust with breath.

Despite the claim of victims and survivors that the Holocaust defies language, words have indeed been sculpted out of its dark center. The silence has been broken by authors such as Alexander Donat, Charlotte Delbo, and Elie Wiesel who oblige us to remember. By sharing their perceptions of reality such as they knew it, they have given a permanent form to the event, which will be transmitted from generation to generation. Because of their writing, the cry that Sartre heard throughout the night still haunts us and has seeped into our collective consciousness. It is a call for help and a call for action. Let us listen to it before it is too late — for we may come to realize that the voice we hear is our own.

Notes

1. Jean-Paul Sartre, Préface à *La Fin de l'espoir* by Juan Hermanos (Paris: Editions Julliard, 1950) in *Situations IV* (Paris: Gallimard, 1964), pp. 77–79.

2. Primo Levi, *Survival in Auschwitz: The Nazi Assault on Humanity* (New York: Collier Books, 1959), p. 135.

3. "Landscape of Screams" is the title of a poem by Nelly Sachs in *O The Chimneys* (New York: Farrar, Straus & Giroux, 1967).

4. Charlotte Delbo, *None of Us Will Return*, trans. John Githens (Boston: Beacon Press, 1968), p. 128.

5. Elie Wiesel, *Legends of Our Time* (New York: Avon Books, 1968), p. viii.

6. Elie Wiesel, *A Jew Today*, trans. Marion Wiesel (New York: Random House, 1978), p. 197.

7. Elie Wiesel, "Why I Write," in *Confronting the Holocaust: The Impact of Elie Wiesel*, ed. Alvin Rosenfeld and Irving Greenberg (Bloomington: Indiana University Press, 1978), p. 201.

8. Primo Levi, *Survival in Auschwitz*, p. 22.

9. Ibid., pp. 112–113.

10. Lionel Trilling, *The Liberal Imagination* (New York: Viking, 1950), pp. 264–65.

11. Lucy S. Dawidowicz, *A Holocaust Reader* (New York: Behrman House, 1976), p. 1.

12. Albert Camus, *Notebooks 1942–1951*, trans. Justin O'Brien (New York: Knopf, 1965), p. 84. Camus says, "Art is the distance that time gives to suffering. It is man's transcendence in relation to himself."

13. David Grober, quoted in Lucy Dawidowicz, *A Holocaust Reader*, p. 7.

14. Emmanuel Ringelblum, *Notes from the Warsaw Ghetto*, trans. Jacob Sloan (New York: McGraw-Hill, 1958). All further references will be noted in the text in parentheses.

15. Chaim A. Kaplan, *The Warsaw Diary of Chaim A. Kaplan*, trans. Abraham Katsh (New York: Collier Books, 1973), p. 29. All further references will be noted in the text in parentheses.

16. Alvin H. Rosenfeld, *A Double Dying: Reflections on Holocaust Literature* (Bloomington: Indiana University Press, 1980), p. 17.

17. Lawrence L. Langer, *The Holocaust and the Literary Imagination* (New Haven: Yale University Press, 1975), p. 3.

18. Mendel Mann, quoted by W. Rabi, "Vingt ans de littérature," in *D'Auschwitz à Israël* ed. Isaac Schneersohn (Paris: Centre de Documentation Juive Contemporaine, 1968), pp. 363–64 (my translation).

19. Lucy Dawidowicz, *A Holocaust Reader*, p. 10.

20. Ibid., p. 12.

21. Alexander Donat, *Jewish Resistance* (Waldon Press, 1964), in *Out of the Whirlwind: A Reader of Holocaust Literature*, ed. Albert H. Friedlander (New York: Schocken Books, 1976), p. 50.

22. Elie Wiesel, *One Generation After* (New York: Avon, 1977), p. 56.

23. Terrence Des Pres, *The Survivor: An Anatomy of Life in the Death Camps* (New York: Oxford University Press, 1976), pp. 29, 38.

24. Alexander Donat, *The Holocaust Kingdom* (New York: Holocaust Library, 1963), pp. 62–63.

25. Charlotte Delbo, *None of Us Will Return,* trans. John Githens (Boston: Beacon Press, 1968), pp. 38–39.

26. Ibid., p. 56.

27. Elie Wiesel, *A Jew Today,* p. 15.

28. Elie Wiesel, *Night,* trans. Stella Rodway (New York: Avon, 1960), p. 48.

29. Ibid., p. 76.

9 POETRY IN THE HOLOCAUST DOMINION

Frieda W. Aaron

An inherent human need is to bring order to chaos, to render the incomprehensible intelligible; hence the primordial mythopoeic compulsion. In the three decades since the Holocaust, a profusion of myths and abstractions of theories has been postulated to explain the carnage. To be sure, an inquiry into the causes of the catastrophe is the proper and necessary subject of history and mimetic art; but what is disquieting is the plethora of social scientists, novelists, playwrights, and filmmakers who trample "where angels fear to tread," misinterpreting evidence, revising history, and perverting the truth.

The frightening phenomenon is that neither the honest inquiries into the causes of the Holocaust nor the reductionisms that exploit it mitigate the suspicion that the edifice, and perhaps even the very foundation of Western civilization, has gone up with the smoke of the immolated Jews. For what is civilization, what are its determinants if not a stream of events generated by the dialectic of antecedent and contemporaneous processes? It is this that produces a continuum within which accepted and established beliefs, customs, and laws are transmitted from one

I wish to express my gratitude to the institutions that granted me research fellowships for my Ph.D. dissertation of which this paper is an aspect. The institutions include the Jack P. Eisner Institute for Holocaust Studies, CUNY Graduate School/University Center; the Memorial Foundation for Jewish Culture; the Institute for the Study of Modern Jewish Life of the City College of New York.

generation to the next, from one cultural type to another. The Holocaust established such a continuum, an archetype against which various bloodlettings around the globe seem to be tacitly measured. Since none exceeds the barbarity of the Holocaust, they are willy-nilly included in the purview of the acceptable and permissible. If the world was initially shocked by the exposure of the concentrationary world, it quickly learned to live in peace and equanimity with the unthinkable.

It seems that the Holocaustal lava continues to erode the foundation of the human community in the third decade after the fact, leaving an increasingly deeper chasm between our feet in which, to echo Dostoevsky, "everything is permissible." This crisis, flagrantly manifested in the licentious policies of great and small nations, in the unconscionable behavior of groups and individuals, is eloquently articulated in the contemporary literature of despair and atrocity.

In view of this one wonders how the condemned, immured in the ghettos and concentration camps, apprehended the cosmic chaos — a scheme in which Dante's imagined "Frozen Lake" was translated into the palpable fires of Maidanek and Auschwitz. One further wonders what kind of literature was produced there and what significance it might have in countering the current vulgarization of the Holocaust.

Role of the Poet in the Landscape of Death

Astonishing as it may be, literary activity was vital and widespread in the ghettos, in hiding, among the partisans, on the "Aryan" side, and even in some of the concentration camps. Indeed, after waves of mass deportations to death centers, those who temporarily hugged life in the various places feverishly turned to writing. Spontaneous literary activity not only continued but actually increased, when one would expect language to evaporate, to turn to ashes in the conflagration of gas chambers and crematoria. As the poet Michal Borwicz writes:

> After each deportation action — when the narrow ghetto streets echoed with a cry of bleeding silence, when the dwellings blew with the emptiness of many thousand martyrs, and the furniture and belongings were confiscated by the Germans — the thresholds, floors, and sidewalks were strewn with tatters and scraps of plundered property. In the midst of it, it was easy to find handwritten slips of paper. Ripped out of drawers and hiding places by the German marauders, these notes, devoid of material value, were trampled by them in utter disdain.[1]

The flowering of literature in the crucible of the Holocaust world reflected an urgent determination to leave a testament for posterity. It was, furthermore, a quest for reaffirmation of traditional values and all that constituted Judaic culture. Hence the greater the threat to the physical and cultural existence of the condemned, the more feverish was their literary activity. What kind of literature did they produce? What linguistic approaches were employed to articulate the unspeakable? What were the dominant themes?

Although the writers availed themselves of the entire spectrum of literary genres, the most popular one was poetry. That this poetry is probably the richest of the Holocaust literature should not be surprising. For poetry — perhaps because it provides, more often than any other literary genre, the most precise correlatives for states of consciousness — was the first vehicle of reaction against Nazi barbarism. Moreover, the poets, writing from "the heart of darkness," reflect an immediacy of experience that is untainted by the remembering processes of memory. Nothing but total recall could unveil the truth articulated in this body of literature. For as Janusz Korczak notes, "Reminiscences hinge on our immediate experience. Reminiscing we lie unconsciously."[2] Yet this naked immediacy of truth has been glaringly neglected by Holocaust scholarship. In fact, little of this work has been translated — perhaps because the bulk of it was written in Yiddish and Polish, both somewhat esoteric languages.

Interestingly, the first to respond to the Nazi assault were the Yiddish and the Polish-Jewish poets.[3] Apparently they knew that the objective chronicler of events needs the complement of a truth that transcends historical fact: the truth of the poet. For it is the poet who explores the thing felt subcutaneously and who lays bare the existential response to life, to hope, to terror, to despair, to heroism, to death. The most cogent articulation of this idea appears in Chaim Kaplan's *Warsaw Diary*:

> Who will immortalize our troubles? The national splendor inherent in religious poetry is not expressed in newspaper reports. . . . A catastrophe that becomes part of poetry . . . spreads among the people and is transmitted to future generations. A poet who clothes adversity in poetic form immortalizes it in an everlasting monument. And this monument provides historic material from which future generations are nourished.[4]

Poetics of Confrontation with the *Anus Mundi*

There is yet another much simpler and more pragmatic reason for the popularity of the poetic idiom. Since paper and pencil were not readily available, especially in the concentration camps, poetry was easier to compose in the mind and easier to commit to memory than was prose.

Often these poems were sung to popular and banal melodies. The juxtaposition between the highly charged concentrationary poetry and the sentimental tunes was startling. The irony was especially corrosive when the carefully wrought poetic diction of despair or hope and moral or political didacticism stood in sharp contrast to a vulgar love tune. This dissonance made more emphatic the chasm between the landscape of endless terror and a world where sentimental love songs were still being crooned in night clubs.

Not all the poetry was marked by the same quality of literary excellence. An abundance of literary neophites, moved by a compulsion to bear witness, resolved to record the apocalyptic events for posterity. Thus occurred a spontanous explosion of folk poetry — a kind of *Urdichtung* as well as balladry, the chief of which was the *kina* or *kluglid* (dirge). The latter is reflected in the following Polish song written and very popular in the Warsaw Ghetto:

The universe collapses in ruins,
Immolated in a vast conflagration.
Nothing can save it,
All drowns in devastation.[5]

Although the young poet witnesses the literal incineration of her world, she cannot fathom it. Nor can she comprehend the vast cosmic silence that envelops her burning world:

O, people where is your conscience?
Where are your hearts?
Where is divine essence?

This simple rhyming lament, devoid as it is of any other aesthetic compulsion, expresses the doubt that the victims could endure the agony and terror much longer. It further affirms the impossible task of recording the suffering. Yet this poet, like all the others, writes.

The dominant idiom, notably among the Yiddish threnodists, derived from the surfeit of Jewish literature of destruction. In the crucible of the Holocaustal world, even such avowed secularists as the Yiddish writing Abraham Sutzkever and Yitzhak Katzenelson and the Polish-Jewish Wladyslaw Szlengel turned to it, seeking in the paradigm of liturgical threnodies a vehicle for expressing the unspeakable. This poetry, therefore, takes its historical analogue, lexicon, and form from the Book of Lamentations and Jeremiah as well as from the iconography of pogroms. Of course the resonances inherent in Yiddish poetry are closer to the liturgical literature than are the poems written in Polish.

Yitzhak Katzenelson's poetry, notably his epic poem, *The Song of the Murdered Jewish People,* resonates with such liturgical influences:

Ani ha-gever, I am the man who watched, who saw
How my children, my women, my young and old were thrown
Like stones, like logs, into wagons
Brutally beaten, rudely abused.[6]

This strophe, one of many, reflects yet another phenomenon: the dissolution of the demarcation lines between personal and communal grief. For the "children . . . women . . . young and old," the poet laments, are not only his two murdered sons and wife, but the entire murdered Jewish people. In this Katzenelson adheres to the traditional Jewish canon that tends to eschew the singling out of the individual victim, but rather invokes the memory of communal suffering.

Moreover, as an eyewitness, the poet of this epic becomes the interpretive mediator whose poetic mimesis produces an abiding fusion of lyricism of agony and objective chronology of events. This jeremiad, like many of its kind, is therefore a synthesis of personal responses to the Draconic laws and detailed documentation.

The structure too is hybrid, combining an identifiable pattern of external archetectonics (fifteen cantos, fifteen four-line stanzas each) with an internal arrangement that defies any known design. Only those who have knowledge of the chronology of the events can decode the inner substance. The disjunctive internal structure is primarily revealed in the dissolution of time. The chronological order of events is suspended in surreal timelessness, and the cantos are held together by the displaced logic of nightmares. The recounting of the sequence of events dissolves in a lament, and the words tumble out in the distraught confusion of uncontrollable weeping. The tension arising from the poem's disjunctiveness and its apparent concern with the primacy of careful documentation heightens its eloquence. *The Song of the Murdered Jewish People* is a monumental elegy and a national testament of the beginning and end of the "Last Jews on Europe's Soil":

> Woe is unto me, nobody is left. . . . There was a people
> and it is no more . . . There was a people and it's . . . gone.
> What a tale. It began in the Bible and lasted till now . . .
> A very sad tale.
> A tale that began with *Amalek* and concluded with the far
> crueler Germans . . .[7]

The torment and the bereavement of the condemned were expressed not only in transtemporal eschatological elegies. A wide spectrum of modernist trends informed the work of many poets, both Yiddish and Polish speaking ones. The bankruptcy of language (intimations of which were already a commonplace in the interwar period) caused them to seek a tongue within the wave of modernist influences, just as it did within the framework of traditional and biblical archetypes. Hence, many poems exhibit unusual patterns that repudiate standard grammatic structures, punctuations, and strophic archetectonics. The poem "Szpital obozowy" (Camp Hospital), written in the Gross-Rosen concentration camp by the Polish Jew Jozef Bau, manifests this predilection. The structure of the poem reveals three strophes of uneven length. The unrhymed verses are marked by a dissonant rhythm and fragmented diction.

> On the shelf-bunks lie
> emaciated, glistening with sweat's enamel
> dying "Mussulmen."
>
> With heavy, monotonous step
> of creaking hours,
> treads
> the length and breadth of the barak-tent
> in the blood-stained apron of a medic . . .
> the "capo-watch"

— and counts the last minutes
— and figures who soon will
be released:
. . . these yes . . . these yes . . . those not yet,
. . . these yes . . . those tomorrow morning . . .

Sees; fever consumes
the not yet lice devoured skeletons
displayed for death to buy,
and stares out the window; — in the nearby
chimney, lightly roasted souls
dance a spectral minuet with the black smoke.
. . . then crosses out the numbers, jots down some footnotes:
"died voluntarily."[8]

Constriction of Language and Image

The convincing verisimilitude with which great poets were able to transcribe the human condition into art derived from the availability of familiar images. However, the kaleidoscope of imagery accrued over the millennia, as well as language itself, was hardly applicable to a knowledge that had no antecedents and no analogues. Nevertheless, the poets knew that language was often all they had in the flood of blood. They also knew that the paradox of language, as Paul Celan expressed it, was that "it had to find sustenance in its own inability to explain. . . ."[9] Sustenance was often found in the adherence to simple, standard devices of versification, in the unadorned, naked language that deliberately eschewed metaphor. Yet, these seeming palimpsests are replete with imagery — imagery, however, that does not lie in the realm of recognizable human experience. Unsymbolic and concrete, unimaginative and *sachlich,* the images mean what they are; for they arise from the spectral reality of the concentrationary world, from "the daily *dread* of experience" — to paraphase James Joyce. An example of this is another of Jozef Bau's poems "Glod" (Hunger) written in Plaszow, a slave labor camp near Cracow:

Flour coagulated into a loaf of cement
— condensed wages for a day's anguish
— that's bread

Eight stomachs creeping through the eyes
divide it into eight even parts,
the exactness of each crumb;
— that's the godhead
to which the thought prays
through the triple barbed-wire wall

. . . and farther beyond that braid
of wires and anguish, apparently a world exists.

But we, check-mated
by watch-tower
machine guns — know it not,
our temples are branded: ''check-mate.''[10]

This compelling articulation of hunger is almost completely devoid of extrinsic imagery. The sole superimposed metaphor is the word ''cement'' to which the daily bread of the denizens in Plaszow is likened. That the coveted bread is metamorphosed into the very godhead by the most excruciating of tortures, starvation, is not an extravagant conceit, but rather a faithful recording of fact. For in the Holocaustal world, a planet expelled from the universe, a slice of cementlike bread was often perceived as the only redemption to which body and soul bowed in reverence and supplication. Indeed, starvation here is so intense that there is a veritable dissolution of selfhood. The austere language has lost one of its essential words: ''man,'' and consciousness is a disembodied sensation of hunger, a stomach ''creeping through the eyes.'' In this godless realm, the victims are condemned to death not only by starvation, but also by the machine guns poised in the numerous watchtowers that dot the triple barbed wire walls. This image, too, derives from the language of concentrationary realism.

The modes of aesthetic stylization used to convey the brutalization and moral chaos suggest that a considerable body of the poetry written in the Holocaust constitutes a new poetic genre, one that evolved from, and is thus peculiar to, the historicity of the apocalyptic events. The register of common language with its accretion of idiomatic expressions was in a continuous process of change, reflecting the growing barbarism. Syntax, style, and symbol were subject to endless changes. Since the self-contained, discrete concentrationary organisms produced their own hierarchy of human relations, they often rendered traditional mores and epistemological modalities obsolete. In the surreality of this world neologisms were a commonplace, and familiar terminology either lost its meaning or else was invested with derisive connotations. Not only was common language informed by Nazi-Deutsch, but by ghetto and concentration camp slang of both Yiddish and Polish derivation as well. Rubinsztajn, the famous Warsaw Ghetto madman-clown and master punster, was particularly adept at coining new words and making droll puns. Here is one of his pithy apothegms in the Yiddish slang of Warsaw:

Ah groshn is goonish,
Ah tsvayer is goonish,
Ah drayer is goonish,
Ah fihrer zol paygern.

(A penny is worthless, twopence is worthless, three worthless, four — which in the Warsaw slang sounded like the Führer — let the fihrer drop dead.)

Cultural and Ontological Divisibility and Creative Integrity

The historicity of the poetry written in the Holocaustal dominion is not only a function of the growing barbarism, but also of the inner vision and, above all, the cultural retina of each poet. Some poets, writing in European languages, straddle two cultures, the Jewish and the non-Jewish. This ontological and cultural divisibility is not the experience of those poets who are indivisibly anchored in the Jewish culture and the Yiddish language. Poets like Czeslav Milosz, who experienced the devastation as Christians, present yet another vision of the violated world.

Polish-Jewish poets often express a bereavement alien to the sensibilities of the Yiddish poets. The assimilated writers, suddenly wrested from their non-Jewish heritage and catapulted into the ghettos, agonize over this cultural truncation. The early poetry is especially replete with adumbrations of this cultural wrench. Later poetry seems to eschew this concern, possibly because of the inverse relationship between the growing atrocities and the intensified sense of Jewish identity. Cogent formulations of these divergent perceptions inform Wladyslaw Szlengel's "Windows Facing the Aryan Side," an early poem, and "Counter Attack," a late one.

"Windows Facing the Aryan Side" establishes the extent to which the Jew, who formerly lived side by side with his Polish neighbor, is now irrevocably separated from the world outside the ghetto. The window of the poet's Warsaw Ghetto room faces not only the Aryan side but also the famous Krasinski Park. Yet looking out the window and feasting his eyes on the Aryan trees is strongly forbidden. He is a "Jewish worm and a Jewish mole," and it is "just and right" that he "should and must be blind." At night, however, the poet rushes to his window, "ravenously gazing and stealing snatches of darkened Warsaw."[11] The poet's longing for his beloved city is intensified and spiritualized by memory. The crescendo cataloguing of the attributes of Warsaw ends on a cadence of bitter resignation and realization that the city and his friends are indifferent to his fervent incantations and invocations. Their ways have parted. Friendship has sunk into an irretrievable swamp, as "Telefon,"[12] another of Szlengel's poems, indicates. The world, the culture, the life, the people he once knew are lost forever.

In "Counter Attack," on the other hand, Szlengel's concern is only with Jewish heritage and the Jewish future. Hence, he is determined to infuse his fellow Jews with renewed pride in their Jewishness. He further seeks to extricate his people from historical causality of acquiescence in the face of atrocity. Since the *sntetl* Jew had little recourse to law or justice, he was often forced to resist total destruction by appeasement. Szlengel now rejects this moral imperative; and his fiery poem echoes the prophetic eschatology of Isaiah. Like the ancient Hebrew prophet, Szlengel, the reborn Jew, rejects redemption through a policy of appeasement. "Counter Attack" becomes a clarion call for armed resistance and reflects the vital political role poetry played in the concentrationary universe. Written after the January 1943 insurrection, it was a vehicle of inspiration of the Warsaw Ghetto uprising in April of the same year. The poem's closing lines lay bare the desperate exaltation and hopeless grandeur of the fighting Jews of the Warsaw Ghetto:

Hear oh German Gods
How Jews in the "wild"[13] houses pray,
Clenching in the fist a stick, a stone.
We beg you, oh God, for a bloody battle,
We implore You for a violent death.
Let us not see, before we expire,
The stretch of the train tracks,
But let the precise aim of the hand, oh Lord,
Stain their livid uniform with blood,
Before the mute groan shreds our throats,
Let us see our simple human fear in their
Haughty hands, in their whip-wielding paws.
From Niska, Mila, Muranowska Streets,
Like scarlet blood-flowers,
Bloom the flames of our gun-barrels.
This is our resurrection! This is our counter attack!
The intoxication of battle!
The alleys of Dzika and Ostrowska
Are our partisan forests.
The block[14] numbers, medals of the Jewish war,
Quiver on our breasts.
The cry, "Revolt," flashes in scarlet
Like a bellowing . . . battering ram.[15]

Crisis of Faith in the Trauma of History

The shock sustained by the victims often produced a crisis of faith, though rarely absolute apostasy. In the works of many poets, God is inscrutable, unreachable, and unaccountable. Terror, chimneys, and death consecrated by divine will are an organic part of the cosmic chaos. In other poetry, the religious despair is transformed into outright blasphemy. The poets express the suspicion that the omnipotent, just, and wise God of their fathers has turned his back on his children either because of their sinfulness or because God Himself has been reduced to craven pusillanimity in the shadow of the hailing Nazi arm. He is, therefore, no longer able to protect his chosen people. In the first case God's wisdom and justice are challenged, for a punishment that calls for living children to be thrown into flames exceeds any conceivable form of sin. In the second case God is charged with bad faith, for He misled his people into believing in his omnipotence and his promise of ultimate redemption. Thus in some poems, Szlengel's for example, the universe is stood on its head, and it is God who, on Judgment Day, is judged by his children. The logic of such an inversion has its antecedents in Hasidic and rabbinic literature.

The right to judge God is implicit in the relationship between God and Israel — a relationship established by God's insistence that Israel accept his covenant. Thus:

> In Jewish law, God can be tried for his crimes because he is a party to an agreement. . . . In this respect he is a "person" in Jewish law. The trials of God narrated by Hasidic literature [and] Holocaust literature . . . are not only aggadically [theologically] defensible, but halakhically viable. As man is required to bear witness before God, he may also bear witness against God.[16]

In his passionately bitter poem, "It's High Time," Szlengel charges God not only with breaking the agreement, but he also accuses Him of handing his faithful and penitent children into the hands of the brutal murderers and into the ovens of Treblinka. That in the distant past, Szlengel vituperates, "God delivered His children from Egypt and brought them to their land will change nothing!" For God cannot be absolved of his terrible sin of indifference when his children were sacrificed on the altars of the world with his name on their lips. Now in a paroxysm of cruelty, God has abandoned them to the terror of the ghetto and death in Treblinka. For this barbarous betrayal and the recantation of the covenant, Szlengel thunders at God:

> We'll pay You back! We'll pay You back! . . .
> And when the executioner will chase and force You,
> Drive and push you onto the gas chamber floor,
> And seal behind you the hermetic door,
> The vapors will choke You, You'll see,
> You'll scream and weep and try to flee —
> And when Your death agony will end,
> You'll be dragged and in a monstrous pit land.
> Then they'll tear out your stars — the gold teeth from Your flesh —
> Then they will burn You.
> And You will be ash.[17]

Although this bitter invective has its roots in traditional liturgy, notably in the right to judge God for his trespasses — his breaching of the covenant — Szlengel's language stands in contrast to the poem's paradigms. He deliberately uses slang, especially ghetto slang, and Yiddishisms to destroy the perfect diction of preconcentrationary poetry. His poems are for and about the condemned, the exhausted, and he makes emphatic the inappropriatness of lofty poetic standards.

Morality and the Metaphysics of Survival

Poetry in the Holocaustal world was a vital and viable means of articulating the entire range of intellectual principles and states of consciousness. These articulations, as indicated, include political, philosophical, and religious concerns. Poetry was also a vehicle of moral and cultural sustenance and an expression of spiritual defiance that helped to keep the spirit of the condemned from dying. Since it articulated for many their thoughts and feelings, this literary genre was often an indispensable means of catharsis. Moreover, it was an expression of moral revulsion and opposition against the oppressor. Above all, it was a vital affirmation of life — an attempt to sunder the walls of an unbearable world and to walk toward the future.

Abraham Sutzkever's "The First Night in the Ghetto" is such an affirmation. For it transcends the moral bewilderment of the young poet whose integrity of youth has been savagely violated. The first night in the ghetto is an evocation of the first night in the grave. The poet is, however, reassured by a neighbor that in the end one gets accustomed even to that. In this, Sutzkever reflects the traditional pacifism of European Judaism, which had to adjust to calamity in order to save the community, the individual, the religion, and the culture. But the poet has it "up to his throat," as he lies near death under a gutter of a building in ruins, a building previously occupied by Jewish tenants, all of whom are now dead. Only he, a piece of "ember betrayed by the last spark precipitously extinguished," is left, and so are "the bricks in the ruins." "Roaring bricks/torn out with chunks of flesh from the walls." Black poison oozes from the gutter drop by drop in the irreality of this world. "Suddenly each drop becomes an eye" and the gutter "a telescope," through which the poet gazes at yesterday's luminous sky and at yesterday's stars, notably at "the after-Sabbath star/that my mother's lips used to bless: *gut vokh*."

Resuscitated by the firmament and his mother's star, the poet declares in existential terms: "I must live, for my mother's good star is alive."[18] This affirmation of life, variously orchestrated in Sutzkever's poetry as well as in that of most other poets of that period, is not only an act of personal survival but one of cultural continuity as well. Such a phenomenology of continuity is the imperative associated with the consecration of life (*kiddush ha-hayym*). In different times the prototypic obligation was martyrdom in the name of God (*kiddush ha-Shem*). The eschatological justification of this shift of imperatives derives from the fact that only a "dying ember" is left of the Jewish community in Europe. The primacy of individual survival is metaphysically linked to Jewish continuity, which is in itself redemptive. Often the struggle to stay alive was less for oneself than for the mother, father, or child who were killed. To reiterate, "I must live, for my mother's good star is alive." The "dying ember" (a central image in "The First Night in the Ghetto"), Sutzkever intimates, will be ignited again; and his dead mother's star "among the familiar, living stars of my town" is a symbol of abiding Jewish continuity that is unextinguishable.

There is yet another purpose in rekindling the "dying ember" — namely, to bear witness lest there be a sweeping and final obliteration of the very memory of

European Jewry. The prototype of the "dying ember" as historical witness is a medieval fragment that, according to Sidra DeKoven Ezrahi,

> has survived from the Hebrew lamentation literature of the fourteenth century, written by a man who returned to his hometown after a trip only to discover that a pogrom had wiped out every inhabitant and destroyed all the holy books, exept one Bible. This one remaining man, who refers to himself as the "last ember," wrote a brief account of the destruction of his town on the pages of the one remaining Bible.[19]

Poetics of Testimony: The Mnemonic Voice

The flowering of poetry even in the darkest of pits has its roots in the tradition of the "dying ember's" sacred duty to leave a chapter of martyrology for posterity. This testimonial or documentation poetry records the community's response to the unfolding destruction. As a day-to-day chronicle, it attests not only to the growing horrors but also to the diverse modes of resistance. This poetry unveils the vitality of the underground culture, replete with clandestine schools on all levels, libraries, theaters, and ingenious support systems without which no survival would have been possible. Even the poems of the children reflect the testimonial purpose of this writing, for they and their adult counterparts, like the biblical poets, knew that it was imperative to leave a record for posterity.

Moreover, poetry was used as a call for assistance from abroad. In the spring of 1944 a slim anthology of poetry entitled *Z Otchlani* (From the Abyss) — containing the works of Czeslaw Milosz, the Nobel Laureate, and Jan Kott, the famous Shakespearean scholar, among others — was smuggled out on microfilm to England by the underground National Jewish Committee. The anthology found its way to New York in November 1944.

The fervid poetic activity was coupled with an equally fervid attempt to save the manuscripts from destruction by depositing them in hermetically sealed containers and burying them in the ground. Abraham Sutzkever's *Kerndlekh Vayts* (Grains of Wheat) articulates this feverish activity. In the imaginative world of the poet, the manuscripts he hides in the earth become grains of wheat sown for an uncertain future. When overcome with despair, he recalls an Egyptian tale about a king who ordered his servants to fill a gold urn with grains of wheat. This urn was deposited in the pyramid built for the king. Nine thousand years later, when the seeds were unearthed, they blossomed into golden wheat. In pensive tones the poet muses:

> Perhaps in destiny's hour
> Even these words may
> Suddenly grow into flower
> In the light of the day.
>
> And like the prehistoric seed
> Transformed into sheafs of wheat —

My words will belong
To my people, the eternal throng.[20]

Indeed, Sutzkever's poetry, written both in the Vilna Ghetto and in the forests where he joined the partisans, saw "the light of the day." Unfortunately this cannot be said for most of the literature written in the Holocaust dominion, although some of it miraculously survived. Most of the poets, however, both well known and anonymous, perished.

Notes

1. Michal Borwicz, "Z otchlani" (From the Abyss), in *Pieśń ujdzie calo . . .* (The Song Shall Pass Unscathed . . .), ed. Michal Borwicz (Warsaw: Centralna żydowska komisja historyczna, 1947), p. 31. Translations of quoted passages and poems from this anthology are this writer's.

2. Janusz Korczak, *Ghetto Diary,* trans. Jerzy Barbach and Barbara Krzywicka (Vedder) (New York: Holocaust Library, 1978), pp. 113–14.

3. Henryk Grynberg, "The Holocaust in Polish Literature," *Notre Dame English Journal: A Journal of Religion in Literature, Special Issue: Judaic Literature: Critical Perspectives,* Indiana, vol. II, no. 2 (April 1979): 115.

4. Chaim Kaplan, *The Warsaw Diary,* trans. and ed. Abraham Katsh (New York: Colliers, 1976), p. 79.

5. This unpublished song was written by an anonymous woman in the Warsaw Ghetto.

6. Yitzhak Katzenelson, *The Song of the Murdered Jewish People,* trans. and annotated by Noah H. Rosenbloom (Israel: Ghetto Fighters House, 1980), p. 23.

7. Ibid., p. 85.

8. Józef Bau, "Szpital Obozowy" (Camp Hospital), in *Pieśń ujdzie calo . . ., op. cit.,* pp. 56–57.

9. Cited in Lawrence L. Langer, *The Holocaust and the Literary Imagination* (New Haven: Yale University Press, 1979), p. 9.

10. Józef Bau, "Glód" in *Pieśń ujdzie calo . . ., op. cit.,* p. 56.

11. Wladyslaw Szlengel, "Okno na tamta strone" (Window Facing the Aryan Side), in *Co czytalem umarlym* (What I Read to the Dead), ed. Irena Maciejewska (Warsaw: Państwowy Institut Wydawniczy, 1977), p. 59. Translations of quoted poems from this anthology are this writer's.

12. Ibid., p. 61.

13. "Wild" houses were empty buildings in which Jews without work permits were hiding out. These people had no right to be in the Warsaw Ghetto, hence no right to live.

14. "Blocks" were designated areas in the Warsaw Ghetto that constituted either several streets or city blocks. The heart of each block was a German factory, a temporary haven for those Jews who were able to secure work permits.

15. Wladyslaw Szlengel, "Kontratak" (Counter Attack), in *Co czytalem umarlym, oc. cit.,* p. 43.

16. Byron Sherwin, "Wiesel's Midrash: The Writings of Elie Wiesel and Their Relationship to Jewish Tradition," in *Confronting the Holocaust: The Impact of Elie Wiesel,* ed. Alvin Rosenfeld and Irving Greenberg (Bloomington: Indiana University Press, 1978), p. 129.

17. Wladyslaw Szlengel, "Już czas" (It's High Time), in *Co czytalem umarlym, op. cit.,* p. 129.

18. Abraham Sutzkever, "Di Ershte Nacht in Ghetto" (The First Night in the Ghetto), in *Di Ershte Nacht in Ghetto* (The First Night in the Ghetto) (Israel: Di Goldene Keit, 1979), p. 10. Translations of all Sutzkever's quoted poems are this writer's.

19. Sidra DeKoven Ezrahi, By *Words Alone: The Holocaust in Literature* (Chicago: The University of Chicago Press, 1980), p. 21.

20. Abraham Sutzkever, "Kerndlekh Vayts" (Grains of Wheat), in *Lider fun Yam Hamoves* (Songs from the Dead Sea) (Tel Aviv: World Federation of Bergen Belsen Associations, 1968), p. 55.

10 HOLOCAUST IMAGERY IN CONTEMPORARY FRENCH LITERATURE

Rosette C. Lamont

On 3 June 1936 a document marked "Top Secret" was being signed in Berlin at the Wilhelmstrasse office of SS-*Totenkopf* Theodor Eicke, inspector general of concentration camps. He signed using only a capital E, followed by the indispensable greeting: *Heil Hitler!* His secretary then picked up the dossier to be forwarded to Fritz Sauckel, *gauleiter* of the region of Thuringia. The matter thus communicated dealt with the permission granted by *Reichsführer SS* Himmler to transfer the concentration camp of Lichtenburg in Prussia to Thuringia, and to build there a camp to accommodate some three thousand prisoners. The cost of this construction, together with barracks for the Second Division of the SS-*Totenkopf*, was estimated at 1,200,000 marks. Such was the monstrous birth of K.L. Buchenwald/Weimar.[1]

Weimar! For the civilized mind the chief town of the land of Thuringia seems to be a privileged locus. This fiefdom of the land-graves of Thuringia became under Karl August and his successors a center of liberalism, and of the German arts. Between 1789 and 1803 a palace was erected on the site of the one that had burned down in 1774; the supervisor of this great *opus* was none other than Goethe. Under the latter's supervision a magnificent theater was erected in 1825, the great hall in which the golden age of German drama was born. The poet also planned a magnificent park, which is considered by some as the finest monument to Goethe's genius. On the edge of that park stands "the garden house," a wooden cottage where Goethe used to spend his summers. Goethe and his friend Schiller lie side by side in the cemetery's ducal family vault.

It was in December 1774 that the "hereditary prince" of Weimar, traveling through Frankfurt on his way to Paris, invited the poet to visit him in Weimar. On November 7 of the following year Goethe arrived in the small capital that was to be his home until his death on 22 March 1832. Although the great poet felt at times confined in "this small residence, which . . . has ten thousand poets and a few inhabitants,"[2] as he liked to define it, he always returned to it with a sense that this was where he belonged. There he completed and rewrote his *Bildungsroman, Wilhelm Meisters Lehrjahre,* composed his purest, most classical poem, *Hermann und Dorothea,* and returned to the work that had accompanied him since early manhood, *Faust*.

In Johann Peter Eckermann's *Conversations with Goethe* one can read a delightful account of a ride taken by the two men to the Hottelstedt Ecke, the most westerly summit of the Ettersburg, a couple of kilometers out of Weimar. On this day (26 September 1827) the weather was warm, and, as the carriage went uphill, Goethe noticed the birds in the hedges and wondered if they were larks. Eckermann drew on his knowledge of ornithology, explaining that they were yellowhammers and sparrows since it is not "in the nature of larks to settle upon bushes" (p. 225). As they reached the top of the hill Goethe suggested that this was the perfect spot for a light refreshment. The two men got out of the carriage, walking up and down among the gnarled oaks while Frederick, the servant, spread a cloth upon the ground and unpacked the lunch. Under the morning autumn sky the view was truly splendid: "on the south and south-west, the whole range of the Thüringer-wald mountains; on the west, beyond Erfurt, the towering Gastle Gotha and the Inselsberg; farther north, the mountains behind Langensalza and Mühlhausen, until the view was bounded on the north by the blue Hartz Mountains" (p. 228). Goethe and Eckermann sat leaning against an oak, enjoying the spectacle of half of Thuringia spreading before them. They feasted on roast partridge and drank a bottle of fine wine poured into a gold cup that Goethe used for such excursions.

Buchenwald/Weimar marks the eerie convergence of the greatest horror known to man and the highest literary achievement of the human spirit. One wonders what Goethe would have thought at the sight of German officers setting aside one of his books, or stuffing it into the pocket of their uniform, in order to proceed to the gassing and burning of women, children, old people, of the crippled, the sick, and those driven to madness. It is almost as though Spinoza's admirer had envisioned his *Walpurgisnacht* as the future quotidian reality of a camp erected in the midst of a forest that sheltered his creative solitude. Were his ghost able to stride through these woods in April 1943, it would have met with the great French writer and statesman Léon Blum whose *New Conversations of Goethe with Eckermann* were published anonymously by *La Revue Blanche* in 1901. France's first Jewish premier, Blum was sent to Buchenwald, or rather to the hunting lodge near the camp, to be kept as hostage for a possible trade or an exchange of prisoners.

In October 1940 Blum was indicted by the Pétain régime and brought to trial on 19 February 1942. This brilliant jurist — Blum had studied law and taken a doctoral degree in philosophy — defended himself so eloquently that on April 14 the hearings were suspended and the accused incarcerated again, only to be taken later to Buchenwald. Blum, who was later joined by his wife and by Georges Mandel, did not realize at first that their place of exile stood on the edge of one of the worst death camps in existence. At times, however, as Blum writes in *Le Dernier Mois,* they smelled something burning, a fetid odor that permeated the rooms at night, when the windows were open; no one knew that this was the smoke of the crematorium.

The Blums's first glimpse of concentration camp prisoners occurred following an American air raid on 24 August 1944. The bombs had fallen on the factory at the center of the camp and on the adjoining barracks. Some of the houses occupied by the SS officers had also been set on fire. Since the pavillion in the forest was close to these residences, Léon Blum saw groups of prisoners called in to make repairs. Some French and Belgian deportees were among them, and the erstwhile premier was able to exchange a few words with them as they passed by. He learned about the existence of the camp and that some of his friends were interned in it; by the same token, the news reached Buchenwald that the Blums were sequestered in a nearby lodge.

The author of *New Conversations of Goethe with Eckermann* did not know that the great beech on which Goethe and Schiller had inscribed their initials and which stood within the camp enclosure had burned down to a stump, hit by an American bomb. He did, however, shudder with horror at the sight of the prisoners walking through the woods once haunted by graceful literary ghosts. Here is how he describes them in *Le Dernier Mois*:

> They were passing by, harnessed like beasts of burden to some cart overloaded with stones and sand, or Indian file, their shoulders bent under the load of a tree trunk, like slaves in Egyptian or Assyrian friezes.[3]

Did the reader of Eckermann remember at that moment Goethe's moving reference to the trees he had planted 40 years before he and his memorialist sat in the refreshing shade of "oaks and beeches . . . impervious to the most potent sun" (p. 53), or the German poet's evocation of his idyllic pastimes in the selfsame woods? This is how Eckermann reports their conversation:

> We took another draught from the golden cup, and then drove round the northern side of the Ettersberg to the Ettersberg hunting-lodge. Goethe had all the chambers that were hung with beautiful tapestry and pictures opened. He told me Schiller had for some time inhabited the chamber at the western angle of the first story.

> "In early times," continued he, "we have spent here many a good day, and wasted many a good day. We were all young and wanton: in the summer we had impromptu comedies, and in the winter many a dance and sledgerace by torchlight."
>
> We returned into the open air, and Goethe led me in a westerly direction along a footpath into the wood.
>
> "I will show you the beech," said he, "on which we cut our names fifty years ago. But how it has altered, and how everything has grown! That must be the tree; you see it is still in fullest vigour. Even our names are still to be traced; but confused and distorted, scarcely to be made out. This beech then stood upon a dry open spot. It was quite sunny and pleasant around; and here, in the beautiful summer evenings, we played our impromptu farces. Now the spot is damp and cheerless [p. 229].

During the two years Blum spent at Buchenwald there was little psychic space for literary musings.

And yet, paradoxically perhaps, literature plays a very important part in the conscious and subconscious life of many camp inmates. When in April 1980 the great Holocaust French writer Charlotte Delbo came to lecture at the Graduate School of the City University of New York, she explained that her purpose in writing about the camps was to raise the image of camp life for all to see. To ensure that these images would pass the test of time so that they would eventually reach readers with no personal connections to the historical event, Delbo, having written *None of Us Will Return* right after her release from camp, put her *poème/récit* into a drawer for 20 years before rereading and publishing it. She explains, whenever she is questioned, that the only way to speak of an event that defies imagination is to recreate it in a series of images so that people can see it, feel it, as though they had been there. Through the use of faithful, evocative details, the poet speaks directly to the mind, heart, senses, of his reader. "Donner à voir," Delbo repeated over and over again in the course of her talk.

In his book, *Versions of Survival,* Lawrence Langer states: "The problem — one cannot repeat it often enough — is to create a language and imagery that will transform mere knowledge into vision and bear the reader beyond the realm of the familiar imagining into the bizarre limbo of atrocity."[4] In the first chapter of his book, Langer proceeds to question the deceptive patterns of language and to explore the ways in which we can invest familiar words with new meaning. When we come to imagery, however, the reverse approach must take place. Images of camp life have nothing to do with the familiar; they are grotesque, profoundly shocking, they belong to the universe of the Gothic novel, of science fiction, or of the genre known in France as *la littérature du fantastique*. Yet this "fantastic," phantasmagoric universe with its absurd rules, its stratified bureaucracy of murder, its Grand-Guignol experiments carried out on living human beings, its inverted social order enforced by former felons and assassins promoted to the positions of *Blockältester, Rapportführer, Lagerältester, Lagerschreiber,* was the everyday reality of millions of victims. How does literature deal with the unthinkable, with the incredible? These are the fundamental problematics of the writer who wants and needs to communicate in a truthful way the situation of man in what the French call *l'univers concentrationnaire*.

With the passage of time the camp's reality begins to fade; it becomes increasingly difficult to realize that these things happened to you. In Jorge Semprun's magnificent book, *Quel beau dimanche!*, the narrator wonders, "Had I dreamt my life in Buchenwald? Or perhaps, on the contrary, my life since my return from Buchenwald had been a dream. Perhaps I had died fifteen years ago and all of this . . . this fragile fabric of political activity which seemed to unravel the moment it was done, was nothing but a dream of grey smoke, a premonition rising over the hill of Ettersberg" (p. 58). In conversation with his friend Barizon, Gérard (the narrator's clandestine name in the Resistance) goes so far as to question the identity of the dreamer. Barizon, who was also in Buchenwald, throws out a question:

> "Camp, do you really remember it as something that happened to you? Don't you have the impression that you dreamt it all?"
> I look at him.
> "Not even that. I have the impression it's a dream, but I'm not sure I was the one dreaming. Maybe it was someone else."
> I don't really say everything I'm thinking. I'm not saying that this someone might be a dead man.
> Perhaps I am nothing but a dream dreamt in Buchenwald by a young man who died at the age of twenty, a man they called Gérard and who went up in smoke on the Ettersberg hill. [p. 97]

Then the conversation comes to an end because it is useless for two ex-prisoners to tell all this to one another. "That's chewing the cud," exclaims Barizon (p. 98). This story must reach those who were never there; you must invent, create your reader.

In 1963 Jorge Semprun published his first novel, *Le Grand Voyage*. The central image of this work is the cattle train taking the prisoners to their unknown destination (Buchenwald). Semprun's novel, however, does not follow a linear, chronological order. He shifts from the trip *to* the camp to the trip *back;* his story — as he envisions the future — is a spiral, a kind of continuous Möbius strip.

Nor does the space of the novel remain unified (the inside of the train, then the inside of the camp). It also keeps on shifting so that "inner" and "outer" become relative concepts. Thus imagination can carry one out of the locked wagon into the surrounding countryside; it can also take one into the past and the future. "Chronology" Semprun writes in *Quel beau dimanche!*, "is neither simple nor realistic. It is an abstraction, a cultural convention, a victory of the geometric mind. One has assumed it to be natural, like monogamy" (p. 113). We detect here, but also in his first novel, the influence of Marcel Proust.

Proust's narrator emerges from sleep in a dark room, one of the many rooms he has occupied throughout his life. It takes a while for this man to ascertain where he is in time and space. His bed seems to move in relation to the walls and windows; the universe, the years form a circle around him, a shifting, elusive element. Outside there are trains in the distance; their whistle describes the curve of their direction and reminds the light sleeper of trips taken to the coast of Normandy, or perhaps to Venice. Proust's narrator will also embark on a long voyage, an exploration of his life and his society, but as he lies cozily in his warm bed he can well afford the luxury of disorientation. Semprun's narrator, Gérard, is in that distant train others hear passing from their beds, but he cannot sit or lie down. He has been traveling with 120 men, standing in the cattle car for "four days and three nights,"[5] or perhaps — he is no longer certain of anything — days have changed into nights. He begins to count on his fingers: "We are moving in the direction of the fourth night and the fifth day. The fifth night and the sixth day. But are we the ones who are moving? We are motionless, pressed tight against one another, and night is advancing, the fourth night, in the direction of our immobile future corpses . . ." (p. 11). And so, in the first paragraph, Semprun leaves the shifting world of time and projects himself into the future, a future where there will be no future, a future when all the men in the car will be motionless corpses, bodies eternally free of enforced travel.

Gérard is traveling with a companion, "the guy from Semur," who will die of a heart attack before the end of the voyage (p. 14). A bond develops between the two men who are forced to stand so close together that for one of them to balance himself on two feet the other must find a temporary equilibrium on one leg. They are luckier than some of the others because they are close to an open slit, and so they are able to breathe in the air of the ambient countryside. "The guy from Semur" informs Gérard that the train is passing through the Moselle valley. Although the young Spaniard was always "indifferent to geography," he is now passionately connected to this bit of French soil they are about to leave (p. 13). By closing his eyes he is able to savor "the dazzling certainty" of the Moselle valley under snow, its tall pine trees, cozy, trim villages (p. 13). Gérard may be inside a cattle car, but his imagination takes him outside. Semprun writes, "My life had escaped out of me, it was soaring over this winter valley, it has become this soft valley, warm in the winter cold" (p. 14). The Moselle region is the last gate to eternal exile, perhaps to death. "They've got a nice white wine," says the guy from Semur, "not quite as good as Chablis" (p. 15). Somewhere outside are vineyards and farmers walking to their homes. The latter stare at the train passing by; it looks like any cargo transport. Meanwhile Gérard is thinking of the Chablis, of the taste of Moselle, a taste he will get to know later, much later, on the return voyage. Once again Semprun takes us into the future, to a hotel at Eisenach where old German waiters are dancing attendance upon American officers and former deportees. This will take place at some point in the distant future. At this moment, however, the prisoners are being conveyed to Weimar.

The image of the inside versus the outside is one of the recurrent images of Holocaust literature. Semprun's treatment is more subtle than most. This former student of philosophy does not have any simple answers; he does, however, raise some questions. For example, in the train Gérard is inside, a prisoner, while the Moselle farmers are free to walk on their roads, to go as they please. But, are they truly free at this moment in history, under occupation? Gérard may be a deportee, but that condition is the result of existential choice, of having opted for the Resistance. He states with fine pride, “I'm on this train. I'm here freely, because it was possible for me not to have been here. It's just a physical sensation: we're inside. There's the outside and the inside, and I happen to be inside” (p. 24).

The dialectic of the Outside/Inside will play itself out most dramatically when Gérard is released from camp. The young man and his group of camp buddies are walking about through the village at the edge of Buchenwald. They notice a comfortable bourgeois house. Suddenly, Gérard realizes that from the upper floor of this house the family must have had an unobstructed view of the entire camp. He decides to go in and meet the owners. “They had box seats” (p. 151) jokes one of his friends, but the rest of the group does not share Gérard's curiosity. Left alone, the young man knocks at the door, first with his fist, then, as there is no answer, by kicking it with his boot. He realizes that his voice is no longer his own, that he is shouting in the voice of an SS: “Aufmachen!” (p. 152). An old, grey-haired women half opens the door. There is a brief exchange; “Ich bin allein.” Ich auch” (p. 152). The strange visitor claims that he wishes to visit the house. The woman accedes to this bizarre request; these are strange times. Quickly he goes through the ground floor rooms; he has one thought only: to get to the top floor. He cannot, will not explain to the woman that he needs “to look from the outside at this enclosure where they went round and round for years. She wouldn't understand. No one from the outside world could” (p. 153). She ventures: “Eine gemütliche Stube, nicht war?” Gérard questions her, “In the evening you used to spend your time in this room?” “Of course.” “Have you lived here long?” “Oh yes, a very long time.” “In the evening, when the flames of the crematorium rose above the chimney, you could see them, couldn't you?” (p. 154). Now the old woman is frightened. All she is able to cast into the tray on her side of the scale is this pitiful sentence: “My two sons died in the war” (p. 155). Semprun writes, “She threw me these two corpses to feed on” (p. 155). He adds for himself alone, and for us, his readers: “All deaths do not weigh the same. No German army corpse will ever weigh this light smoke weight of my dead comrades” (p. 155). Gérard runs down the stairs, out into the small garden; he races in the direction of the camp where his friends are waiting for him. For a while the inside of the camp, now that it has been freed, is his home. Soon they will all be leaving forever, leaving for their real homes.

The concept Inside/Outside can also be applied to the hidden face of society. When Gérard walks into a German village to drink at a public fountain, he senses that, although no one is to be seen, people are hiding behind every curtain, in every house. They are looking at the stranger, the outsiders. Semprun states, ''I came to the sudden realization that this village was not the outside, that it was merely another side, the inner side of the society which had given birth to concentration camps'' (p. 161).

Parallel to the Outside/Inside dialectic lies the Before/After. The farmers who reside in the small village where the former convicts are now free to walk have continued to live as they always did; they are still in the Before. For these staid, unimaginative people, the dirty prisoners signify some kind of guilt, some unknown, unknowable crime. They have never posed themselves the question of the prisoners' existence, of the problem this existence posed them. They were not philosophers, intellectuals. Now that the prisoners can drink from their public fountain, walk through the streets and central square, a threat has invaded their quiet world, the universe of the Before — a reality which, until a short while back, was punishable by death. For them the familiar world of habits, of moral assumptions, has come crumbling down. They are projected violently into the After, the time following their nation's defeat. As to the prisoners, one could wonder why they have entered the village. Could it not be that they are also seeking something that no longer exists: the Before of things even if that Before used to exclude them, to deny their very right to existence. The life outside, the life before, these are illusions that have come to an end. Nothing will ever be like before, not for anyone. No one will ever be the way he was *before*. In fact, even identity is a myth.

So-called reality is shown to be an illusion. During the long voyage, the narrator loses his sense of reality, of proportion. Actually, most of this had already taken place in the course of the many months of jail preceding deportation. Later the feeling would be intensified in the camp. ''The unreal and the absurd were becoming familiar,'' writes Semprun, and he continues, writing as the philosophy student that he was: ''In order to survive the organism has to adhere to reality, and reality was precisely the unnatural world of prison and death'' (p. 70). What is this new reality, this unacceptable fact which one has to live with if one hopes to survive: it is the world of the flaming furnaces, of the crematorium working full time through the night. Only at the time of air raids did the officers order the crematorium to be stopped, the lights put out throughout the camp. From the watchtowers, over the loudspeakers, come the guards' orders: ''Krematorium, ausmachen!'' (p. 37). Then all is dark.

The obsessive, central image of the Holocaust literature should have been that of the crematorium chimney, yet, strangely enough, it is not mentioned or described as frequently as one would imagine. It is almost as though the mind could not face the horror of this image. There is of course the evocation in Elie Wiesel's *Night*. Wiesel prepares us gradually to receive this image, as if we were made to follow the horrifying process in the boy's consciousness. In the early part of *Night,* we are introduced to two characters who are believed to be insane:

Moishe the Beadle and Madame Schächter. The first, having been deported from Sighet (Máramarossziget) with some "foreign" Jews, escapes from mass slaughter and makes his way back to the small town. He is the bearer of such a horrifying tale that no one believes him. He shouts to the Jews of the town, going from one house to the other, "All I ask is that you listen to me. I ask neither for money, nor pity. Only please listen."[6] He tells of his companions being taken off a truck after they crossed the Hungarian border into Poland, of having to dig a large common grave, of being shot at the edge of the gaping hole while infants, tossed up, were used as targets for skeet shooting matches. The story is beyond anything the quiet population is ready to receive, to accept as even remotely possible. Even the narrator does not believe this man from whom he learned so much about Jewish mysticism. "They think I'm mad," Moishe whispers, his tears flowing slowly down his cheeks, "like wax" (p. 20). He is the messenger whose message will not be heeded in time, but, unlike Tiresias, he has had no need of a third eye, an inner eye; his two eyes told him all there is to know. The people of Sighet, however, choose to blind themselves, to stop their ears until it is too late.

Madame Schächter on the other hand is a Cassandra. Wiesel's description of the train journey in the company of this woman who wakes at night to shout "Fire!" (p. 37) has a mythic quality. Having been left behind — her husband and two elder sons have been deported earlier — she has lost her reason. Yet, clearly, her unreason takes her to a zone of reality far deeper than that reached by those who use only rational means. Like Cassandra she has a clear memory of the future. When the train reaches Auschwitz all the deportees see the tall chimney spitting fire and dark smoke. At that moment, Madame Schächter grows strangely quiet, as though her mission were accomplished, and she returns to the corner in which she had been crouching.

When the narrator of *Night* is faced with a gaping hole in which babes are being burned, he knows that the two "fools" were right, and yet it seems impossible. It is as if the mind recoiled from what the senses revealed. Wiesel writes: "Little children, babies! Yes, I saw it, with my own eyes . . . Children in the flames" (p. 44).

Semprun also tells a story of the death of Jewish children. Sixteen years have passed, and he feels that he can now tell this story not as something that happened to him, the witness, but as the story of these children, who, had they lived, would have reached womanhood and manhood. The heartrending tale, as it is presented, shows us another train arrival, this time from Poland. "It was the final winter of the war," Semprun writes, "the coldest winter of a war that played itself out in the ice and snow" (p. 163). The Soviet offensive was at its height, and the Germans were beginning to evacuate the Polish camps. Convoys were arriving daily from Poland to Weimar. One gray afternoon a train arrived carrying some two hundred people compressed into each car. Most of the adults had died of the cold, and their corpses stood stiff, frozen solid. As the doors were pulled open, the bodies fell, tumbling down upon the platform. Others had to be pulled out. There they lay, like trees stripped of their bark. In between the stiff bodies some 15 small children, alive, were found. The youngest was probably eight, the eldest twelve. Even the SS did not know at first what to do with these tiny survivors, until the realization dawned on them that they could play a game of death and blood. They set the group upon the grand boulevard leading to the camp entrance, the boulevard bordered on each side by columns topped by an eagle. Next they brought out their dogs, held upon a leash. At first the dazed children did not catch on; they assumed they were being escorted in the direction of the gates. The SS started to club the children in order to make them run, and the children ran, still unaware of what was to follow. Semprun depicts with vivid clarity this nightmarish scene: "The children ran with their visored caps pulled down over their ears, and their legs moved awkwardly, in a slow, broken rhythm reminiscent of silent films, or as in nightmare when you run as fast as you can without being able to move a step, and whatever is chasing you follows you, catches you, and you awaken, covered with cold sweat . . ." (p. 165). This was no dream, however, no nightmare from which one can awake; it was the children's death. Two little ones, one taller than the other, were still racing hand in hand. Soon the guards caught up with them, beating them down to the ground. Now no one stood on the avenue. Retracing their steps, the SS guards shot each prostrate body in the head. "Hitler's eagles looked on with empty eyes" (p. 166) writes Semprun.

How does one commemorate such suffering? Does one build monuments? Semprun rejects this idea. He feels that it is best to let nature take over, cover the camp site. Goethe's forest ought to grow over this blood-soaked earth. In *Quel beau dimanche!* Semprun suggests that wooden planks and huts should be allowed to fall apart, to become nothing but wood again, and iron utensils be returned to their mineral origins. In the minds of men, in their memory, the camp's image must live on, be transmitted, but the obscene spot ought to be obliterated. Nature is stronger than brick and stone, nature can bury the infernal invention of the human mind.

If the site disappears from sight, what will make it live in the memory of the survivors, in the consciousness of future generations? Images translated into words, literary language, will prove far more eloquent than monuments of bronze or stone. No one illustrated this point more clearly than Charlotte Delbo in her novella, *Spectres, mes compagnons*.

This short, powerful work is written in the form of a letter addressed to Delbo's friend and "patron" Louis Jouvet. For a number of years Delbo worked as the great director's assistant and the faithful recorder of his classes at the Conservatoire. Jouvet discovered the young woman's ability to transcribe his mode of speaking when the philosophy student came to interview him for a student paper. When the interview appeared he was astonished to find that his spoken text had been captured to perfection, and that somehow his manner of delivery also came through in the transcription. (At the time the tape recorder had not yet come into being.) Jouvet contacted Delbo and invited her to work for him. She accepted, giving up her Sorbonne studies, and she never regretted this decision.

Spectres, mes compagnons starts with the address: "Cher Louis Jouvet . . ."[7] It begins as an evocation of the many walks Charlotte Delbo took with Jouvet through the countryside surrounding Vallauris. The great director enjoyed discussing novels and plays with this intelligent, sensitive woman. They spoke of Stendhal, Dickens, of Giraudoux's *Electre,* and Molière's *Misanthrope*. One of the questions they raised was that of the difference between a character in a novel and a dramatic character. Jouvet thought that the *dramatis persona* can be defined only by his acts, that he is an essence defying introspection. This, the director pointed out, is what allows for so many interpretations of the same character, so many incarnations on the stage. As to theater, it was life, but heightened, both deeper and wider. Later, in camp, Charlotte recalled her master's teaching as she recreated for the women of her *blockhaus* the plays she had seen Jouvet direct, or as she told them in her own words the great novels she had read. At night, despite a day of murderous work, the women, who had discovered Charlotte's gift for story telling, begged her to indulge them, and she was happy to be their Woman/Book. She had always enjoyed committing to memory both poetry and dramatic texts; now she was able to recite for her friends whole plays, acting out the various characters. In this way. Molière, Racine, Giraudoux, came to life again within the walls of the *blockhaus*. Charlotte also evoked the life of the Paris theaters: *La Comédie Française, l'Opéra, L'Athénée*. A theater space is a magic kind of place, a place for magic: the excitement of *les coulisses* (the wings) and the dressing rooms, the thrill and heart throb of the actors about to enter the stage, the apprehension of the director at the sight of his inner vision coming into being, the particular mood of a first-night audience. Many of Delbo's block mates had never had a chance to go to the theater, nor the time to read a novel. They listened entranced, filling themselves with this greater life, promising their story teller that, were they to survive, they would read all these books, see all these plays; they wanted to survive in order to return not only to their familiar and familial existence but to discover for themselves the world being uncovered for them. Paris rose before them within the narrow confines of their prison: the gilded, painted ceilings of the theaters, the red velvet seats and tiny *strapontins,* the chandeliers glowing like the diamonds on the bare arms and necks of lovely women. These images of grace and elegance, however, did not unleash class envy — Charlotte herself had belonged to *La Jeunesse Communiste* at the time of her arrest. The women knew that museums and theaters belonged to the people; the oasis of peace was not a mirage, only a distant memory, a future possibility.

Delbo's personal story is one of heroic courage, loyalty, and profound love. During the war she found herself with the Jouvet company on tour in South America. One Sunday in September 1941, as Delbo tells it in *Le Convoi du 24 janvier,* she was sitting in a public square in Buenos Aires, reading a paper. She read that a young architect she knew had been arrested in May by the French police; the paper reported that he had been guillotined for terrorist acts. Delbo ran to Jouvet and declared her determination to return to France. "I can't bear to be safe while our friends are being guillotined. I'll never dare look anyone in the eye after this.''[8] Her husband, Georges Dudach, a resistance fighter, was in France. Jouvet tried to talk the young woman out of her resolve, but she was determined to make her way back. She left the company at Rio de Janeiro, catching a Brazilian ship on the way to Lisbon, and arrived in France on 15 November 1941. After meeting her awaiting husband in Pau, they traveled to Paris by different routes. In the occupied capital they lived under secret identities. On 2 March 1942 the police broke into the apartment and arrested them. Georges Dudach and Charlotte were incarcerated in La Santé. There Georges was given the choice of going to Germany in the ''volunteer'' labor force or being executed; he chose the latter. Charlotte was taken to his cell for a final farewell, not out of sentimental feelings on the part of the police but in the hope that she might persuade her husband to renege. But Dudach was a man of principle; he was shot at the Mont-Valérien on 23 May 1942. The following day Charlotte was taken to Romainville, where she met some of the women who were to share her *blockhaus* at Birkenau.

It was while she was in solitary that Charlotte Delbo began to be visited by literary characters. In *Spectres, mes compagnons,* the writer speaks of her utter solitude:

> At first I found myself locked up in a high room where nothing reached me except voices without faces, a pallid light that projected shadows upon a wall spotted by humidity. . . . Thoughts and objects existed only as shadows on the wall. Shadows of my thoughts, shadows of my life, shadows of my love were projected upon the screen of my memory, this wall, while their palpable past eluded me. [p. 12]

At this time she is visited by Stendhal's hero, Fabrice del Dongo, the protagonist of *La Chartreuse de Parme*. He is the perfect cell mate because he spent much time in a dungeon. Delbo tells us that Fabrice enters her cell by means of a rope, the perfect daredevil act for this adventurous, gallant young man. We understand that this is a metaphor for the charitable offering of a woman fellow prisoner confined to a cell directly below that of Charlotte, who, for some absurd prison regulation, is allowed to use the prison library, which is forbidden to Delbo. Charlotte tells us that she has fashioned a slender rope from the threads of her blanket. Now, having lowered this string through her window, she is able to pull up the precious volume. The book, and its protagonist, become the companions of her solitary imprisonment.

When the time comes for leaving her jail to enter the train that will take her to camp, neither the book nor the hero of the novel can accompany her. As to the charming, civilized Fabrice, he is hardly the companion one would choose for a cattle car. By now, however, Delbo has learned to summon literary characters, to make them come to life. On the train she believes, for a while, that she is alone, alone with all her fellow prisoners, until a voice sounds in her ear. It asks, ''Why are you so frightened of solitude? It is often far richer and less disappointing than any company'' (p. 20). Delbo recognizes the ironic, bitter voice of Alceste, the Misanthrope. He seems to have left Jouvet, who lent this character his own voice and aspect on the stage, and is now living up to his own cherished dream of flight from all the hypocrites, flatterers, and coquettes who turn Paris into a living hell. Yet, when the train reaches its final destination, and the doors open upon the ravaged site, Alceste is unable to recognize the desert he thought he was seeking; this wasteland is too bare, too horrifying even for him. He slips away, hastening back to Louis Jouvet.

Who will endure then the horror of camp life? What literary character can share this exile? Charlotte is certain at first that she is doomed to solitude. At that very moment she catches a glimpse of Electra standing at the edge of "a line of reeds, with nothing but marshes in the background" (p. 28). Electra's smile is "proud and resolute" (p. 28). Other "resurrections" (p. 28) will follow that of Electra: Giruadoux's Ondine, Molière's Don Juan, even Proust's Oriane. Now these ghosts made of words will be able to live side by side with women whose flesh is melting from their bones, turning them into ghostlike creatures. Words can be as palpable as flesh; they can lend dignity to those who have been stripped of pride and hope. In a recent piece written for *Le Monde* (15 October 1981), Delbo writes:

> Characters in novels and drama, creatures of fiction, are nevertheless real. They are alive. They live in our minds and are part and parcel of our private universe in the same way as our intimate friends, or the members of our family we feel closest to. Some are so dear to us that we are in love with them, that we love them. This is the case for Tolstoy's Natasha and Prince André, for Fabrice and Lucien Leuwen, for Bérénice and Violaine. We share in their passions, identify with them, we refer to their feelings when we wish to give expression of our own. They are endowed with a magnified kind of life, a dimension far greater than the human.

Charlotte Delbo tells her reader that the books we delve in, the plays we see, can assist us in the hour of our greatest need. When we study the literature that has issued from *l'univers concentrationnaire* we realize that great art helps us survive because survival is often a matter of spirit, of not losing hope, of not losing the memory of a better past so that we can look forward to shaping a future.

The triumph of the spirit over the most dire of circumstances is celebrated by Eugene Ionesco in the opera libretto he wrote in 1982, *Maximilian Kolbe*. With music by Dominique Prost, this one-act opera is to be performed at the Opéra de Paris in 1983. *Maximilian Kolbe* deals with the same material as Rolf Hochhuth's *The Deputy*, but whereas the latter focused on the Pope's failure to denounce Nazi mass murders, Ionesco's libretto introduces us into the cell where Father Kolbe is dying, together with nine other fellow prisoners. Father Kolbe, who has been canonized in Rome, was the priest who volunteered to take the place of a concentration camp inmate condemned with nine blockmates to a slow death by starvation and thirst. This punishment was meted out to serve as an example for the rest of the inmates following an unsuccessful escape attempt by a member of the ten men's block. One of the victims, faced with this irrevocable condemnation, cried out, begging to be spared so that, were he to survive his camp experience, he might return to join his wife and children. Free of family ties, the Catholic priest offered himself in place of the family man. Strangely enough, his sacrifice was accepted. Most of the ten prisoners, already weakened by camp labor, died in a matter of days. A couple, however, sustained by Father Kolbe's spiritual fervor and courage, lived on beyond the expected time limit. So did Father Kolbe, and, finally, the camp commander sent in a guard to inject the stubborn survivor with an acid that would put an end to his flickering life.

By choosing to dramatize the sacrifice of a Christian saint, Ionesco, who is known as the creator of the typical antiheroic protagonist, opted for heroism. The tag "theater of the absurd" has prevented most people from discovering Ionesco's profoundly philosophical and mystical side. He is the creator of what we prefer to call "the metaphysical farce." Ionesco spends a good deal of time reading Plato, Plotinus, *The Tibetan Book of the Dead,* and other contemplative and visionary works. Although Ionesco did not live through the camp experience, he fled a fascist country. A self-proclaimed apolitical writer, he is nevertheless profoundly *engagé*. *Rhinoceros, The Killer,* and *Man with Bags* testify to the dramatist's need to make a statement. *Maximilian Kolbe* reveals what has been present all along, although undetected: Ionesco is an important Holocaust writer.

Holocaust imagery will continue to live on in the consciousness of future generations through testimony, and, to a greater degree, through the works of art that will raise an indelible vision of the camp. In a recent talk at Columbia University, Elie Wiesel said, "We were exiled from space but we took the space with us." Is this not the writer's noble task: to make and remake his own space and, by so doing, to create a space for our existence as fully conscious human beings?

Notes

1. For a detailed description of these events, see Jorge Semprun, *Quel beau dimache!* (Paris: Bernard Grasset, 1980). All subsequent references to this book will be incorporated in the text. The quotations have been translated by the writer of this essay.

2. Johann Peter Eckermann, *Conversations with Goethe,* trans. John Oxenford, ed. J.K. Moorhead (London: Everyman's Library, 1930), p. 105. All subsequent quotations from this book have been incorporated into the text.

3. Léon Blum, *Le Dernier Mois* (Paris: Editions Diderot, 1946), p. 7. The quotation was translated by the writer of this essay.

4. Lawrence L. Langer, *Versions of Survival* (Albany: State University of New York Press, 1982), p. 12.

5. Jorge Semprun, *Le Grand Voyage* (Paris: Gallimard, 1963), p. 11. All subsequent quotations from this novel have page references within the body of the text. The quotations have been translated from the French by the author of this essay.

6. Elie Wiesel, *La Nuit, L'Aube, Le Jour* (Paris: Editions du Seuil, 1969), p. 20. All subsequent quotations from this book have page references within the body of the text. All the quotations have been translated from the French by the author of this essay.

7. Charlotte Delbo, *Spectres, mes compagnons* (Lausanne: Maurice Bridel, libraire, 1977), p. 7.

All subsequent quotations from this book have page references within the body of the essay. All quotations have been translated from the French by the author of this essay.

8. Charlotte Delbo, *Le Convoi du 24 janvier* (Paris: Les Editions de Minuit, 1965), p. 101. This quotation has been translated from the French by the author of this essay.

11 THE GENOCIDE BOMB: *The Holocaust Through the Eyes of a Survivor*

Jack P. Eisner

Two unprecedented events in the early 1940s have changed the course of human history: the atomic bomb and the Holocaust. Both were mutations, yet the Holocaust is the greater and more likely peril to humankind. Its implications and consequences are enormous. It has changed forever the relationship of man to man; it has changed the relationship of Gentile to Jew. It introduced the specter of mass national insanity; it elevated genocide to an ideology, an aim, a policy, and *not* a consequence or an instrument of policy. It has confirmed that man is neither good nor bad but both good and bad, depending on the circumstances. Most important of all, by example it introduced the idea that the fastest way to restructure, to remake, to "beautify" the human race is through killing, through death factories.

Is the Holocaust just another tragic example of bestiality, brutality, and genocide? Or was the annihilation of six million Jewish men, women, and children a unique phenomenon? Can it happen again? Can it happen to non-Jews as well? What are the implications, lessons, conclusions for the present and future generations?

For more than 35 years since my liberation from the Nazis, I have watched in amazement and dismay how the world, the media, and even some within academic circles have distorted that epic era. Humankind has yet to grasp the Holocaust's immense importance for Jew and non-Jew alike, even though some 40 years have passed since it began.

The Holocaust is so very complicated and horrifying an epic that it took humankind more than 30 years even to begin debating it. Only recently, since the late 1970s, has a new generation been courageous enough to inquire, "How was it possible and why?"

I was born in Warsaw among half a million Jewish people who dwelled amidst two million Gentiles. A product of a middle-class, traditionally Jewish family of the late 1930s, I remember as a boy of 12 sitting in my small room contemplating the fate of my birth. "I'm so very lucky that I wasn't born in the Dark Ages, the eighth or twelfth centuries. How fortunate I am to be born in the twentieth century, the age of science, of technology, the century of progress." The world that I grew up in did not know of Auschwitz. My children and your children and the generations to come will never again be as innocent. Civilization can never be as innocent; we now know the names of Auschwitz, Treblinka, Buchenwald.

For five thousand years of recorded civilization, man's relationship to man when at its worst had always been one of exploitation, subjugation, and domination. Some conquered in order to exploit others economically, militarily, geographically. Some conquered for national, racial, or religious reasons. All through the ages man killed generously to prevent domination, enslavement, exploitation, or conversion. But the Holocaust was the first time in the history of humankind that the victims could not avoid the tragedy through such simple devices as conversion to another faith or system of beliefs. There was no choice to be made. We could not choose to escape to another country or another continent as was the case so often in Jewish history of two thousand years in diaspora. The choice had always been there: Convert or be expelled. In the Holocaust there was no such choice. We couldn't even exclaim, "I accept slavery but just let me live so that my grandchildren may, someday, be free." No choice.

We were condemned to perish without recourse. Being without a choice was a new phenomenon, a new relationship of man to man. Each was condemned not for what he did, not even for what he was, but for what his grandparents were. Guilt through heredity. Near my backyard in Warsaw lived one of my best friends, a teenaged Catholic boy. When he became angry with me, he would often call me a "dirty Jew." But when Nazi Germany occupied Warsaw, they promptly discovered in the city archives that his grandfather had, 60 years earlier, converted from Judaism. The Nazis declared him and his entire family to be Jewish and moved them into the ghetto. They subsequently perished in one of the death camps; their conversion failed them in the end.

The Holocaust was not just a period of discrimination or persecution. The Nazi philosophy transcended anything humanity had ever known or had ever experienced. The Nazi philosophy aimed at the reconstitution of humanity, the remaking of the human race through death factories. The Germans called it the "beautification" of the human race, not through life but through death.

The Jew, Western civilization's traditional scapegoat, was only the first of the victims. Had Nazi Germany been victorious, the gas chambers and crematoria might still be working full blast on additional millions of unwanted people. Once the Jews were eliminated, the system of restructuring humanity would have continued with the blacks, the Slavs, the mentally ill, homosexuals, and other non-Jews as the victims. Obviously the Holocaust is not just a Jewish problem; its ramifications are universal. With the advent of the Holocaust, a new philosophy began to govern the relationship of man to man. Subsequent events have shown the human propensity to annihilate those who stand in opposition; genocide to some has now become an objective, a goal of human endeavor and behavior, not a consequence of it. That is a cardinal and radical departure, perhaps made less shocking by the grim standards established by the perpetrators of the Holocaust.

Myths About the Holocaust

Among the most infuriating things to a survivor of the Holocaust are the myths that are perpetrated and perpetuated about this unique man-made catastrophe. The first such myth is that a few hundred or at most a few thousand Germans were responsible for the immense slaughter that included more than a million infants and children. No one who was there, as was I, could possibly believe that the systematic extermination of millions could be carried out without the complicity of many millions of Germans and the participation or criminal acquiescence of virtually the entire population of 70 million people.

In a sense, a whole nation went insane in accepting a program for the elimination of entire races and regions of humanity. This age of mass communications and mass psychology, with the ability of psychotic leaders to lead millions into mass insanity, represents a new and complex threat to human survival. If such mass insanity could occur among 70 million Germans, could it not happen among the French, the Americans, the Soviets?

This revelation is new to civilization. The Holocaust has acquainted us with the first encounter of mass insanity on an enormous scale. The chances and conditions for this new phenomenon are growing and expanding, due to the constant introduction of new advanced scientific methods for wholesale brainwashing, especially through the methods of mass communication.

The modern potential for mass organization and mass communication offers a tremendous, deadly potential for the mobilization of the most vicious, evil instincts in man. The Holocaust showed how far such mass insanity could go. We have found that the range of human actions is enormous, from the most noble and heroic to the most vile and criminal, within an individual and in a whole people.

The Nazi philosophy is not dead; Nazism is alive. Nazi Germany's military might was destroyed, but one cannot expect to destroy an ideology, especially one that has been enthusiastically and wholeheartedly embraced by tens of millions of people so recently as a generation ago. And so, Nazism is slowly but clearly emerging in many countries around the world.

Under different labels the Nazi theory can readily be adopted by any fanatical nation, race, or society that claims its superiority through "divine" or technical rationalizations or, perhaps, that has nationalistic or economic reasons that precede the restructuring of the human race through mass murder. We can see why the example set by the Germans in the Holocaust is indeed terribly serious and dangerous for all humanity — not only for Jews.

Another persistent myth is that millions of Jewish people did not resist the Nazis, that millions of these people went passively to the slaughter. The question is always asked in a negative manner: "Why didn't those millions resist?" The truth is that most fought valiantly, courageously, heroically, as any people or nation would under similar circumstances. The media have failed to portray adequately and accurately what really happened. Organized warfare was waged against us. Nothing was improvised by the Germans; everything was planned. Hundreds of Nazi officials, including psychiatrists, sitting in Berlin, in Frankfurt, and in Hamburg were planning our destruction. First they attacked us spiritually, then morally, then through hunger and disease, and at the very last through physical annihilation.

The resistance took many forms. Who is to say what form was most courageous? Each would say his own was. Was mine because at the age of 15 in 1943 I confronted a German tank with a Molotov cocktail in the Warsaw Ghetto Uprising? Or was my father braver who through all those years insisted, "I shall never degenerate and become a barbarian like they are. I believe in a sane and ethical world"? This man — who on his last journey, his passage to the gas chambers, in the crush of a cattle car — I watched in amazement as he still managed to hide one of his favorite books and squeezed his way through the crowd to the little window where the moon was shining in, so he could study a few more pages of Spinoza's *Ethics*. For he wanted to preserve his world of ordered culture around him, to the last moment of his life. Perhaps my father was more courageous and heroic in resisting barbarism than I.

Or was a 15-year-old girl named Halina more courageous when she silenced half a dozen storm troopers with her last and only grenade, exclaiming ecstasy, "My God! Their blood is as red as ours!" As Jewish boys and girls, we were brainwashed by the Nazis every hour, every day, every week, every month, every year, to believe that we were inferior, not worthy to be crawling on this earth. More worthless than rats. We didn't know whether the so-called master race, supermen, could bleed as we did. Could they have pain? Could they hurt? Halina and I were just two among many thousands of young Jews who resisted militantly in the Warsaw Ghetto and elsewhere, against a mighty modern war machine, against impossible odds. We fought day and night, year after year.

Or perhaps the most courageous was that Jewish mother I saw in front of the gas chambers, refusing life when it was offered to her and insisting, "If my little girl walks in there, I'll follow her." And she did. Let no one ever dare to imagine how he or she would behave in front of a gas chamber. To me that mother is the ultimate of courage, for it takes much more to refuse life than to take life.

And what about my grandma Masha; was she courageous? Did she resist? I can tell you that she saved my life. At the age of 70 she went to her death with her Bible in her hands and with a smile on her face. For she outsmarted those Nazis, having saved the last of her 20 grandchildren by hiding him beneath her old Victorian bed.

Yes, courage and resistance take many forms, and each of us resisted in his own way. Let no one tell you that the Jews went passively to their deaths. That is vile and untrue. It is a scurrilous myth.

The most vicious myth of all is the attempt by certain pseudoscientists and propagandists to argue that there never was a Holocaust, that it was all a lie invented by Zionist or other Jews seeking sympathy in a world of Gentiles. This vicious and flagrant campaign, devoid of evidence and in violation of the most basic human decency, is not even worthy of debate.

The only survivor among 31 first cousins, I saw the massive, organized slaughter with my own eyes, as did thousands of other survivors — though numerous, they were only a tiny fraction of those who passed through the Nazi death machine. The testimony of the Allied armies and even of former Nazi officials is further proof, beyond any shadow of a doubt, that there was indeed a man-made Holocaust, the most dehumanized campaign of genocide in history.

Another misleading idea frequently advanced by those in the public eye is the conclusion that our concept of the Holocaust should embrace several million non-Jewish civilians who perished at the hand of the Nazis along with the six million Jews. No one can deny the millions of non-Jewish victims, least of all those who lived, suffered, shared, and witnessed the starvation and slaughter of thousands of non-Jews in Majdanek or Flossenberg or Dachau or Buchenwald. Yet there is a crucial difference: As non-Jews they were not part of a race targeted for total extermination; that is the significance of the Holocaust.

Yes, millions of non-Jewish Frenchmen, Poles, Russians, Yugoslavs, Dutch, Greeks, Czechs, and even some Germans perished in those Nazi camps. We must never forget them. Their struggle and death was a consequence of their refusal to submit to the Nazi philosophy of domination, exploitation, and subjugation. They fought back against tyrants who planned to enslave them and relegate them to second class citizens, inferior human beings. Their heroism is yet another example of valiant resistance against tyranny that has recurred through the ages and always has been a part of man's relation to man.

Their deaths were the consequences of their behavior. Had they behaved in conformity with their adversaries' design, those concentration camps would have been empty of all except the Jews. Only the Jews had no choice whatsoever to escape punishment and annihilation. Only the Jews were subjected to this new philosophy of genocide, a first in human behavior. Only the Jews were the victims, without recourse, debate, or appeal.

The fundamental reasons to punish both the Jew and non-Jew were profoundly different; the consequences were and had to be radically different as well. Although many of the non-Jewish victims were incarcerated in concentration camps and subjected to inhuman treatment, at least 30 to 40 percent survived. In fact, those "lucky" Jews who were not immediately gassed had a survival rate similar to that of non-Jews. Thousands of today's Jewish survivors of the Holocaust are almost all former inmates of these camps — Majdanek, Auschwitz, Flossenburg, Dachau, Buchenwald. However, there are scarcely any survivors of the Nazi death camps like Birkenau, Sobibor, Treblinka, Belzec, and so forth, built especially for the extermination of the Jews. Those insisting that the non-Jewish victims of Nazi oppression were also targets of the Holocaust are completely ignorant of the significance of this event, its uniqueness, and its lessons for humanity's future.

In my last concentration camp, Flossenburg, I became very friendly with a Polish teenager, a staunch Catholic who found himself incarcerated because he refused to obey the Nazi German demand for forced labor. We were liberated by U.S. tanks on the same day, 23 April 1945, while on a death march somewhere on the side roads in the Bavarian hills. Because we were young and aggressive, we regained our physical health and strength within a few months. Both of us had been born in Warsaw, and so we set out on foot, hitchhiking on military vehicles, hanging on to speeding locomotives or to railcar roofs, on the road back to our home town 1,500 kilometers east of where we were liberated.

In postwar Warsaw, decimated and near total destruction, my non-Jewish friend promptly found his family and friends. The house he last lived in was destroyed by the retreating German Army during the brave September 1944 Warsaw Uprising. His father was arrested and deported to Auschwitz, where he perished. Yet, most all that he remembered and loved was still there to greet him with enthusiasm.

My non-Jewish friend came home with scars, of course, but he found his family and friends war-torn but alive! Their reunion was one of hope and laughter. He hugged and embraced his grandmother, stroked with joy the now old and pouchy Irish setter he remembered so well, smiled broadly gazing over the pages of his family album, hugged and kissed his younger cousins, exchanged greetings and kicked a soccer ball with an old school friend. He even stared with nostalgia at his old worn-out sweater that he tried on again after a three year absence.

I too came to Warsaw, my home town, but I was greeted by no one, received with silence, and found nothing and no one that I loved, remembered, or cherished. My grandma Masha had 20 grandchildren, my grandma Hannah had 11, 31 cousins in all, boys and girls — some blonde, some brunette, and some redheaded — smiling, crying, hoping to grow up. Their ages were 2 to 12 when I left them. When I returned not one was alive to greet me, to hug me. I, alone, of 31 had survived. That reality was even beyond my non-Jewish friend's capacity to comprehend. My entire world of happiness, love, nostalgia, was completely and absolutely destroyed, not by accident or improvisation, but by an organized methodical plan to eliminate everything that is Jewish — its people, old and young, its homes, its synagogues, its schools, its libraries and newspapers, even its cemeteries. I and my world was part of the Final Solution; my Catholic friends were not. The difference between us was monumental and profound, even though we both suffered at the hands of the same oppressor. We, the Jewish survivors of the Holocaust, are a unique species, for we experienced a unique historical catastrophe.

Other immense psychological differences separate my experience from my non-Jewish friend's ordeal. Both of us, living in normalcy and prosperity in the years that followed, can and do forget and forgive much of the personal physical hardships, torture, and even psychological trauma. Both of us can recall and sometimes even laugh at some of the ridicule, hunger, agonies, and lashes our backs absorbed. Time and years of comfort sometimes make those experiences seem remote. But I, unlike my non-Jewish friend, was subjected at a young formative age to watching the ridicule and slaughter of my grandma, my sister, my father, my best boyhood pal, and so on. Unlike him, I witnessed the agony of my uncle trying desperately to protect his three young children from the cattle cars and the subsequent journey to the gas chambers. When my uncle failed, he hanged himself.

I, the Jewish boy of 13, was forced to endure the immense mental strain and psychological nightmare of witnessing the pain and oblivion of all that I loved and cherished. All that surrounded me with security was destroyed before my eyes. That is what makes me different from the non-Jewish survivor or any other survivor from any other calamity. Only my experience and my world, with its unique drama and tragedy, is the Holocaust. To equate other sad World War II or other experiences is to water down the meaning and depth of the Holocaust's uniqueness and demonstrates the failure to grasp its implications of a new relationship of man to man.

Finally, there is the myth that the pre-Holocaust survival techniques of Jews could have saved them. For centuries Jews used tactics of assimilation, minimum visibility, lying low, not rocking the boat, and compromising with the oppressor.

These philosophies and tactics that had served Jewish people well over the centuries and in many countries died in the Holocaust. They all went bankrupt. We must realize this fact. Assimilation was one system that evolved over the centuries, starting with the age of Enlightenment, "Haskala," and promptly turning into the age of assimilation. Assimilate with your neighbors, be like them, imitate them, integrate with the Gentile majority, intermarry, adopt their customs, their traditions, and anti-Semitism will disappear forever. You will live in peace and in harmony with the world around you. That was utopia, that was an illusion. Assimilation came to its final and formidable climax and test with the Holocaust.

In 1933, when the Nazis came to power in Germany, the majority of German Jews were perhaps more and better Germans than the Christians. Did it save them, did it help them? Quite the contrary. Precisely in that community, where assimilation was supposed to have solved discrimination and anti-Semitism, the greatest tragedy to Judaism arose — in a country where a relative handful of Jews resided, 600 thousand amidst 70 million. Assimilation died in the Holocaust, hopefully never to be reborn as a philosophy for Jewish existence anywhere in the world.

Another philosophy that went bankrupt or died in the Holocaust was the galut or diaspora mentality. This philosophy was prevalent among East European Jews. When in the early stages of the Holocaust my father was confronted with it, he promptly tried to apply his old bag of experiences and tricks. After all, it worked all through the ages; it must work right now as well.

What was that system that worked so well in the past? Negotiate and compromise with the enemy, bribe the enemy, sacrifice the few for the majority, educate your children, and wait for the oppression to pass. My father was stunned and shocked; his system, proven for thousands of years, suddenly didn't work. He had no one to negotiate with, to compromise with; he had no one to bribe; he could not sacrifice the few. The Nazis wanted all. He saw the face of a new and vicious enemy, not seen in thousands of years. He was stunned! So he withdrew; he isolated himself. He could not understand how humanity had changed so radically and rapidly.

The Need to Face the Truth

The myths surrounding the Holocaust divide and polarize humankind and thus deny society any chance to acknowledge the facts and to proceed with common efforts to prevent their recurrence. The majority of people are unable to cope with this unique event and are simply ignoring it, pretending it was no different from any of the numerous massacres that plagued humanity, often as a consequence of war.

Long before World War II the Nazi philosophy was clearly outlined in Hitler's book *Mein Kampf,* with a complete description of the future racial division of humanity and the new Aryan society without Jews. Tragically, the world did not take this insane, deadly ideology seriously then. World War II was only the method of fulfilling some of the Holocaust's objectives and not its source or its origin. The war was the consequence of the long-range plan to restructure the human race, not vice versa.

Some argue that the Germans, unlike the rest of the Western nations, are a vicious, cruel people, singly capable of perpetuating such a monstrosity; therefore, let's condemn them and absolve the rest of humanity. All these theories classifying the Germans as bad or good people are false. The Holocaust exposed humanity as a whole and not just individuals, races, nationalities, or creeds. The truth has been revealed to us that the Germans as well as all of us — Americans, Russians, Italians, Christians, or Jews — are neither good nor bad. We are, each of us, both good and bad. We possess the passions of love as well as of hate. Neither religion nor formal education has prevented humanity from degeneration.

Nazi Germany had one of the most advanced systems of education with one of the lowest illiteracy rates in the world and the most prestigious university system. Yet the SS, SD, and the Gestapo counted in their ranks thousands of people with Ph.D.s; the medical profession did not hesitate to fully support the experimentation program of the Nazi concentration camp system.

Among its victims a similar phenomenon occurred. In the Warsaw Ghetto the ranks of the Jewish bestial police were swollen with the best academic element from among Warsaw's Jewry. Yet, on the opposite side, the underworld element became the saviors of the starving population through their daring food smuggling operations. Moreover, in the heroic uprising of April 1943 in the Warsaw Ghetto, the remnant of underworld figures fully cooperated with the Jewish fighting organization. In fact the famous Mila 18 bunker, the underground headquarters was originally the chief underworld hideout, which the criminals voluntarily surrendered while joining with the Jewish fighters to serve the resistance.

These examples merely support another Holocaust truth: that both the more as well as the less educated classes possess the same elements of beauty and ugliness, only circumstances bring out these contrasting faces into the open.

The Holocaust and the New Jew

It was we, the youngsters, the teenagers who were not as closely tied to the old traditions, who took to the streets and engaged in a hopeless militant battle. The leader of the Warsaw Ghetto Uprising, Mordechai Anieliewicz, was only 23 years old. Not that we were geniuses and our fathers were wrong. Their system applied to a pre-Holocaust society; they were its products, reflections of a pre-Holocaust civilization. The boys and girls who rose up to fight in the ghetto streets, in death camps, and in the forests were the beginning of a new Jew. We are the products of post-Holocaust civilization, the reflection of a new environment. Yes, a new Jew was born in the Warsaw Ghetto!

Often I am asked, "Why did you not embark on a mission, to enlighten and to educate people to the Holocaust years ago? Why? Weren't you ready?" And I promptly respond, "I was ready, but you weren't. Your parents and grandparents weren't ready." They did not want to listen to us survivors, to our accounts of the Holocaust. They did not want to confront it. They had a feeling of guilt and shame because they and their leaders were passive and silent, while their brothers and sisters were being slaughtered across the ocean. We did not see hundreds of thousands of Jews marching, screaming, demonstrating, in the streets of New York or Chicago. We did not see thousands fasting on the steps of the White House trying to influence the administration perhaps to do something. Why? Did they not care? I would never be that cynical. Of course they cared, but they had the diaspora mentality; they and their leadership were too timid to act boldly, to be heard.

"Be silent, keep quiet, perhaps it won't come here," was their mentality. "Let's not awaken the Jew hater in this country; the evil won't come here." But the truth is quite the opposite. The Holocaust has taught us a lesson. The more quiet, silent, passive you are, the faster it will come to your doorsteps.

Yes, a new Jew was born in the Warsaw Ghetto and all the other ghettos and camps in the Holocaust: A Jew that from now on will declare boldly to neighbors, "I am Jewish!" And just as boldly declare that "I am proud of it." And a Jew that will not hesitate to announce to the world around him, "I shall defend it, with all means at my disposal." That new Jew will continue to carry the book and the Torah in one hand, as was done for thousands of years, but will not hesitate whenever necessary to carry the gun in the other hand. That type of post-Holocaust philosophy, so well exemplified by the State of Israel, is the only one that fits with the post-Holocaust world and that will be respected.

That new Jew is a reflection of post-Holocaust society, just as the old Jew was a reflection of pre-Holocaust civilization. Neither one is right nor wrong, nor courageous nor cowardly. They are both merely the products of different ages and their respective gentile environments.

Yes, the new Jew is the reflection of a post-Holocaust society. Not that we Jews are safer or more secure, quite the opposite. I would have preferred to continue with the diaspora mentality in a pre-Holocaust society. I was equipped to deal with it; I had the experience of centuries. Then I always had a choice and my chances to survive and flourish as a Jew, although with hardships, were reasonably good. I would have preferred my father's world of yesterday, the world of discrimination, to the world of annihilation, the world where I was not a hero, but a survivor. But in the post-Holocaust world we no longer have a choice. In a world where the ideology of annihilation has taken root, the centuries old tactics of the diaspora will not work. Only boldness, education, enlightenment and the willingness to fight when necessary have a chance.

Yet the Jews, no matter how courageous, cannot win the struggle for survival by themselves, for they constitute only a tiny fraction of humanity. Their safety lies not only in their own efforts but equally in the sanity, generosity, and tolerance of the rest of humanity. If great masses of non-Jews are infected with the disease of the Holocaust, with virulent anti-semitism, Jews alone cannot overcome such organized masses gone insane.

Yes, the Jews must be ready to fight for their survival but the main struggle must be a struggle for truth, education, and sanity. We must all, Jews and non-Jews, work for a world in which evil forces aiming toward a new Holocaust will find little fertile ground.

A Program of Action

What then must be done? Here are a few practical suggestions. First, we must study and understand the Holocaust thoroughly through the use of the unique resources of the survivors. These people can provide a dimension no one else can. They must be joined by other investigators who possess different Holocaust perspectives and experiences.

Humanity, and especially us Jews, has paid an enormous price. The lives of a third of our people — six million men, women, and children were lost — yet we are not using that most potent weapon in our arsenal to enlighten and educate society: The truth and knowledge of the Holocaust is our best means to prevent a recurrence. The Holocaust can serve as an example of how a nation can go insane.

Often I am asked whether I am bitter, or angry. Not at all! Nor do I have difficulties remaining sane; quite the opposite. My experiences in the Holocaust have brought me much closer to understanding the true human being. I now know how to deal with the weakness in him and what to expect of him. This knowledge makes me able to be more honest with myself and to be a better guide to understanding these events for the benefit of those who care to listen and learn from this survivor.

To me in particular, the Holocaust is a most intense lesson. It represents the essence of human existence: humanity's loves and hates, beauty, and ugliness. Its past and its future are all mirrored there if I have the courage to immerse myself thoroughly and deeply. In its ugliness I found much optimism; in its insanity I found tranquility. I turned despair into hope, nightmares into visions, dilemmas into solutions, disappointments into calm. I became shockproof by acknowledging humanity's ugliness and hate alongside its love and beauty. The stronger and more personal was my encounter with what Elie Wiesel called "the kingdom of night," the more resistant and impregnable I became to humanity's shocks.

And in such a state of reason, serenity, and calm I am more capable of diagnosing the Holocaust's truth without hate, rancor, revenge, or complexes.

Only in such a state of mind can you and I diagnose our new malady and offer remedies in order to minimize and prevent another Holocaust. It is a state of being without illusions, one thoroughly realistic, yet sane enough to acknowledge insanity, to recognize its symptoms and to work for a cure.

Often I feel as one orbiting the planet earth in a satellite, looking down at billions of people going about their lives on this planet. I still see vividly the cattle cars packed with humans in agony arriving at the railcar sidings in Auschwitz, only minutes away from the gas chambers, only minutes away from their Final Solution, an end that they do not expect nor imagine.

I can see and even smell an entire city going up in smoke, thick black clouds mushrooming miles up into the sky, while beneath thousands of people scramble for breathing space in an underground bunker or they jump from burning collapsing houses or struggle in rat-infested flooded sewers. One can recall young mothers risking their lives climbing to the top of the ghetto wall with a bundle in their arms, an infant, seeking someone on the Aryan world willing to receive it, raise it, give it life. These were the scenes in the Warsaw Ghetto during its suicidal uprising where, of a half a million Jewish inhabitants, less than one thousand survived; more than 99 percent perished. I can also see the pigs corner in Flossenburg concentration camp, where hundreds of still breathing 60-pound corpses are piled up waiting for their turn to be consumed in the crematoria.

But I also see my Grandma Masha offering her life to save mine; Franek, a Christian, who could have lived quietly in the Aryan world yet offering his life to save the life of a Jewess, my sister; Major Stockman, the Jewish commander, the kapo, who used his power to save my life and numerous others from the hands of the sadistic storm trooper Feiks, and who eventually sacrificed his own life on the altar of decency.

Yes, the survivors have seen the vilest and the noblest of human behavior. We know that, within each human, is the potential for the most vicious bestiality and the most generous of humaneness. After 30 years of silence the survivors have only recently begun to speak, to talk about the Holocaust experiences. It is the duty and responsibility of the media, the arts, the publishing industry, historians, and society as a whole to encourage, to listen, and to record all that has been conveyed to us.

Soon after the event, most survivors were eager to tell their story, but they soon discovered in shock and disappointment that no one cared to listen; the world was eager to forget that it ever happened. The Holocaust became the survivor's exclusive domain. Only they commemorated it; only they talked about it when with other survivors; only they recalled it in nightmares.

The subject was an embarrassing one to raise in public, or even among nonsurvivor friends. Consequently, the survivor withdrew into a world of pain. Soon, upon seeing this world of indifference, indifferent during the event and indifferent after, they began suppressing the past through an eagerness to build a new life, a new family around which one's own emotional security would evolve. But, for how long can these people manage to bottle up within themselves experiences of this magnitude?

Obviously, if the survivors are honest, now that in middle and old age, now that a new life has been formed with a new family, now that the survivors have accomplished and fulfilled new careers, they will now turn these pent-up emotions loose. This suppressed secret is growing into an explosive boiling volcano that must be unloaded, exposed for reasons of self-therapy, as well as for obligations to society, not to mention one's responsibility to children and grandchildren. And now, so many years after the event, all people, Jews and non-Jews alike, should at long last be ready to face the truth and learn from it.

The few Holocaust themes shown on the screen have been made without actively consulting survivors. In some cases, so-called Holocaust experts were consulted, but they were really experts on Jewish affairs. Assuming that experts on Jewish studies are also experts on the Holocaust is wrong. They often are reluctant to confront the issues of the Holocaust, for they tend to feel comfortable only when dealing with raw statistics and documents. They have been known to back away from acquiring firsthand information from the survivors of the Holocaust, those who experienced it and witnessed it. Their relationship to these primary sources of historical information is that of avoidance.

Part of their fear derives from the awareness that the Holocaust and the actions of the world toward Jews as well as the responses of the Jews do not fit into the theoretical models that explain Jewish history. The Holocaust was a unique event not only in Jewish history but just as much so in world history.

Every study of the Holocaust must employ a number of eloquent survivors. Only then can people come closer to knowing the truth. The world of art, historians, and academicians must study and listen to the survivors with much more zeal and interest, because they are the best, in fact the only, sources from whom to obtain the truth and avoid distortions.

It is understandable and to be expected that a flood of material will be pouring out from the survivors in the next few years, and a certain amount will be repetitious, wasteful, and of inferior quality. That result is unavoidable and rather a small price to pay considering the value of the survivor's contributions.

The real inquiry into the facts of the Holocaust, its interpretations, and meaning for civilization is just beginning. One can be quite certain that in another 20 or 30 years much will be written, argued, and philosophized, and that more plays, lectures, motion pictures and symposiums conducted than ever before. That fact is unavoidable; the coming generation's appetite to inquire, to want to know, and to learn from this new pattern of human behavior will never be sufficiently satisfied. And from these dialogues new formulas of prevention will be attempted by Jew and Gentile. Whether they will be successful is not for us to speculate, but we survivors have the obligation to assist.

Above all we, the witnesses, must set the record straight and, before we pass on, make certain that humanity has established the right and true diagnosis of what happened in the Holocaust. That is the minimum legacy for us to contribute to the next generation.

The second most pressing endeavor is to establish Holocaust centers of study in every university and college across this world. This will encourage the training of thousands of qualified instructors who can teach the lessons of the Holocaust to millions of young boys and girls during their formative years. These centers must develop full academic programs, including master's and Ph.D. degrees, a serious and comprehensive science of the subject. This would encourage thousands of young academicians to seek careers in the field of human survival.

The last and most important aspect of prevention is to inaugurate comprehensive courses on the Holocaust in all high schools, so that the youth may fully acquaint itself with humanity's weaknesses and strengths. The young must spend several hours weekly in absorbing the possible dangers of hate, genocide, and mass insanity. These precious hours of study of the Holocaust will counter the negative influence from the adult world outside, the already poisoned environment offered to the young.

A long-range, systematic study of the Holocaust would acquaint the students with their own temptations and prejudices and prepare them to deal with these forces. The attractive novelty of new "secret" philosophies will cease to excite the students since they will no longer be new and revolutionary; they were all tried in the Holocaust with negative and tragic results.

On a recent lecture in a leading Manhattan high school, I stunned the crowded auditorium when I picked out a neat, bright-looking 16-year-old student as the future barbarian. "In 10 years from now you may become a professional killer of infants children and old people." I pointed at this innocent looking boy, who, considering it a clumsy joke, reacted in bewilderment. "It's unbelievable, impossible, ridiculous. Is that what you think?" I continued.

"Now imagine the year 1930 and not 1981 and the place is Berlin and I am addressing a hall full of German students your age, as clean, neat, bright, intelligent looking as you. Well, 16-year-old Hans is reacting the same way as you do to my suggestion that he may become in 10 years a barbarian and killer, a commander of a death factory. I assure you his disbelief would be as genuine as yours."

The Holocaust reveals to us that none of us is exempt from mass madness. The place and time to prevent the affliction is in the high school or even earlier. For we can innocently be captured by evil and then slowly progress in the participation in cruelties until it becomes mechanical, scientific; then we can "justify" it with confused morality or insane idealism to satisfy our conscience.

Dangers Ahead

I am certain that the dangers of another man-made Holocaust are more real and acute than the threat of an atomic Holocaust. In an atomic confrontation, both sides are powerful enough to destroy each other; consequently, they will abstain from mutual annihilation, from suicide. Man is basically a survivor with an immense addiction, a desire to live, to continue.

The psychological and historical truth is that man will coexist longer and more durably out of fear than out of kindness. Such a coexistence is rather a permanent struggle, yet these are the facts of man and life. Coexistence to be derived from tolerance, understanding, and generosity, however, requires a much greater effort. But it is possible and it is a goal humanity must never, ever abandon.

The passions, ideas, and philosophies that changed the relationship of man to man are more dangerous and more likely to recur because they always confront a minority. The masses blinded by passions of superiority and righteousness are the powerful adversary of their victim, who is always in the minority and so much weaker. It is precisely the Jew and other minorities that serve as a springboard to Nazi-like societies. Since the Holocaust is humanity's greatest danger, the great task for the coming century is the battle for the human mind, for the preservation of sanity.

The germs of a new Holocaust have been spread, like seeds in the wind. We must spare no effort to build healthy, sane societies resistant to this deadly disease which can threaten the extermination of whole peoples. The Jews, the first victims, the traditional scapegoats, and the most threatened, have the most direct and immediate interest in a world of sanity, tolerance, and generosity that is so essential for their survival. As Edmund Burke said, "The only thing necessary for the triumph of evil is for sane men to do nothing." The Baal-Shem-Tov put in in a more philosophical context: "Remembrance is the secret of redemption. Forgetfulness leads to exile."

Contributing Authors

Frieda Aaron is an Adjunct Lecturer in the Department of Comparative Literature at Brooklyn College of The City University of New York. She is enrolled in the Ph.D. Program in Comparative Literature at the Graduate School and University Center, completing her dissertation titled "Literature of the Holocaust: Poetry Written During the Holocaust." Her writings have appeared in *November Review* (Spring, 1970) and *Centerpoint* (Spring, 1980).

Yitshaq Ben-Ami was educated at the Hebrew University of Jerusalem. He joined the *Irgun* in 1932 and from 1937 through 1939 served as its commander of the European Rescue Operation. He also served as Executive Director of the American Friends for a Jewish Palestine and of the American League for a Free Palestine. His semi-autobiographical book — *Years of Wrath, Days of Glory* — was published by Robert Speller and Sons in 1982.

Leslie Berger is a Professor at Queens College of The City University of New York. He is the author of a number of studies that have appeared in *Psychophysiology, Journal of Projective Technique, Psychological Report,* and *Journal of Comparative Psychology*.

Randolph L. Braham is Chairman of the M.A. Program in International Relations and Professor of Political Science at The City College of The City University of New York. He also serves as Director of the Jack P. Eisner Institute for Holocaust Studies at the Graduate School and University Center of The City

University of New York. He is the author, co-author, or editor of 20 books and has contributed to 13 others. He has also published about two hundred notes and articles in various encyclopedias and professional journals. His two-volume work, *The Politics of Genocide,* was published late in 1980 by Columbia University Press.

Jack P. Eisner is the author of *The Survivor* (William Morrow, 1980). As president of the Holocaust Survivors Memorial Foundation, he made possible the establishment of the Institute for Holocaust Studies that bears his name at The Graduate School and University Center of The City University of New York. He is also the founder of the Warsaw Ghetto Resistance Organization (WAGRO).

Ellen S. Fine is an Associate Professor of French at Kingsborough Community College, The City University of New York. She is the author of *Legacy of Night. The Literary Universe of Elie Wiesel* (State University of New York Press, 1982). Her scholarly studies have appeared in a number of professional journals, including *Centerpoint, Midstream,* and *Shoah*.

Jonathan Helfand is Assistant Professor in the Department of Judaic Studies at Brooklyn College, The City University of New York. He is a specialist on "French Jewry During the Second Republic and Second Empire, 1848–1870." His studies have appeared in a number of scholarly journals, including *Archives Juives, Jewish Social Studies,* and *Judaism*.

Rosette Lamont is Professor of French at Queens College and a member of the doctoral faculty in the Ph.D. Program in French and the Ph.D. Program in Comparative Literature at the Graduate School and University Center of The City University of New York. She is the author of several books, including *Ionesco* (Prentice-Hall, 1973), and *The Two Faces of Ionesco* (Whitson, 1978). She also has contributed chapters to a number of books and articles to a variety of professional journals.

Franklin H. Littell is Professor of Religion at Temple University, Philadelphia, and a Corresponding Faculty Member of the Institute of Contemporary Jewry, Hebrew University, Jerusalem. He is the author or editor of 20 books, including *The German Church Struggle and the Holocaust* (Wayne State University Press, 1974), *The Crucifixion of the Jews* (Harper & Row, 1975), and *Religious Liberty in the Crossfire of Creeds* (Ecumenical Press, 1978). He has also published over 275 major articles or chapters of books. Professor Littell is a member of the U.S. Holocaust Memorial Council and of the International Council of Yad Vashem.

Alan Rosenberg is a Lecturer in the Department of Philosophy at Queens College, The City University of New York. He is the author or co-author of a number of studies that have appeared in a variety of journals, including *Triangle, Main Currents in Modern Thought, Cross Currents,* and *European Judaism.*

Stanley L. Rustin is Associate Professor and Counselor to students at Queensborough Community College, The City University of New York. He was formerly associated with a number of medical and psychological centers, including the Kings Park State Hospital. He is the author or co-author of many studies that have appeared in such professional journals as *American Journal of Orthopsychiatry, Journal of Contemporary Psychotherapy,* and *Journal of Family Counseling.*

Ruth Zerner is Associate Professor of History at Herbert H. Lehman College, The City University of New York. Her articles have appeared in a variety of scholarly journals, including *Fides et Historia, Jewish Social Studies, The Journal of Ecumenical Studies,* and *Austrian History Yearbook.* A specialist on Dietrich Bonhoeffer, she also contributed chapters to a number of books, including *Lion's Handbook to the History of Christianity* (Aslan Publishers, 1977).